THE TRAGIC MASK

A Study of Faulkner's Heroes

THE TRAGIC MASK

A Study of Faulkner's Heroes

By

JOHN LEWIS LONGLEY, JR.

Chapel Hill

THE UNIVERSITY OF NORTH CAROLINA PRESS

#167458

for my mother and father

PREFACE

SOME PAGES of this book were written as early as 1956; some of them were finished as late as July, 1962, on the banks of the Dreisam in Freiburg im Breisgau as I finished the process of changing "is" to "was" and "has" to "had." Chapter 5 of the book appeared in somewhat different form, under the title "Faulkner's Byron Bunch," in the Summer, 1961, issue of *The Georgia Review*. Chapter 13, also in somewhat different form, appeared under the title "Joe Christmas: The Hero in the Modern World" in the Spring, 1957, issue of *The Virginia Quarterly Review*.

In view of the several serious book-length studies of Faulkner's work which appeared in the years shortly before his death, this book should begin with a brief statement of its purpose and scope and a brief justification for its being done at all. The great bulk of previous Faulkner scholarship has consisted of studies of individual works or the establishing of thematic patterns. It occurred to me, however, that there would perhaps be some profit in undertaking instead an analysis and assessment of the various characters—individual human beings—in the Faulkner canon. This approach could be justified on the obvious ground that many Faulkner characters appear in more than one book. More important, Faulkner asserted on many occasions that he was more interested in "people"—the human heart—than he was in literary technique as technique.

In the past, far too many commentators have ignored the radically empirical nature of Faulkner's content and method. The result is all too often a pontifical, sweeping assessment of behavior and morality in Yoknapatawpha. Action and character in "real" life are governed essentially by cultural responses, whether with or against the grain, and Yoknapatawpha is a culture which should be known at first hand before analysis is attempted. The same difficulty infects many discussions of form and technique. In spite of Faulkner's own readily available comment on his own education, training, and working habits, many interpretative studies are obviously based on the unconscious assumption that Faulkner was of necessity committed to the same criteria of value and procedure as is the critic and that his literary education was not essentially different from the critic's own. The present study makes no effort to correct these errors directly (that would be another book entirely). It undertakes instead one change of direction and emphasis which the author hopes will ultimately be of some value.

ii.

Many persons have been vital to the completion of this book. Here I wish to single out Miss Charlotte Kohler, editor of *The Virginia Quarterly Review,* and the advisory editors of the *Review* for their very real encouragement and generosity in awarding me the Emily Clark Balch Prize in 1957. Gratitude is due also to:

Robert Daniel, the late John Bernard Emperor, Clarence Pendleton Lee, Oscar Cargill, William M. Gibson, and William Riley Parker; who at various times and places tried to teach me what literature is.

My colleagues in the University of Virginia, particularly the members of the Department of English of the School of Engineering; for their advice and encouragement.

Walter Slatoff, who offered many detailed suggestions.

Linton Massey, President of the Bibliographical Society of America, for his encouragement and constant exhortation to "get it done."

Miss Miriam Brokaw of the Princeton University Press, for her constant encouragement, kindness, patience, and tolerance.

The Old Dominion Foundation and its secretary, Monroe Bush, for an Old Dominion Foundation Fellowship which made possible the drafting of this book.

Chief Boatswain's Mate Sidney Toller and SC2 James Wernicke of the Oak Island, North Carolina, Station, United States Coast Guard; for making our stay on Bald Head Island so pleasant, safe, and secure.

And certainly for myself and for many others there is no adequate way to speak of the gratitude we feel for the years in Charlottesville which William Faulkner gave us. The gift of himself was unstinted; this book, for instance, would not have existed without that gift. There must have been times in those years when his kindness, patience, tolerance, and leisure were sorely tried, but they were never, to my knowledge, exhausted.

TABLE OF CONTENTS

THE TRAGIC MASK
A Study of Faulkner's Heroes

1.

INTRODUCTION

THE HEART HAS its reasons, said Pascal, of which the reason is unaware.

In the Nobel Prize address, William Faulkner, after a lifetime of writing, affirmed that the only thing worth the agony and sweat of the creative effort is ". . . the old verities and truths . . . of the human heart in conflict with itself." In his two recent sessions as writer-in-residence at the University of Virginia, the gist of his remarks and comments upon his own work was: "I just tell stories. . . . I just write about people."

Any work of criticism which wishes itself to be taken seriously must establish within itself its own justification. What the present study proposes is a change of both pace and direction. Few experts would deny that a sweeping reassessment of all Faulkner criticism is long overdue and may already be underway. Major re-evaluation is needed first of all to wipe out forever the hostile and vituperative early misinterpretations, which are far from dead. Even more urgent is the need to screen carefully the tidal wave of generally enthusiastic but often uninformed and unreliable interpretative studies. The present book does not propose to make such an assessment but does hope to avoid compounding the confusion. In view of the several recent books on Faulkner (some of them excellent in many ways), there is less need for further analysis of themes, ideas, and motifs, or individual novels and stories as such. Therefore this book will present a consideration of the individual human beings who are Faulkner's fictional characters—that teeming multitude of heroes, villains, clowns, and saints who inhabit the mythical kingdom of Yoknapatawpha.

Such an approach could be justified entirely on the basis of inclusiveness—the interlocking structure of the Yoknapatawpha Chronicle, which in presenting the saga of various dynasties causes many characters to appear in two or more books. The real necessity for doing such a study is far more serious and fundamental. If the general tendency of Faulkner's own remarks in recent years is any indication, his central concern, his primary awareness as man and writer, has always been Mankind, rather than the making of books. The sole point I am trying to nail down is that Faulkner's essential concern is not with form or style or technique, however brilliant his accomplishments with them may be. The central concern is with Man—his folly, his heroism, his tragedy, his comedy—or more specifically, that inward arena where love and honor and pity and pride and compassion and sacrifice create themselves: the human heart. The outward unity of the Yoknapatawpha Chronicle exists in the fact that it is all a part of the history of Yoknapatawpha. The inner unity lies in the fact that all of it centers in humanity, which causes it to transcend the accidents of locality and period and moves it toward the realm of the great literature of all time. I want to suggest that Faulkner's remarks about humanity ("people") be taken seriously. I should like to suggest further that the comment of a major author on his own ideas, content, and working methods may not be beyond all question worthless.

No purpose is served by rehearsing the melancholy and incredible history of Faulkner criticism. By now it has become customary to state simply that until George Marion O'Donnell's "Faulkner's Mythology" in 1939, there was no responsible American criticism of the work at all. Critics and reviewers were engaged largely in searching out deviations either from their own particular sub-Marxian theories of socio-economic determinism or from that view which insists that all is for the best in this best of all possible worlds. Such deviations were not difficult to discover, and sometimes the critics were able to embrace both objections at once, difficult as that may seem. They could even dismiss the writing entirely, as "pure event without implication."

Faulkner, they said, was the leader in the new "cult of cruelty" school. He was one of those engaged in "a rather profitable literary business with unmitigated cruelties and abnormalities as their regular stock-in-trade." "The world of William Faulkner echoes with the hideous trampling march of lust and disease, brutality and death." ". . . there is nothing, we feel, behind his atrocities, no cosmic echoes; each gamy detail exists for itself alone." "To read these books is to cross a desert of terrifying nihilism." Finding "no predilection for 'ought,' no interest in 'why,' " these critics resorted to the same kind of treatment accorded Hardy and Proust: for the crime of having reflected the condition of the world too well, Faulkner was accused of having single-handedly caused it all to happen.

But the tale of all this impercipience has been told too often. Since the O'Donnell essay in 1939, that cluster of brilliant articles by Warren Beck and Robert Penn Warren in 1941, the Cowley *Portable* in 1945, and particularly since the Nobel Prize, the current of praise has swelled. Disparagement, with the exception of that from a few die-hard Marxists, has dwindled to a trickle. Now we are faced with a phenomenon almost as bad. Old, established journals and new journals lately sprung up among us are flooded with articles highly enthusiastic but largely speculative, and we are even treated to sly and sinister book-length psychological exposés of Faulkner's inward life, based largely on minor points in the less important fiction.

The greatest advantage a critic can have is hindsight: by a fairly simple analytic process, he can compare the literary text to the critical commentary and determine with some precision which techniques have proved fruitful and which have not. In dealing with a special region and climate of temperament and culture, such as Faulkner's South, all the cautionary safeguards that are customarily applied in historical scholarship must be used. Sincere, earnest, and competent critics have all too often been mistaken about Faulkner's work, especially in its social and cultural significance. Almost always the error can be traced to an interpretation which is a projection of the Intentional Fallacy. Consciously or unconsciously, the critic ignored what could be learned about the intention of the novelist, and the work was distorted past all recognition to fit it on the rack of some a priori theory or belief. Sometimes a younger critic trained in some fashionable Method of interpretation or the other had a probably not even conscious belief, as a part of that training, that the Method was infallible, regardless of the nature of the work under consideration. He went ahead and applied it, even in the face of an invincible ignorance of those qualities in the work of the writer which make his work distinct from any other. In a very real sense, such ignorance is innocence—an innocence as radical as that of Thomas Sutpen. Precisely as with Sutpen's innocent ignorance of the dynamics of morality, these commentators on Faulkner seem powerfully convinced that their assessments of significance deal with nothing more complicated than ". . . the ingredients of pie or cake and once you had measured them and balanced them and mixed them and put them into the oven it was all finished and nothing but pie or cake could come out."[1]

Nor are the more traditional methods of scholarship very much more helpful. One thing that is constantly embarrassing about Faulkner's work is the way in which it defies easy generalization—the slapping-on of a ready-made label which will enable the work to be filed away and forgotten. All of it so conspicuously lacks the neatness, the prim reduction of scale and easy fragmentation, so beloved by the bureaucratic academic mind. "Facts" about Faulkner's ancestry and career are being discovered here and there but do not lead to very much that is useful. The history of his family has been published in a popular magazine; we know now that his great-grandfather in several ways resembled the fictional Colonel Sartoris, but no one has so far been bold enough to assess with precision the exact degree to which the use of this matter has made for better or worse fiction. The places in the Yoknapatawpha Chronicle where names and dates do not agree are being carefully tabulated, but all this effort is negated by the small note Faulkner placed at the beginning of *The Mansion* in which he states that he is aware of the discrepancies but hopes that they represent growth and understanding of the human heart rather than simple carelessness.[2]

By the same token, that happy hunting-ground, the search for "sources," also seems pointless—for two reasons. One: the evidence of the influence and attitudes of such writers as Keats, Swinburne, Mallarmé, and Wilde is most obvious in the period of Faulkner's immature apprenticeship. When he pulled a Symbolist turn of phrasing or even an overt time-shift from what he called his "lumber-room," it was probably no more and no less conscious than Coleridge's thinking "Bartram" when he needed crocodiles. At any rate, whatever was borrowed was so altered in the process of passing through Faulkner's imagination as to be practically unrecognizable. The source of his major tradition and theme did not have to be found in books. It was as much a part of his early life as the air he breathed; it came directly and orally from his own family, the town and the region where he grew up. Anyone growing up in a large Southern family (before World War II, at least) was treated to the same half-conscious, half-heard process, like Quentin Compson growing up in a barracks full of ghosts. Secondly, there is Faulkner's notorious inability to tell a story the same way twice. He was so incorrigibly creative that a major episode in his work may be told two or three times and be presented in a different version in each. When asked at Virginia if he had ever contemplated an autobiography, he replied: "No sir, . . . for two reasons. One because I am such a congenital liar that I could never tell it the way it happened, and two, because any writer worth his salt is convinced he can create better characters than Godalmighty ever made." When we can with fair certainty point to something taken from an older writer, that taking may very well be deliberate, since Mr. Faulkner has also remarked that a writer has to steal where he can.

William Faulkner was notorious for his indifference to what people said about him and what pundits and professors thought of his work. Even though he never cared to discuss his work, even with interested persons, he gave several fairly lengthy interviews concerned in whole or in part with his reading preferences, working methods, and intentions; some of these exchanges took place several years before his two sessions as Writer-in-Residence at the University of Virginia.[3] With the publication of *Faulkner in the University*, the transcript of his many public appearances, interviews, and classroom sessions was made available to anyone interested in the author's own commentary. Even before this volume was issued, ample evidence existed concerning his literary training and background. Malcolm Cowley has summed it up this way: ". . . Faulkner . . . had less of a formal education than any other good writer of his time, except Hart Crane—less even than Hemingway, who never went to college, but who learned to speak three foreign languages and studied writing in Paris from the best masters."[4] Faulkner confirmed this estimate by stating that he taught himself to be a writer largely by "undirected and uncorrelated" reading of everything he could find, even pulp-paper trash of all kinds.[5] This attitude is further confirmed by his statement that the only book he ever attempted to write by means of elaborate notes and outlines was *A Fable,* which he does not consider one of his notable successes.[6] With *The Reivers,* Faulkner had published some twenty-six books, some of them very uneven but the best of them equal to anything since the best work of the great Russian novelists. This very unevenness further underscores the fact that he was not a "schooled" writer. His achievement is not explained by his training, education, or working methods. We are more or less compelled to explain the power and impact of his work by a summation something like that made twenty-odd years ago by Warren Beck, who is still in many ways the best critic of Faulkner: "A reader whose sensitivity and courage approach Faulkner's own . . . will rather experience that catharsis of pity and terror which comes only of great literature, and which can be conveyed only by a temperament of genius, proceeding from a humane point-of-view, and employing a comprehensive grasp of a significant section of life."[7]

At last the word is out. We might as well admit the term "genius," with all it implies about anarchy, unevenness, excess, the shading-over of classifications, and downright inconvenience, because in the long run the use of this term is probably the easiest way out. This done, I want to suggest that Faulkner's remarks about his own literary training and working habits be taken seriously. I propose that we abandon for the moment even those methods of close examination which work so brilliantly when applied to the fiction of such highly self-conscious artists as Flaubert, James, or Joyce. It is not that Faulkner cannot write as they did when he wishes: witness the highly experimental novels of the period 1929-36. It is simply that his temperament, his genius, his habits of mind, are more congenial to the narrative, the epic, the bardic attitudes in the creation of literature. What he has done in creating the mythical kingdom of Yoknapatawpha is to establish the myths and epics of his particular place and people—both past and present—and then by the alchemy of genius to convert myth and epic into history, a history both particular and universal. Thus, the Yoknapatawpha Chronicle more nearly resembles *The Odyssey* than *Ulysses*.

Seen in this way, as the long perspective of history, Faulkner's world-view becomes classic and classically simple, however swollen, rhetorical, or grotesque the surface of the printed page of his work may be. In general, the cosmos of Yoknapatawpha is the cosmos of the orthodox Christian: God made the world and saw that it was good. He created Man and placed him therein, giving him dominion over the earth, placing him higher than the animals but lower than the angels. Through disobedience and the willingness to listen to temptation and collaborate with the devil, Man fell; he became subject to sin and death, lost Eden, and was doomed to labor for his livelihood forever after. The complexity of human nature and the monstrous uncertainty and ambiguity under which all mankind lives are part of the heritage of sin and death. More specifically, Faulkner's Yoknapatawpha is a county in northern Mississippi, existing in the present but with a past extending back before the coming of the white settlers. To a greater extent than other regions of the nation, Yoknapatawpha, by being in the South, is conscious of its past. The passion and suffering of that past are palpable in the present, often affecting the attitudes and actions of both individuals and groups. The individual may respond to this heritage in several ways. He may ignore it entirely, as does Flem Snopes. He may, with irony and detachment, take it as it comes, as do Ratliff and Will Varner. He may destroy himself attempting to gain acceptance inside it as does Charles Bon or destroy himself attempting to repudiate it, as does Charles Etienne St. Velery Bon.

ii.

At various times in the past thirty-five years, Faulkner has been labeled with varying degrees of accuracy as a Primitive, a

Naturalist, or a Decadent.   Each of these designations contains a particle of appropriateness; the Primitive probably in his mystic affinity for the wilderness and his creation of the various Indians, Boon Hogganbeck, and Sam Fathers, as well as of his various children and idiots.   The Naturalist label is more understandable if we assume a critic already strongly biased toward scientific determinism, who may easily mistake the subject matter for significance, as in such a book as *Sanctuary*.   The Decadent tag might have been used appropriately, especially if applied to the early poetry in an attempt to relate it to a specific historical literary movement, but I suspect that those who used it had something more lower-case in mind.   It is now more or less agreed that the term which comes as close as any is Traditionalist.   George Marion O'Donnell described Faulkner as a traditional moralist; this hybrid term requires sharp qualification.   He is, in the sense already described, a traditional moralist who is also a modern writer.

Aside from being so in the obvious sense that he was writing up until the recent present, and frequently on subjects as timely as the morning's headlines, there is the outward evidence of modern forms and techniques: the Joycean word-linkages and, in the novels of the period 1929-36, the restless and often brilliant experiments in time-shift, point-of-view, surrealistic presentation, and structural manipulation.   For better or for worse, modern fiction is obsessed with technique, certainly more so than the literary effort of any period in the past.   Symbolism, intense subjectivity, the interior consciousness, and free association are legitimately established as standard literary techniques of our time. Occasionally, a first-rate literary artist will be able to do without most of them, but it is again redundant to say they are as firmly established in the texture of the times as, for instance, television is.   Precisely as the poems of a modern poet are apt to be "difficult," the matter, the method, and the meaning of a major Faulkner novel are apt to be difficult—to be presented in a way that is oblique and implicational rather than direct.   To take one simple example, there is the technique of presenting the protagonist at a distance, allowing the reader to view him through the consciousness of one or several narrators, as in much of the work of James or Conrad.   This process complicates the form and allows us to see significance only as it comes altered by the subjectivity of the "reverberator." Still, with reference to the terrifyingly complex world we live in, it is hard to see how the writer who is sensitive and aware, and above all, honest, could present existence in any other way. Now that the control and manipulation of mass opinion are reaching scientific precision, the individual man, obsessed with his vision of the truth, will know the uneasy suspicion that it is his version only. "Well," Strether might have said, "here we are." After all, Conrad and James did not invent the Twentieth Century; it invented them. Perhaps the best the writer can do is to call it as he sees it.

As we constantly rediscover, this sense of complexity and subjectivity, the manipulation of action and reaction, of shift and change in Man and his cosmos, is the most essential sense in which Faulkner is a modern writer. This assertion also must require some clarification. Skillful treatment aside, there is the question of temperament and attitude. More than one critic has complained that the Present often seems to suffer when contrasted with Yoknapatawpha's more noble and glamorous Past. Brilliance of treatment again aside, it is hardly a secret that Faulkner was not very well satisfied with the Present as he saw it, but then who is? In the spatial sense, and perhaps even in the spiritual sense, his major activity in thirty-five years of writing was the construction of that mythical county loosely located in northern Mississippi. But in the temporal sense, and certainly in the spiritual sense, his work has consistently demonstrated the *present-ness* of the Past, as an influence, and as a measurable factor in shaping the Present. For one example, the boy Ike McCaslin is listening to Sam Fathers tell about the old times of the Old People:

And as he talked about those old times and those dead and vanished men of another race from either that the boy knew, gradually to the boy those old times would cease to be old times and would become a part of the boy's present, not only as if they had happened yesterday but as if they were still happening, the men who walked through them actually walking in breath and air and casting an actual shadow on the earth they had not quitted. And more: as if some of them had not happened yet but would occur tomorrow, until at last it would seem to the boy that he himself had not come into existence yet, that none of his race nor the other subject race which his people had brought with them into the land had come here yet. . . .[8]

During the two recent spring semesters (1957, 1958) when Faulkner was Writer-in-Residence at the University of Virginia, he often read to literature classes from his own works and answered questions put to him by students, faculty, and townspeople. Often these questions were highly complicated, multi-level ones about sources, influences, allegory, symbolism, and theories of composition.   It was in response to these questions that he returned his usual reply about just telling stories and just writing about people.   In response to a question about difficulty in sustaining creative effort, he replied in effect: "If the character the author creates is any good, then all the writer has to do is set him up on his feet and then run down the road behind him with a notebook and pencil, taking down what he says and does."   This is not, as Allen Tate once remarked in a different connection, as much another one of Faulkner's outrageous lies as it seems.   For a writer who has created the rich and varied cast of characters that Faulkner has, his people must have been very real and vivid to him and during the process of creation must in truth have seemed to carry on a life of their own.   Who since Dickens has created such variety?   This rich and varied creativity is one result growing out of the central concern with humanity, which is central even in those lyric passages where Faulkner describes the weather or the wilderness—which however beautiful in its own right is still the *mise en scène* for man's comically futile or tragically successful attempts to dominate or encompass or destroy it.   This is the case also in his creation of such mass phenomena as war or religious frenzy or mob hysteria; the narrative, the telling, the focus, is not on the thing itself but on the human beings who are swept up in it, either as participants or observers.   The concern is with the individual's response to the crisis—what he accepts and rejects— the tensions set up between the event and the emotion inside the human heart.

As noted earlier, Faulkner often used the matter, manner, and the techniques of naturalism without accepting any of its basic presuppositions.   His view of the life-process sees Man as considerably more of a free moral agent than does the usual naturalistic theory. Nature is amoral, but Man has been condemned to be moral or take the consequences. "Man creates," says Faulkner, "engenders so much more than he can bear." These destructive processes which Man engenders with particular reference to the world of Yoknapatawpha include first of all the cutting, burning, and destroying of the wilderness. The land became cursed when people began to abuse it. Coeval with this destruction are the twin evils of greed and usury. Negro slavery, the curse and outward symbol of evil in the South, culminated in the War Between the States and the enforced penance of Reconstruction and remains as the current acute race problem. These crises exist in the various periods of Yoknapatawpha history, in addition to the problems normally besetting human existence. All these destructive processes produce pressure on the individual. What Faulkner has done in creating his imaginary world is to depict all kinds and conditions of men under all kinds and conditions of life situations. Many of his figures are human beings who, under internal or external pressure, or both, go to extremes. When this extremity of commitment causes harm or destruction to themselves or to others, the result is tragedy. When it harms only themselves and the effect is humorous, the result is comedy. When the human figure engages in extremes of conduct without any emotional or personal commitment or involvement, the result is villainy.

Under these circumstances, the world of Yoknapatawpha becomes infused with both the classic tragic and the classic Christian paradoxes: even though the human man is predestined to some pitiful and terrible fate, that fate is justified by the actions the human man performs, chooses to perform, because he is, paradoxically, free to choose his actions and in choosing precipitates his fate. It is paradox also when we observe such cold, rational madness as that of Joanna Burden or Percy Grimm, or remember those fanatic, furious creatures like the young Mink Snopes or Old Doc Hines, who drive their hot hearts against the immovable mass of circumstance or personal inadequacy until they are destroyed or go mad, and we say they are as they are because they wish to be. Yet it is just so; whatever the obsession: pride, money, sex, hatred, or the simple self-created image of the Self without which life would be intolerable, they have it because they have willed it into being.

Because of this freedom to choose, responsibility is inescapable. There is no way to escape responsibility for actions taken or not taken. This view places Faulkner in company with the Existentialists, if on that one point alone. In this attitude he differs sharply from the majority of twentieth-century humanity, who have gladly adopted those theories of self-exculpation formulated out of the folklore of the social sciences, which excuse everything on the theory that no one is free to choose to do or not to do anything. Even acts of goodness and benevolence carry dangers which must be guarded against. What seems to a comic hero like Byron Bunch or Gavin Stevens an act of the purest and most disinterested human kindness on their part may contain the element of self-serving and self-interest which corrupts it.

In view of all these factors, the principal effort of the present study is a consideration of Faulkner's fictional characters, that various gallery he has created, though not of "types" because his people are not types, they are each one sharply differentiated individuals. For the sake of convenience, this book (but not the people) will be divided into the sections "Comic Heroes," "Villains," "Tragic Heroes." One thing the modern world seems to have rediscovered from the ancient world is the way in which comedy and tragedy merge into each other at the absolute limits of human experience. The modern world is a world of extremity, and being a part of the modern world, Faulkner exhibits an awareness of this fusion. This study will take due care not to push any character into a single pigeonhole. It is my hope to demonstrate Faulkner's ever-present love for and concern with humanity—however humane or abysmal a given character may be. Even when there is nothing left to love, the work is still infused with that elegiac and brooding regret for what Man might have been. My effort will be to show meaning and significance, to say what I can (with the aid of Faulkner's own statements and those of other commentators) about what each character seems to stand for, or to imply, and to relate that significance to the larger meaning of the entire corpus of Faulkner's work—to tear aside the comic or tragic mask to show the living, human creature underneath.

1. William Faulkner, *Absalom, Absalom!* (New York: Random House, 1936), p. 263.

2. The note says in part: "... there will be found discrepancies and contradictions in the thirty-four-year progress of this particular chronicle; the purpose of this note is simply to notify the reader that the author has already found more discrepancies and contradictions than he hopes the reader will ... due to the fact that the author has learned, he believes, more about the human heart and its dilemma than he knew thirty-four years ago; and ... having lived with them that long time, he knows the characters in this chronicle better than he did then."

3. The most solid coverage of these matters is of course found in *Faulkner in the University* (ed. Frederick L. Gwynn and Joseph L. Blotner [Charlottesville, Va.: University of Virginia Press, 1959]), which covers eight months on the grounds of the University of Virginia. Other, earlier interviews, covering periods from a few minutes to several days, can be found in the following: Annie Brièrre, "Faulkner Parle," *Nouvelles Littéraires,* No. 1466 (October 6, 1955), pp. 1, 6; Loïc Bouvard, "Conversation with William Faulkner," trans. Henry Dan Piper, *Modern Fiction Studies,* V (Winter, 1959-60), 361-64 (the interview reproduced here took place in Princeton, N.J., on November 30, 1952, and was published first in *Bulletin de l'association amicale universitaire France-Amérique* [January, 1954], pp. 23-29); A. M. de Dominicis, "Scrivo perchèmi piace, dice William Faulkner," *La Fiera Letteraria,* IX (February 14, 1954), 1-2 (for de Dominicis, see also "An Interview with Faulkner," trans. Elizabeth Nissen, *Faulkner Studies,* III [Summer-Autumn, 1954], 33-37); Cynthia Grenier, "The Art of Fiction: An Interview with William Faulkner—September, 1955," *Accent,* XVI (Summer, 1956), 167-77; Robert A. Jelliffe, *Faulkner at Nagano* (Tokyo: Kenkyusha, 1956); Lavon Roscoe, "An Interview with William Faulkner," *Western Review,* XV (Summer, 1951), 300-4; and Jean Stein, "The Art of Fiction XII: William Faulkner," *Paris Review,* XII (Spring, 1956), 28-52 (reprinted in Malcolm Cowley, *Writers at Work: The Paris Review Interviews* [New York: Viking Press, 1959]).

4. Malcolm Cowley, ed., *The Portable Faulkner* (New York: Viking Press, 1946), p. 2.

5. *Ibid.* See also the interviews listed in n. 3, especially Roscoe, "An Interview with William Faulkner."

6. See the listings under the heading *"A Fable"* in the Index of Gwynn and Blotner, *Faulkner in the University.*

7. Warren Beck, "Faulkner and the South," *Antioch Review,* I (1941), 94.

8. William Faulkner, *Go Down, Moses* (New York: Random House, 1942), p. 171.

2.

FAULKNER AND COMEDY

Aristodemus said that . . . he was awakened towards day-
break by a crowing of cocks, and when he awoke, the others
were either asleep, or had gone away; there remained only
Socrates, Aristophanes, and Agathon, who were drinking out
of a large goblet which they passed around, and Socrates was
discoursing to them. Aristodemus was only half awake, and
he did not hear the beginning of the discourse; the chief thing
which he remembered was Socrates compelling the other two
to acknowledge that the genius of comedy was the same with
that of tragedy, and that the true artist in tragedy was an artist
in comedy also.

SEEN IN THE LONG perspective from *Soldiers' Pay* to *The Reivers,*
the literary achievement of William Faulkner seems ready for
assessment. One problem to be faced in dealing with the extensive and varied writings of the author is the mass of commentary
from the past, much of it obsessively wrong-headed. There seem
to have been many ways in which Faulkner forever prevented himself from becoming a great writer. Aside from the attacks on
his inadequate sociology and his tendency to write on unpleasant
subjects, one of the most persistent forms of carping has been the
assertion that the work is obscure, difficult, prolix, extravagant, or
needlessly redundant. Worst of all is the suspicion that he did
it all on purpose. Such peevishness often means that the reviewer
experiences difficulty in finding what he already knows the work
should say, or difficulty with the manner of presentation. But,
as Randall Jarrell recently remarked to the nation, the objection to

the "difficulty" and complexity of modern literature is like showing General Eisenhower a picture of a man in full armor on horseback and saying, "Now there's what a *real* soldier looks like!"

Those who demand such simple-minded reduction are at heart apostles of the Positive Power of Wishful Thinking. A passionate commitment to realism (or truth, or the responsibility of the artist) demands a constant pressing to encompass and express the complexity of a universe filled not merely with the confusion of meaninglessness but a pervasive and Manichaean evil which can be seen in part in the momentary threat of nuclear vaporization and a scientifically precise control over the minds of men. What seems the strained exaggeration of nightmare may be worse when we awake. It was Kafka who said that he wanted to exaggerate until everything became clear. Kafka died in 1924, and in 1955 the present writer learned from a footnote that in 1943 the three sisters of Kafka passed through the gas chambers of Auswitz. Whatever else this sequence of dates may show, it is a comment on the element of fantasy in modern literature.

Part of Faulkner's prolixity can be put down to temperament, and this does him no discredit. Temperament is one aspect of genius. Another aspect of such genius strongly aware of complexity is that it creates and uses ways of seeing and knowing which pedantry has not yet classified. Later chapters of the present study will demonstrate how certain works of modern literature have transcended the dogmatic restrictions and requirements which the historians of literature have imposed. One such air-tight compartment is labeled Comedy. Our concern at this point is to consider Faulkner's diverse and versatile creation of comedy and the comic hero.

One striking thing about the comedy of the twentieth century is its difference from the comedy of Molière, Congreve, or even Goldsmith and from the theoretical prescriptions for comedy set out by Meredith and Bergson. In content, breadth, and diversity, the present Idea of the Comic is far closer to the violent and merciless spirit of Aristophanes. This greatly intensified and extended sense of the comic is a direct reflection of the climate of opinion which has produced it.

Comment on Greek and Elizabethan tragedy has been brilliant, and none of it more so than that written in the present century. One rediscovery brought about by the work of Jane Harrison, Cornford, and the others of their period was the psychological and social aspect of the tragic experience: its relation to the darker and more sinister underside of the group and individual consciousness. A somewhat similar process has occurred to extend our definition of the Comic. As we know, the Comic has always included a heavy content of the element which is loosely called "social," as in the sane and sophisticated comedy of Molière and of the eighteenth century. In the twentieth century the sense of the Comic has spread far beyond the narrow and civilized limits prescribed for it by Meredith, into that whole spectrum of personal, social, and cosmic awareness which is Man's conviction of his own absurdity.

If the psychologists are correct, the ultimate common denominator of laughter is the dirty joke. The dirtiest joke of all is the cosmic posture present-day Man has created for himself. On every side Man sees himself reflected as a buffoon, a worthless and degraded animal. Every force has been brought to bear to convince Man of his absurdity and to persuade him that he likes it, not merely the fatuousness of the "entertainment" media and a public education system dedicated to the fostering of mediocrity but the whole series of mechanisms devoted to stultifying Man's own sense of his dignity and importance: the cynical use of "motivational research" psychology to turn the processes of his own mind against him and the totalitarian technique of brainwashing, in which a systematic degradation of the individual is always the first step, to break down even the rationale for fighting back. It is not fear of hurricanes, floods, famine, or pestilence that drives Western Man to schizophrenia. To paraphrase Faulkner again, all other anxieties are swallowed up in the simple question: when will I be blown up? All the terror, the nihilism, the disgust, which disturb the present scene are man-created and man-sustained, not only impending atomic vaporization but also totalitarianism, the concentration camp, the ever-growing distaste for and fear of freedom itself, and the "lust for irresponsibility" which seems to seize nations and individuals alike. In our time, when the estimate of these conditions has grown from a largely ignored and discounted

minority report into the very fabric of the world-view itself, the
moral problem of the artist becomes acute.

The artist, of all men, must be the most aware. Of all the
areas of sensitivity, the truly great artist must possess a powerful
moral sense. Unquestionably, the most noble dedication an artist
in any medium and any age can undertake is the refusal to accept
the idea that Man is finished: to assert Man's essential nobility
even in a period of regression like the present; to press back against
the pressure of "reality" and to resist what has so aptly been
called "the suction of the Absurd."* The writer must do this in
an age of skepticism—not merely the half-baked sophistication
which asserts a belief in nothing but a society which proudly
asserts a total ignorance of anything (". . . the only people on
earth who brag publicly of being second-rate . . ."). In an era
when nothing is certain, the artist must somehow descend into
the lonely region of his own integrity and from that reservoir
draw the stubbornness and persistence to go on affirming, even in
the morass of what Man does, Man's essential nobility and the
categorical importance of his human responsibilities.

ii.

In an age of militant complacency, the function of the comic
artist is to be the Socratic gadfly; to strip naked as gently as
Goldsmith or as savagely as Swift the affectations or crimes of his
fellow men. The comic dramatist has and must have the majority
of opinion with him, but when the entire society is in need of a
purgative, the artist may be forced to the extremes of negative
example resorted to by Voltaire or Swift. If his disgust with
what man does to man is strong enough, he reacts with a savagery
which must be sufficient to express that disgust and still maintain
a reasonable degree of honesty, realism, and integrity.

* I recall with particular vividness one occasion on which Faulkner met a
class of mine. During the previous weeks, the reading assignments and the discussion had centered on works of modern literature in which the concept of the
Absurd figured or was implied. One young man asked: "Mr. Faulkner, is Mankind absurd?" More sharply than any reply of his I can remember, the answer
came: "No sir; he is not. Mankind is not absurd." I take this to mean that,
while Mankind is not inherently absurd—God not creating him so—many individual men engage in absurd behavior, ranging from the hilarious to the tragically destructive. Men can and do become absurd, or wicked, or foolish, or
weak, when the pressure of circumstances or their own wishes makes them so.

But this reaction is only one side of the coin. The other side of the Problem of Evil is the problem of goodness, and that problem for the artist is not so much how to recognize goodness as how to depict it. The condition of goodness is often completely static, beyond the accidents of the human condition. The difficulty lies in finding a way, still within realism and truth, to present a goodness that is dynamic and dramatic in an essentially do-nothing world. The diverse spectrum of Faulkner's comedy ranges from the gentle and sunny tolerance of "Was" and "Shingles for the Lord" through the tragicomic quixotism of Gavin Stevens and the dynamic moral force of Ratliff to the mechanistic Absurdity which the protagonists endure in *Pylon*. Yet in all these examples, whether the case be amusing or desperate, the evil is opposed by an element of active goodness. This dynamic of goodness may assert itself anywhere in the scale, between the easy and quietly amused chastisement of affectation, as in "My Grandmother Millard . . ." to the total (if totally ineffectual) and far from disinterested effort of the reporter in *Pylon* and the stoic commitment of Roger Shumann in the same novel. In some of the short stories, where nothing more is at stake than a comedy of manners, the moral comment may simply be presented from the author's third-person point of view. Where the situation contains what is sometimes called Natural Evil—in the form of tornadoes, floods, and so on—Faulkner seems not to consider these phenomena as evil at all, since they are a part of nature. But when the evil is purely human—what Man does to fellow man, even when at times this human evil seems aided by a malignancy which is almost Manichaean—there always seems to arise one of those quixotic and *manqué* Galahads like Byron Bunch, like Gavin Stevens, like V. K. Ratliff, who impose themselves between the innocent helplessness and the evil. In a brisk skirmish or in the long attrition of war, the outcome is seldom better than a draw. I have designated these men of stubborn good will as Faulkner's comic heroes.

3.

FAULKNER'S COMIC HEROES

THE FIRST FAULKNER COMIC hero is found in *Soldiers' Pay* (1927); two major comic heroes round off their long careers in *The Mansion* (1959). Evidently Faulkner attached some importance to the labors of the comic hero. As noted earlier, he viewed the human condition primarily in classic Christian terms: life is a deadly and ceaseless struggle between good and evil, light and darkness. In the Faulkner canon, the abstraction (theological or otherwise) must become action and the word become deed. To state again the major thesis of the present book: the great eternal constants of human existence, which are existential both as theological theory and human flesh, must be presented dramatically, as realism, in human terms expressed in human action. As a man's heart is, so he does. The emphasis is on the action; mere passive goodness is not enough. This can be seen once a few simple distinctions are made.

A systematic reading of the Faulkner canon leads to many discoveries: one of these is the surprising quantity of innocence contained there. This innocence is not to be confused with simple ignorance or dullness or with naïveté, which is a polite term for that quality in persons which causes them to go through life without seeing what is before their own noses. It is rather innocence in the pristine, theological sense: innocence which can move through malice and evil without being stained or corrupted. There is the innocence of some children, like the five-year-old Wall Snopes who trots unscathed and unafraid under the flashing teeth

and slashing hooves of the spotted horses. There are the several virgins (or even un-virgins) who move unmolested through all sorts of violence, as though by troops of unicorns defended: Lena Grove, Drusilla Hawk, and Patricia Robyn, the heroine of *Mosquitoes*. Or there are the boys and youths, like young Ike McCaslin, Bayard Sartoris and Ringo before they grow up, and Chick Mallison and Aleck Sander.

Perhaps all human life is an irremediable progress toward corruption. Certainly, ordinary human innocence cannot hold out against the corrosion of temporal life. Faulkner documents his awareness of this process by the quietly bitter way in which he presents his estimate of unfallen innocence: in Yoknapatawpha the most truly innocent creatures, whose inward hearts remain most completely unchanged in the passage of time, are the feeble-minded: Tawmy, Isaac Snopes, and above all, Benjy Compson.

The afflicted in mind have often been regarded with reverence. Both primitive people and sophisticated artists have an interest in them. Dostoyevsky once attempted to create the heroism of innocence in his "holy innocent," Prince Myshkin. Most critics today agree that *The Idiot* is a major novel in many ways but that it fails to make innocence heroic. Myshkin can remain innocent only because he is defective. Faulkner is far too much the major artist to pretend that innocence can remain undefiled. Children grow up; Lena Grove evades her obvious responsibilities in the aimless, careless pursuit of the worthless Lucas Burch; Drusilla marries John Sartoris and with him becomes corrupted by the lust for violence. The young men will grow up with their innocence drained away by the demands of the world as it is. Only the idiot escapes completely. This kind of purity is like virginity, and virginity, Mr. Compson said somewhere, is unnatural, because it is a state of non-fulfillment. Innocence is reserved to saints and idiots—those touched by God—and neither saints nor idiots can, by definition, become heroic, since the one has already surpassed the human level and the other can never reach it. Thus the major artist cannot project very much from a foundation of total innocence. What is wanted is not innocence but virtue. Virtue is used here in the sense defined by Aristotle, and by Milton when he dispraised that ". . . fugitive and cloistered virtue, unexercised

and unbreathed, that never sallies out and sees her adversary, but
slinks out of the race, where that immortal garland is to be run
for, not without dust and heat. Assuredly we bring not innocence
into the world, we bring impurity much rather; that which puri-
fies us is trial, and trial by what is contrary."

Thus the Faulkner comic hero, to be a hero, must be more
than passively a man of good will. He must wrestle with evil.
When tumbled into the dust, he must be willing, though bruised
in body and soul, to fight again. But, in another of those paradoxes which a searching, far-reaching consideration of morality
sooner or later uncovers, a further threat is revealed: in this very
willingness to aid the helpless and to tilt at whatever windmills
present themselves, there lies the seed of corruption and defeat.

Aristotle noted that the man who is exceptionally virtuous will
not serve as a tragic hero, and Louis L. Martz has recently reminded us that a figure on the side of the angels is not tragic. The
Faulkner comic hero is always on the side of the angels. But,
being neither saint nor holy idiot, he is merely human, with human
limitations and abilities. Since always and in all respects, Yoknapatawpha reflects the realistic and the actual, the human man is
never entirely free from the taint of human corruption. The
heroic figures in the work of Conrad (Lingard, Kurtz, Jim,
Heyst) often perform acts of benevolence and kindness or announce grandiose projects for the future, but usually their benevolence contains an insidious germ of self-interest or simple egoism,
however disinterested and charitable the action may seem to be.
By the preliminary use of a very broad generalization, we can
say that the Faulkner comic hero is subject to roughly the same
dangers; he will be successful only so far as his action is untainted
by self-interest. In the typical Faulkner pattern, the comic hero
is subjected to human temptation somewhere in the process of his
moral action, and if he succumbs to this temptation, he nearly
always fails in his endeavor.

In a typical instance, Horace Benbow fails to save Lee Goodwin, primarily because of his own incapacity and innocence. But
in both the formal and profoundly deeper senses, his failure is
rooted in the response of his own personality and his own guilty
relationship to the various women who figure in the Goodwin trial

and in his private life. Gavin Stevens fails at first—and it is a moral failure—to estimate the actual situation in *Intruder in the Dust* because he responds to the accusation against Lucas Beauchamp with his professional and sectional reflexes (the "professional rigidity" of Bergson), thus blocking for the time any effective sweep for that moral consciousness of his which is usually so sensitive. In the later novels, Gavin fails to protect Eula Varner Snopes and her daughter from Flem, from De Spain, and from the indignation of the town simply because he loves them both, and this love, however essentially pure and virtuous, represents Gavin's "conflict of interest."

In *Light in August,* it is much the same story with Byron Bunch, that ascetic and unworldly employee of the planing mill who has avoided the blandishments of the flesh and the devil for more than thirty years. Byron tells himself that he is providing food and shelter for Lena Grove and medical care for her when her illegitimate son is born only in a spirit of charity long after he knows he is in love with her.

Ratliff, the most able and most adroit of the Faulkner comic heroes simply because he is the most intelligent, the most perceptive, the least deceived and self-deceived of all, is nevertheless brought to his downfall in *The Hamlet.* He loses his running conflict with Flem Snopes when he is trapped by one of the oldest tricks in the world. So long as he does not succumb to the temptation of material goods, he is at least equal (if only that) to anything Flem can devise. His entirely human desire to get something for nothing brings him into the trap Flem has set.

Thus, each of the comic heroes commits himself to a struggle of some sort; for the major figures it is usually a protracted and continuing struggle to protect the innocent and helpless from the powers of evil. Within this virtuous action there is the interaction of temptation and self-interest, which brings about a greater or lesser degree of failure. The chapters to follow will relate each of the comic heroes to this pattern of commitment and involvement just defined and will attempt to establish to what extent each protagonist is in the pattern, as well as his significant differences from it.

ii.

Some Minor Figures

The Faulkner comic hero has now been defined as the man of good will—one who performs acts of kindness and benevolence even though this means self-denial and sacrifice or perhaps even personal danger.   In the fiction of Dostoyevsky, the most outwardly depraved of human monsters have a way of suddenly reversing themselves completely; a Raskolnikov or a Dimitri Karamazov from whose hands blood still drips will unexpectedly exhibit genuine depths of human feeling and concern.   Perhaps this inconsistency proves that Dostoyevsky was neurotic or merely demonstrates the notorious instability of the Russian national personality.   By contrast, Faulkner's characters are far more consistent, in the Aristotelian sense.   His monsters, such as Popeye or Jason Compson, never show a tendency toward amendment. Flem Snopes becomes outwardly respectable when the people he exploits (who are entirely predictable, if consistently irrational) seem to require respectability as a major condition for his uninterrupted rise to legitimate wealth and power.   Therefore, even at some expense and inconvenience, he carefully maintains respectability.   Such tragic figures as Sartoris, Sutpen, and Christmas remain tragic because they drive on in the most essential of tragic virtues: the persistence in a chosen line of conduct.   But tragic heroes are like meteors; they flare to incandescent heat in the violence of their fall and burn out suddenly.   There then remains in the Yoknapatawpha chronicle what more than one critic has commented on: the less intense but more enduring recollection of episodes and character; the qualities of serenity, affection, loyalty, and goodness.

Faulkner is an "atmospheric" writer. This term usually means that a writer so described achieves certain effects and to some extent ultimate ends by the over-all mood or emotional feeling which the work conveys over and beyond its actual "intellectual" content.   If it is not a contradiction to say so, Faulkner's work contains not one but several atmospheres, often within the same work and sometimes almost simultaneously.   There may be the "glamorous fatality" of the Sartorises, the hopeless sense of impending disaster in *Pylon,* or as in different parts of *Sanctuary,* the felt menace of Popeye or the uproariously vulgar sequence of Red's funeral and the ensuing exchange between Uncle Bud and the three madams. But under these, like a minor strain of music, there is the prevailing atmosphere of goodness.

Aside from the major comic heroes like Ratliff and Gavin Stevens and minor ones like Chick Mallison, all of whom appear throughout the length of more than one book, the atmosphere of goodness is sustained also by those good and decent people who appear for only one episode or scene or in a short story. It is one more evidence of Faulkner's ability to create character that these briefly-seen individuals stick so firmly in the mind. A typical example is Henry Armstid's wife, Martha,* in *Light in August.* Martha views Lena Grove's unabashed condition of unwed pregnancy with all the cold and furious outrage of her rural, fundamentalist Protestant upbringing, but she gives Lena the eggmoney she has painfully scraped and saved, even though she will not hand it to Lena herself or even talk to her. *Light in August* alone would provide a half-dozen or so such people, each shown once but vividly, in the act of helping others. The stories in *Knight's Gambit,* for instance, involve Gavin Stevens. In most of them he is the county attorney bent on seeing justice done and as such is more often a spectator and commentator than a protagonist. Yet in each of these stories, particularly in "Hand Upon the Waters" and "Tomorrow," as distinct from the ordinary detective story, there are authentic human creations, people who are caught up in love and hate, altruism and greed; in short, all the passions of the human heart.

iii.

Joe Gilligan

Typical as these briefly glimpsed figures are, they do not represent an extension or a development, as do such minor heroes

---

* I am aware, as everyone is now, that Henry's wife is called Martha in one book, Lula in another, and is nameless in a third. Not only do thirty years separate the events in *The Hamlet* from the events of the other two books, but her character is profoundly different. Also, Henry is demented and crippled *ca.* 1907 but friendly, vigorous, and unmarked *ca.* 1930. Is it possible there is more than one Henry Armstid? (Southern hill people tend to be prolific.) The interested scholar is directed to Mr. Faulkner's little note at the beginning of *The Mansion.*

as Joe Gilligan or the reporter in *Pylon*. *Soldiers' Pay* is Faulkner's first novel and has certain obvious faults that any first novel
is apt to have. It is different from a typical Faulkner work primarily because it seems to express or imply so little below the
surface of things. Plot, motivation, and characterization are
adequate and convincing, if no more than that. The novel becomes
interesting when it is seen as adumbrating the three types of
figures considered in the present study: comic hero, villain, tragic
hero. The tragic hero is Donald Mahon, a World War I combat
pilot who is being sent home, shattered in mind and body, to die.
The villain is Januarius Jones, a draft-dodger and amateur woman-
chaser. The comic hero is Joe Gilligan, a hard-drinking, un-
reconstructed and unabashed goldbricking enlisted man who discovers Lieutenant Mahon on a train with only the overworked
porter to look after him and who appoints himself, without any
particular noise or heroics, as watchdog and guardian to the dying
man, who obviously is unable to care for himself.

Gilligan is joined in this effort by Margaret Powers, a young
war widow. Joe performs the usual actions of the comic hero:
protecting the helpless from cruelty and exploitation. He eases
the pitiful remnant of life that Mahon has left. He fends off
Jones's efforts to seduce Margaret and protects Emmy, the maid,
until the very end of the book. Some time before Mahon dies,
Joe has come to realize that he is in love with Margaret and asks
her to marry him, but like Byron Bunch or Gavin Stevens, whom
he clearly foreshadows, he is rejected. Like many comic heroes,
he is not particularly successful in what he tries to do. Margaret
Powers also carries out many of the functions of the comic hero
and does so with more success than Gilligan. She knows how to
protect Mahon from any and all forces that would disturb him: his
bumbling father, his worthless fiancée Cecily, and the heedless
actions of the rest of the townspeople.

iv.

Horace Benbow

Horace Benbow is characterized early in *Sanctuary* as a man
"given to talk and not much else." There is almost no field of
human endeavor at which he has not failed—as a lover, as a

husband, as a stepfather, as an attorney, and even as a Red Cross worker in the war. Present-day psychology has much to say about the role of the subconscious in the dynamics of self-punishment and the wish to fail. Without delving too deeply, it can be said that Horace might have made a reasonably successful life for himself if it had not been for his fatal tendency to throw himself into the troubles of others. His part in *Sartoris* is not an important one, but he is seen there as closely, perhaps too closely, involved with his sister Narcissa (who is very different from the Narcissa she will become later) and unable or at least unwilling to free himself from the seductive influence of Belle Mitchell, who is married but with whom he is involved. In *Sanctuary,* he becomes emotionally involved in the situation of the Goodwins as soon as it comes to his attention. The combination of innocence, ineffectuality, and emotional involvement clearly designates him as the comic hero but as one who is an almost total failure.

On the literal level of his performance as defense counsel for Lee Goodwin, Horace's failure is so abysmal that his innocent client is not only convicted but is hauled away and burned to death by a mob. But Goodwin's fate, dreadful as it is, is not our point of interest here. Lee is convicted on the perjured testimony of Temple Drake, but the ambitious and unscrupulous prosecutor is steered to Temple by Narcissa, Horace's sister, who is determined to punish Horace and bring him back into line for having involved himself (and hence the family name) in the "disgraceful" events and publicity of the Goodwin trial. On the surface, Horace is guilty of nothing more than failing to realize that perjury and malice can be used to convict an innocent man. But in the deeper sense—this being the modern age—Horace fails to estimate Narcissa and Temple accurately and take effective countermeasures precisely because they are women and because of the self-accusation in his relationships to women in general: the adultery with his wife before she became his wife and the semi-incestuous feeling which he accuses himself of having toward his stepdaughter. Central to the immediate action is his feeling for Ruby (Lamar) Goodwin, the common-law wife of Lee. Precisely because his moral energies are enervated by his feeling of guilt and his attention distracted by it, he cannot see what Temple and Narcissa are going to do until it is too late.

It should be pointed out that Horace has not committed any overt action for which he should feel guilty, with the possible exception of taking Mitchell's wife (to whom he is now married). His weakness is that he allows women to make him think that he *ought* to feel guilty. He does not have any carnal designs on Ruby Goodwin—not consciously and perhaps not even unconsciously. The great bundle of guilt that this hapless hero carries about with him is after all only grafted onto his basic ineptitude.

To pass moral judgment on Horace is pointless. He is inept and perhaps weak in a number of ways, but he is neither a moral nor a physical coward. It would be possible to say that any lawyer, even an inexperienced one appointed by the court, might have done better for Goodwin, but even the best lawyer cannot beat perjured testimony if he has nothing concrete with which to refute it. To attribute all Horace's effort to a simple lust for Ruby, even an unconscious one, is to deny him credit as a man and as an attorney for doing what he can to defend a client he is convinced is innocent.

v.

Wilbourne and the Convict: Two Aspects of Eros

One type of hero that is conspicuously absent from the present study is the erotic hero, the hero as romantic lover, someone like Romeo or Tristan, who finds his fulfillment in the expression of his love for a woman, on a grand and usually tragic scale. Critical comment has noted that Faulkner has not chosen to deal with this subject often and almost never in what might be called the full romantic vein. The many destructive, consuming relationships that we find, such as those between Christmas and Miss Burden or Quentin and Caddy, can hardly be described as "romantic." Whenever Faulkner has shown us the young man in love, he is usually the lover as clown—"horribly in love." No lover escapes this comic agony entirely—from George Farr in *Soldiers' Pay* to Gavin Stevens in *The Town* and *The Mansion*. In this attitude Faulkner is much nearer that of the Greeks, who

saw a violent attachment which overwhelms balance and reason as
a terrible affliction rather than something to be sentimentalized.

In the sense just described, there is perhaps no single erotic
hero in all the Faulkner canon (unless we count Manfred de Spain,
who doesn't amount to much). A clear understanding of this
distinction of types is vital. There are the clown-like types just
mentioned, and the present section of this study deals for the most
part with men who fail in moral endeavor because of various kinds
of involvement with women. Byron Bunch and Gavin Stevens
go through considerable inconvenience for the women they love.
But the hero who flings down honor, career, and even life itself in
the conviction he is proving something is rare: the only example
is Harry Wilbourne in *The Wild Palms,* a book fairly well established as not the best in the Faulkner canon. The twin heroes of
this diptychous novel present an instructive contrast. The tall
convict is far nearer the usual pattern of the Faulkner comic hero;
Wilbourne is more atypical. Only passing attention will be given
to Wilbourne's case, primarily for the purpose of ironic contrast,
which is also his function in the novel. Even so, Wilbourne seems
to have a deep subconscious unwillingness and regret throughout
his tortured relationship with Charlotte.

Critics have often complained of the lack of essential structural
relation between the Charlotte-Harry *Wild Palms* and the "Old
Man" half of the same novel. It is true that the two halves have
been published separately and that the two sets of characters never
encounter each other. But they are linked by a similarity of
subject matter; they are the two halves of Faulkner's ironic consideration of the conflict between love and duty.* Harry Wilbourne and Charlotte Rittenmeyer give up everything (including
Harry's medical career and Charlotte's husband and children) to
escape the toils of bourgeois respectability and convention, to try
to live entirely in the perilous freedom of their love for each other.
The tall convict in the "Old Man" section is by accident given
freedom and a chance to live with the woman he has rescued but
turns it all down to go back and serve out his sentence at Parchman. Harry throws over duty and responsibility for love, the

* The structure of *The Wild Palms* has been ably defended, notably by Olga
W. Vickery in *The Novels of William Faulkner* (Baton Rouge, La.: Louisiana
State University Press, 1959), p. 156 ff.

tall convict throws over the woman he rescued for duty and responsibility; they both end up in jail. Properly speaking, Harry Wilbourne's case is more nearly tragic than comic, since the totality of his commitment leads inevitably to the death of Charlotte.

The tall convict (otherwise unnamed) represents a rigid, lonely, and austere morality which can be compared to some extent with that of Byron Bunch and Ike McCaslin, but with an interesting difference. Byron and Ike each find in time that moral imperatives are in conflict with love for the woman in their lives; the tall convict lives through an agony of impatience and frustration in order to be free of the woman he has rescued. In several interesting ways he prefigures the subsequent life of Mink Snopes. Like the young Mink, his severe and crippling inadequacies mark him as a distinctly atypical human and hero, almost enough so to remove him from consideration as a hero at all.

The thing the fat convict finds hardest to believe in the tall convict's story is that he would be ". . . toting one piece up and down the country day and night for over a month . . ."[1] and do nothing about it. Yet this is precisely the case. He is no plaster saint: he does have women on the journey back and is an accomplished crap-shooter. He resents and complains about his enforced role of nursemaid and caretaker. But none of this stands in the way of his own sense of integrity, however cramped and limited that sense may be. His sense of duty tells him to return to the levee where he started and serve out his sentence.

To sum up, he has most of the virtues. He is taciturn rather than cheerful, and certainly is ignorant and naïve, but in the social emergency of the flood he does what he is told and attempts to carry out orders promptly and completely. This same persistence is what takes him on his incredible trip down the river. His orders were plain: take the boat, pick up a woman in a tree and a man on a cottonhouse, and bring them back. His response is plain also. Throughout the nightmare experiences on the river and on the small island covered with snakes, his one effort is to carry out those orders. He shows endurance, courage, resourcefulness, and restraint. He had forgotten, he says about one episode, how good it is to get money in exchange for hard, back-

breaking work, such as the cotton-farming he does at the peni-
tentiary. Yet he uses this money he has earned himself to get
back up the river not only with the woman and the baby but with
the boat as well. It would have been much easier without the
boat, but it never occurs to him simply to let the boat go. Even
when the woman makes it plain that she would like to stay with
him, he does not swerve from his purpose. As soon as he can
find a peace officer at the point where he started out, he sur-
renders himself formally. His comment at this point sums up
the man himself very well, with all his severe virtues and severe
limitations: "All right. . . . Yonder's your boat, and here's the
woman. But I never did find that bastard on the cottonhouse."[2]

The final irony is the disposition of his case. Ordinarily, one
supposes, such fidelity and integrity, not to mention the saving
of human life, might be rewarded by a reduction in sentence or
even a pardon. The convict had been declared dead when he failed
to return after a few days, and because of political machinations
and red tape, it is decided that the only way out of the bureaucratic impasse is to add ten years to the convict's sentence for
"attempting to escape."

This austere and ascetic man has one great failing that must
not be overlooked: his refusal (for it is that) to accept a commitment to the human condition. He does not want the involvement,
the impediment, the daily wear and tear of living with a woman
and children. It is not that his return to prison prevents his
taking up life with the woman—it is exactly the opposite; he has
turned his back on the prospect of life with the woman with something amounting to revulsion: "He remembered it: how there
were times, seconds, at first when if it had not been for the baby
he might have, might have tried. . . . But they were just seconds
because in the next instant his whole being would seem to flee
the very idea in a kind of savage and horrified revulsion; he would
find himself looking from a distance at this millstone which the
force and power of blind and risible Motion had fastened upon
him. . . ."[3]

To the extent already mentioned, Harry Wilbourne is an
erotic hero. In traditional theological terms, the relationship he
and Charlotte share is both love excessive and love perverted.

Constant reference is made throughout this half of the novel to Harry's rigid Protestant background; his passive reluctance and ultimate tragic bungling can be explained by his inability or unwillingness to shake off the awareness of guilt.

vi.

Charles Mallison and Aleck Sander

Like his uncle Gavin, Charles Mallison appears in several books of the Yoknapatawpha series. With some simplification it can be stated that he appears as comic hero in only one of them, *Intruder in the Dust,* in company with his partner in crime, Aleck Sander. This novel turns out to be more Chick's book than Aleck Sander's, simply because Chick's problems are more complex. Aleck Sander's heroism is genuine, and the tasks he undertakes are full of very real physical danger. Both he and Chick know that Beat Four and the Gowries are inclined to lynch any Negro they can find at the moment, much more a Negro caught messing with Vinson Gowrie's grave. Nevertheless, courageous and demanding as it is, this action is all that is demanded of him. There is none of the guilty, agonizing reappraisal of culture and self that Chick must fight his way through. Simply because Lucas is the same color, Aleck Sander does not have to define himself in relation to Lucas Beauchamp. Lucas, though forbidding, Olympian, and austere, is for Aleck Sander simply an older and highly respected member of the Negro community.

As seen here, Chick offers an interesting contrast to the normal pattern of the Faulkner comic hero. In the usual pattern, the hero begins by assuming that he works from the purest and most altruistic motives; only later does the guilty awareness of self-interest begin to creep in. Chick begins with a powerful awareness of resentment and an unwelcome sense of obligation in his relationship to Lucas. Four years before, when he was twelve years old, Chick had fallen through thin ice while hunting, and Lucas had pulled him out. Chick ignorantly (and childishly) attempts to "pay for" his life with several of the cheap and easy expedients which are customarily used on Negroes, but Lucas eludes the gesture each time without apparent effort and Chick is left angrier and more beholden than before. When Lucas is

arrested for the murder of Vinson Gowrie, Chick quickly seizes
the opportunity to help, to save Lucas' life in turn, and be free of
his obligation. Chick is only sixteen years old, but he is morally
sensitive enough to realize that his first response to the emergency
is painfully close to the attitude of the red-necks who want to lynch
Lucas: at last this uppity, high-nosed old nigger is going to get
"if not what he deserved then at least what he had been asking
for" for so long. Under the sting of this shameful realization, he
is able to work his way to the realization that within the human
condition all are responsible for all and the process of "paying off"
debts is illusory.

The moral maturing of Charles Mallison is, of course, the real
content of *Intruder in the Dust* and not the hocus-pocus of the
various burials and disinterments of Vinson Gowrie. The matter
of this element is not major Faulkner. The humor is not so outrageous as in *The Hamlet,* and the quality of grotesqueness is
not powerful enough to be elevated to the condition of art, as it
has been elsewhere in the Faulkner canon. What is important in
the novel is the very real moral, social, and racial comment the
novel has to offer. Chick has to define himself in relation to
Negroes, the law, his nation (the United States), his region (the
South), and the mores of that South, including the custom of
segregation. With the active help of Aleck Sander and Miss
Habersham and the belated collaboration of his uncle and the
sheriff, he is able to save Lucas from lynching, if only by proving
that someone else did the murder.

Gavin Stevens (as he tends to be under pressure or tension)
is his most garrulous self in this novel, expressing estimates of
American civilization, segregation, the patterns history makes, and
the South. He offers his solution to the current race problem (a
solution Mr. Faulkner was to repeat on his own ten years later,
in an address before the Jefferson Society at the University of
Virginia).[4] But most important of all, Gavin is the source of
advice and illumination to Chick when Chick is trying to resolve
his own attitudes. Chick feels the mixed emotions that he does
because he is a Southerner, which means that he is part of a
section and shares a historical heritage that is distinct if not
unique. Because of this distinctive history, the awareness of which

is charged with emotional overtones and undertones, he has inherited also certain cultural and social points of view, some of
which he must affirm and some deny: the problem is to know
which is which. He is thus both more lucky and less lucky than
the American from almost any other part of the country who is
far less personally involved in the tension between past, present,
and future of a particular part of a particular region. This tension
is, of course, one of the great ground themes of Mr. Faulkner's
work: place and people, social history and segregation, the plantation system and Pickett's charge, all compressed into one
instantaneous, continuous moment, all working powerfully on the
individual in the present:

"It's all *now* you see. Yesterday wont be over until tomorrow and
tomorrow began ten thousand years ago. For every Southern boy
fourteen years old, not once but whenever he wants it, there is the
instant when it's still not yet two oclock on that July afternoon in
1863, the brigades are in position behind the rail fence, the guns are
laid and ready in the woods and the furled flags are already loosened to
break out and Pickett himself with his long oiled ringlets and his hat
in one hand probably and his sword in the other looking up the hill
waiting for Longstreet to give the word and it's all in the balance, it
hasn't happened yet, it hasn't even begun yet, it not only hasn't begun
yet but there is still time for it not to begin against that position and
those circumstances which made more men than Garnett and Kemp-
ner and Armstead and Wilcox look grave yet it's going to begin, we
all know that, we have come too far with too much at stake and that
moment doesn't need even a fourteen-year-old boy to think *This time.
Maybe this time. . . .*"[5]

The essence of this statement is that the individual must go
on, over and over, attempting to define both himself and his relation to history. On this one occasion at least, a dynamic effort
toward goodness has succeeded. Within the limit of the few days
covered by *Intruder in the Dust,* two teenage boys and an old
lady are completely successful in their effort to save Lucas Beauchamp. This success sets them apart from any other comic heroes
in the Faulkner canon. But as Chick also learns, one success does
not make a summer, much less a lifetime. His uncle tells him,
" 'Some things you must always be unable to bear. Some things
you must never stop refusing to bear. Injustice and outrage and

dishonor and shame. No matter how young you are or how old you have got. Not for kudos and not for cash: your picture in the paper nor money in the bank either. Just refuse to bear them. . . .' "[6]

These words by Gavin Stevens might serve as one version of the code of the quixotic comic hero. They will serve also as a bridge from those comic heroes thus far considered—who, because of a more restricted scope or less serious opposition have been designated "minor"—to those who are designated "major."

1. William Faulkner, *The Wild Palms* (New York: Random House, 1939), p. 334.

2. *Ibid.*, p. 278.

3. *Ibid.*, pp. 334-35.

4. *Faulkner in the University*, ed. Frederick L. Gwynn and Joseph L. Blotner (Charlottesville, Va.: University of Virginia Press, 1959), pp. 209-27.

5. William Faulkner, *Intruder in the Dust* (New York: Random House, 1948), pp. 194-95.

6. *Ibid.*, p. 206.

4.

THE COMIC HERO:
GAVIN STEVENS

WHAT GAVIN STEVENS STANDS for in the fiction of William
Faulkner and what he is in himself may seem ambiguous or
inconsistent, but they are not, once an adequate prespective is
taken. This chapter hopes to demonstrate that Gavin's complex
behavior and turgid rhetoric are simply the complex response of
a sensibility grounded in a point of view that is unified and even
consistent. Gavin turns up in as many places as Conrad's Marlow
and in the nature of his personality and profession is apt to observe or be involved in anything that happens in Yoknapatawpha.
His profession is that of attorney; his hobby is observing human
beings, their motives and feelings, and speculating on the content
of the human heart. His relaxation, when the noise and pressures of the world become too great, is translating the Bible into
classical Greek. His faults are that he sometimes jumps too
hastily to conclusions and that he talks too much—the occupa-
tional disease of the legal profession. His fatal flaw is an imperfect sense of ironic detachment; he has such a sense, but it seems
to operate either too well at the wrong time or not at all. The
result is often laceration of heart and spirit.

Gavin appears so often for the same reason Marlow does: he
is intelligent and literate and given to speculation and comment
when something interests him. He has the speculative sort of
mind which, in talking out a situation, helping himself to understand it, also explains it to the reader. Horace Benbow is one
clear prototype for Gavin, even with all their differences of weak-

ness and strength.   Relating Gavin to Marlow suggests comparison with another Conrad figure, a comparison so obvious that it
should go a long way to explain Gavin.   In the words Stein applied
to Lord Jim, Gavin is romantic.

This incisive comment cuts to the heart of what Marlow's
speculation had only clouded.   Jim's romanticism allows him to
see himself as "a fine fellow," far nobler and braver than he is,
and in this belief he attempts to act.   Gavin's romanticism is
somewhat different, and it is of at least two kinds.   One is like
Jay Gatsby's extraordinary gift for hope—a heightened sensitivity
to the promises of life.   Within this romantic readiness, Gavin's
sense of irony is adequate if no more.   Unlike Jim, he does not
often overestimate his own abilities and usually knows when he
is going to be defeated; still he is never deterred.   The other romantic quality is more unconscious, more subtle and pervasive,
and hence more fatally destructive.   It is the constant tendency
to overestimate the goodness and decency of others.   On the level
of conscious speculation, he is capable of wit and irony, in viewing
the antics of the Snopeses, for instance.   Evidently this irony is
only cerebral; on the unconscious level he never remembers that
many people would not be gentle and compassionate even if they
could.   He wants to believe that people want to be better than
they are or seem to be, and on this basis he acts.

We lack the precise adjective for this quality.   "Quixotic" and
"foolish" are often used, yet Gavin is never self-deceived or a fool.
It is a matter of degree of excess, and excessiveness is the key to
it all.   Excess is authentically and indisputably the essential attitude of the comic hero: the quixotic determination to defend whoever and whatever he decides must be defended, whether defending
is requested or even desired or not.   In Gavin's case the results
are often worse than merely painful.   To cite his early career,
there is the twin fiasco of the Cotillion Ball and the abortive im-
peachment of Manfred de Spain.   Throughout his career there
is his inability to anticipate the deviousness of Flem's motives
and rapacity.   Paradoxically, he fails even more tragically on the
rare occasions when he underestimates virtue, as in his last interview with Eula.   Thus Gavin is weakest when strength is most

needed, is most nearly correct when imputing goodness to the truly good.

ii.

Gavin has many parts to play in the Faulkner canon, from the purely "surface-level" appearances in such detective stories as "Smoke" and "An Error in Chemistry" to his role as the grief-stricken, all-but-helpless defender of humanity who tries to stand between Flem Snopes and the two women who are, legally at least, Flem's wife and daughter. For the present writer, there is something not quite convincing about the part Gavin plays in the novella *Knight's Gambit* and in *Requiem for a Nun:* he is too much the master of the situation, too much the unflustered stage manager who not only knows what is best for people to do next to obtain the ends of truth and justice but even knows, without any anguish at all, exactly how he is going to make them do it. It is not that he is less a good man, or even less a human and understanding one; it is only that he is less interesting. Above all, in *Requiem for a Nun,* he is distinctly not the comic hero that we know, with all his anguish and passion. There is anguish in that play/novel, but it is the anguish of Temple and Gowan, and the passion is the lonely immolation of Nancy Mannigoe. To be sure, Gavin is as bent on justice, but he functions as a sort of infallible *deus ex machina* and is seemingly no more anguished than the governor is.

There are other contradictions also. Between *Knight's Gambit* and *The Town,* which, in part at least, cover the same span of years, there are radical differences in fairly important matters of fact; these would not be cleared up until the publication of *The Mansion.* The other stories in the *Knight's Gambit* collection, though not major Faulkner, are usually well worth reading in their own right. Most of them are older than *Knight's Gambit* and at first glance seem to present the same uncomplicated image of Gavin that the novella does. But there is a difference. I have used the term "surface-level" to describe the part played by Gavin himself in these detective stories based on Gavin's career as county attorney. Some of them, particularly the one called "Tomorrow," have a great deal to say that is true and permanent about the human heart; still it is the hearts of the murderers and those who love or hate them that are put under scrutiny. Gavin is usually able to establish an acceptable degree of justice in his legal cases, even though sometimes the law itself must be fairly roughly handled to bring that justice about. Even when Gavin is not the central focus of interest, some generalizations can be drawn from these stories about his career as county attorney. He exhibits three major areas of concern in carrying out his duties. These are, in the order of increasing importance: (1) enforcing ideal justice rather than the letter of the law, if the two conflict; (2) speculation on what justice is; (3) speculation on the ultimate motives of the human heart.

Intruder in the Dust is a rather special book in the Faulkner canon, since both heroism and justice triumph, at least during the few days covered by the story. Gavin's actions as comic hero are special also, reversing the usual pattern. He begins by being in the wrong, sees his error, then bends every effort to see justice done. Gavin's initial behavior is interesting as a clear example of the Bergsonian "professional reflex." Lucas Beauchamp has been accused of shooting a white man in the back. He has been found standing over the body with a freshly fired pistol, his own, in his pocket. So far, the only thing that has saved Lucas is the fact that it is the week end, and the Gowries never lynch on a Sunday. Lucas has always been "high-nosed and stiff-necked" and has a calmness and self-sufficiency which is at least half-consciously arrogance. He has simply never bothered to conceal the casual contempt he feels for most people, particularly the rednecks. Half-felt, rather than stated, the thing white Yoknapatawpha will never forgive Lucas for is neglecting to "act like a nigger." Gavin and Chick feel, along with the rest of the white people and most of the Negroes, that Lucas is about to get ". . . if not what he deserves than what he has been asking for all these years." Gavin does not refuse to take the case, even though he says: "I dont defend murderers who shoot people in the back."

To give Gavin his due, it must be stated that the evidence looks absolutely cut and dried and that most of his exasperation grows out of Lucas' arrogant and absolute refusal (as Gavin sees it) to tell anything directly—he will never bother to deny that he did the shooting, for instance. After Chick and Aleck Sander and frail little old Miss Habersham have gone in the middle of the night and dug up the body, the way is then cleared for the re-establishment of Gavin as the acutely sensitive moral agent he usually is. His understandable exasperation with Lucas only helps remind us he is human, rather than an insufferable prig who is always right about everything. This recovery of his moral sensitivity is firmly established by the instant rapport between himself and Miss Habersham, when he and Sheriff Hampton are going to open the grave legally. The Gowries allow themselves to be shown what is actually in the grave, and Beat Four is quickly able to forget Lucas and leave the real murderer to his own family. It well may be that nothing permanent has been accomplished, except that old high-nosed, stiff-necked Lucas Beauchamp is still alive and comes strolling into Gavin's office to pay off his lawyer. Sixteen-year-old Charles Mallison has learned something, and perhaps his uncle has too, who can say: " 'I said it's all right to be proud. It's all right even to boast. Just don't stop.' "

iii.

Before the publication of *The Town* in 1957 and *The Mansion* in 1959, Faulkner had not presented a fully developed, chrono-logical history of Gavin's career centered in Gavin's own con-sciousness—that is to say, an account of Gavin's own moral de-velopment. In *Knight's Gambit* and *Intruder in the Dust,* Gavin is seen as commentator or chorus, and the action covers a rela-tively brief chronological span. In contrast, *The Town* presents the twin spheres of Gavin's heroism in an account which spans not merely days or weeks but decades. One sphere of his life is love for Eula and Linda; the other is his position, shared with Ratliff, as the defender of Yoknapatawpha against Snopesism. To some extent the public and the private spheres are separable, but more and more the reader senses the process of merging, of growing into a single mode of being.

Gavin's relation to Flem Snopes and Snopesism in *The Town* (and that of Ratliff also) is different from the relation of Ratliff to the same evils in *The Hamlet,* largely because of the very great difference in the aims and aspirations of Flem himself. In

The Hamlet, Flem is amoral rapacity personified, and the reader is forced ultimately to realize that, in the most absolute of terms, Flem has not learned to care what people think of him. In *The Town,* Flem has begun to discover that respectability is an absolute requirement for getting to the top, and inconvenient as it may be, he must modify not only his own behavior but also check that of his more outrageous relatives. At the beginning of *The Town,* only Ratliff, fresh from his major defeat, is in a position to appreciate the danger which threatens. Gavin, from the vantage point of class, education, and profession, is inclined to view the antics of the red-neck *arrivistes* with little more than amusement. After the "Centaur in Brass" episode, Gavin's amusement changes to alarm, and he realizes that Snopes-watching is a full-time occupation. The water tank that contains the scraps of brass stands as one of Flem's enduring public monuments, a specific object in the growing Snopes mythology. The skirmish of the stolen brass was only a skirmish, resulting only in Flem's being forced to resign as superintendent of the power plant. This can be seen in retrospect as a turning point in Flem's career, the point at which he discovered respectability and began eliminating the cruder Snopeses on his own, thus leaving Gavin and Ratliff with little to do in the public sector.

As the years bring their changes, even the need for such a guardian of the public weal will diminish. What Gavin is never free of is his commitment to Eula Varner Snopes and her daughter Linda. In the long history of his agonizing defeats and Pyrrhic victories, this constancy will be often frustrated but never absent. In all he does in what he calls his "belated and clowning adolescence," his intentions are consistent and clear to him. Ratliff says of him: "It was his fate and doom . . . to been born into . . . that fragile and what you might call gossamer-sinewed envelope of boundless and hopeless aspiration Old Moster [gave] him." His ineptness and the pathetic humiliation he endures in public are simply an ineptness of means, not ends. In the early years his efforts result in a public scandal so funny as to border on the grotesque; in later years he will not know what to do, and the result will be tragedy.

Like every other local male between nine and ninety, Gavin

has seen the way Eula looks and moves, and his response is basic and disorganizing. In Gavin's case we can see that it is more than simple lust; he is quixotically convinced that he alone can fully apprehend Eula's magnificent and so-far dormant potential. For Gavin, the summons to action is imperative; he wants to see Eula accepted as an equal by the ladies of Jefferson. In a series of what he hopes are subtle maneuvers, Mrs. Snopes receives her invitation to the Christmas Cotillion. Gavin knows perfectly well that Eula is Manfred de Spain's mistress; this action throws down the gauntlet to Manfred, and the result is what Chick's father calls the "great Rouncewell Panic." This episode constitutes a bawdy and mock-heroic public duel between Gavin and his rival. All the strategy and tactics with the flowers, de Spain's red roadster with its cutout, the rakehead, the fist fight, and the corsage with unmentionable components make up a comedy of manners which is exquisitely funny to the reader and excruciating to Gavin. Gavin is hopelessly outmatched, but he cannot seem to stop caring. More than this, he is keenly aware that the entire situation is magnified (if that is possible) in the attention it gets, and that his family and professional status makes it even more the property of the public at large. He has tried to express his love for Eula in the only practical way he can think of and the result is to confirm and underscore what everyone had suspected all along.

After the fiasco of the Cotillion Ball and the fist fight, there is the further spectacle of the futile attempt to have De Spain impeached. Gavin is not sure what he is charging Manfred with, but he wants him charged with something. In all the uproar, Eula asks Gavin to meet her privately at his office. She offers to give him then and there the thing she has assumed (along with the rest of Jefferson, he now realizes) must be the one thing he wants from her. It is not the bluntness of Eula's offer of her body which repels Gavin, nor even her promiscuity; it is the lack of importance she attaches to giving it to *him*, the casual indifference with which the offer is made. If the agony of Gavin's *"Don't touch me"* seems excessive, we should remember that his response is not merely that of the *cavalier servente* who finds his lady only soiled flesh after all. It is the total response of that fragile, gossamer-sinewed, boundless aspiration. Gavin has been proceeding energetically on the assumption that this blunt-spoken and uncomplicated young woman not only can be but wants to be elevated to some sort of abstract status on par with Helen and Isolde and that the transformation can be accomplished by Gavin's unaided will.

He senses at once that Eula would not have made the offer on her own. Simple ego would cause him to decline Eula's explanation that she dislikes unhappiness and uproar and has decided to take a few minutes off to pacify Gavin. He cannot delude himself that Manfred is frightened enough to send her. It can only be that Flem has sent her, to put an end to the uproar. Out of this newer agony, he can say: ". . . nothing can hurt you if you refuse it, not even a brass-stealing Snopes. And nothing is of value that costs nothing. . . . Don't worry about your husband. Just say I represent Jefferson and so Flem Snopes is my burden too." He sends her away. Gavin does not renounce his love for Eula—he will never do that—he simply faces and accepts her simple inability to feel for him anything like his feeling for her. He has been made powerfully aware of Eula's honesty and the sexual directness she inherits from old Will Varner: *"I am, I want, I will and so here goes."* He overreaches as usual in his reaction: he tends half-consciously to see this non-romantic directness and readiness as a spiritual and even moral coarseness in Eula. He gives up the woman but retains the dream. All his subsequent behavior—what Ratliff calls simply "not losing Helen" —can be explained in terms of this dream. In every sense except legal and physical fact, Gavin is married to Eula—not *the* Eula that is, but the Eula Gavin imagined, and he has married her for better or for worse. Having married the Snopes named Eula, he has married that ". . . whole damned entire connection she married into" as well. This is the basis also of his private myth concerning Linda. Linda is not, could not be, the child of Flem. Since Eula is not Gavin's wife in fact but should have been, then Linda is not his child but ought to be, hence she is. This myth explains much of his subsequent behavior toward Linda—why, for instance, he resists the idea of marrying her.

The history of Gavin's devotion to Linda can best be described by Ratliff's description of him as "the man that was still trying to lay down his life for her maw if he could jest find somebody that wanted it." In Linda, Gavin at last finds the appropriate field for his quixotic and heroic impulses: he will save Linda Snopes from Snopesism. As he says, to save Jefferson from a Snopes is a duty, but to save a Snopes from a Snopes is a privilege, an honor, a pride, a joy. Once more Gavin is willing to risk being thought ridiculous (or worse) by attempting to help a woman he loves. He wants for her what a father should want, the best that can be had. She must be freed not merely from Flem but from all of it: "It was Jefferson itself which was the mortal foe since Jefferson was Snopes." Gavin's bustling plans to send Linda to a good school brings on a series of devious counter-moves from Flem. According to Ratliff, once Linda is married and has a name of her own, Flem's power to blackmail Eula and the Varners will be gone, and with it Flem's last chance for the Varner money and the de Spain bank. Once more Eula summons Gavin and tells him to marry Linda. Gavin cannot believe that he should, even when Eula tells him that Manfred and old Will are not meekly going to give Flem everything. In the anguished days that follow, Gavin has an agony of regret for many things. One is the memory of his "frank" and sophisticated conversation with Eula concerning her adultery with Manfred and her plans to go away and abandon Linda. What Gavin could not know was that his refusal to promise to marry Linda may have brought on Eula's decision to save Linda from Flem in the only way she can, by killing herself, to leave Linda "a mere suicide for a mother instead of a whore."

Eula's suicide can be seen as Gavin's ultimate failure, since he did not foresee it and was unable to prevent it. Perhaps too, as Ratliff suggests, she was bored. Gavin buries his anguish in his busy round of activity—arranging for Linda's move to Greenwich Village and setting up the trust fund to be administered by the bank, not Flem. For the memory of Eula, there is the last action a romantic and hopeless love could perform: the harrying of sculptors and Italian consuls about the medallion of Eula's face, which is to be set into her monument. Gavin does not rest until he is convinced the medallion is perfect, since it must stand for all that Eula could have been for him.

iv.

Structure in *The Town* and *The Mansion* is even looser and more episodic than in *The Hamlet*. Structure in the modern sense of that term is almost non-existent. The later volumes are made up of monologues delivered by the various characters, that often repeat and modify what has been told before. Unity and coherence are achieved in another way, by bringing the disparate parts, themes, and conflicts of the trilogy into a cohered focus at the end. The major intent of the work is thus fulfilled in the perspective of all three volumes: the rise and eventual fall of the red-necks, as exemplified in the career of Flem Snopes. In the impact of Flem on Jefferson and Jefferson on Flem, there is the classic progression of thesis, antithesis, synthesis: the onslaught, absorption, and termination of Snopesism. Near the end of *The Town* there is mention of a highway that leads from Jefferson to the world. *The Mansion* will be concerned in part with figurative passages along that highway, the opening out from the confined spaces of Jefferson to the figurative and literal stages of the great world itself: New York, Spain, and the first truly global war. Of even more importance is the transformation and universalization of character, role, and significance. Linda changes from a beautiful, confused, and insecure teen-ager into an austere, implacable, almost abstract avenging Fury. Mink is transformed from a vicious little murderer who kills from ambush into a humble and determined instrument of justice. Gavin is almost sixty years old at the end of the trilogy.

Like Ratliff, Gavin will be more and more limited to observation and comment on Snopesism and occasional companionship with Linda. Gavin's part in fighting Snopesism is surely diminishing, and just as surely the whole great pattern of rise and fall, injustice and punishment, exploitation and retribution, is being reabsorbed into the Snopes family, being taken over by people who are themselves named Snopes—provided that "Snopes" is given its full ironic meaning when applied to Linda and especially to the man Mink has become at the end.

If Gavin's greatest failure is his failure to "save" Eula in any sense, then his greatest success is in freeing Linda, not merely from Flem, Snopesism, and provincial Yoknapatawpha, but finally

from her dependence on him as well. Gavin might well qualify
as comic hero for this one sacrifice alone. Yet in this action, this
decision to allow Linda the fullest possible scope for development,
she becomes the self-sufficient woman who will take the final
action against Flem. At one place in *The Town,* Gavin states
that to be involved with a Snopes at all is to lose an arm or a leg
any time you get within ten feet of him. Ratliff defines Gavin's
relation to the Snopes family as "like that one between a feller
out in a big open field and a storm of rain: there aint no being
give nor accepting to it: he's already got it." Linda has learned
much from the men who have formed her mature character: Flem,
whom she hates, and Gavin, whom she loves. Her passion for
justice and the underdog has been learned in part from Gavin, in
part from Barton Kohl, and finds its outlet in whatever comes to
hand: the Spanish war, Jim Crow schools, or riveting in a war-
time shipyard. She makes Gavin promise to marry, not herself,
but someone. After the war, when she is settled down in apparent
idleness in Jefferson, Ratliff tells Chick with the utmost seriousness: "She has done run out of injustice. . . . So she will have to
think of something."

Thus, when Linda asks Gavin to draw up the documents for
Mink's release, he does so. He fears what Mink may do, but
both he and Ratliff clearly see they have no choice: if Gavin does
not draw up the petition, Linda will simply employ another lawyer,
perhaps an unscrupulous one. Mink will be out in two years in
any event, clear and without restriction. Gavin pins all his hope
on the conditional nature of Mink's early release—he will be freed
only if he agrees never to return to Mississippi. Gavin's personal
passion for justice makes him want to see Mink released, and his
attorney's passion for red tape, contracts, and paper work makes
him believe the agreement will work. Ratliff warns him that he
is flirting with *hubris,* trying to eat his cake and have it too. He
wants to keep himself clear of what Mink may do to Flem, yet he
is personally circulating the petition. He replies: "I not only believe in and am an advocate of fate and destiny, I admire them;
I want to be one of the instruments too, no matter how modest."
Having requested the warden to telephone if Mink refuses the
money and pardon, he has a revealing moment of relief before

he discovers the voice is Ratliff's. *"So I am a coward after all. When it happens two years from now, at least none of it will splatter on me."* A moment later, he is told that Mink has not kept the money and realizes he has known all along the scheme would not prevent Mink from killing Flem. This is agonizing to Gavin; he knows that both technically and morally he may be an accessory before the fact to murder. This crisis is only the latest of the maelstroms involving Gavin and a woman named Varner or Snopes. Now we see the point of all Ratliff's rambling discourses on Eula and Linda as natural cataclysms of some sort which snatch up Hoakes and Gavins for the moment's needs and then discard them again.

Gavin has not wanted to believe that Linda has coldly planned Flem's death, yet when he sees the brand-new Jaguar which he learns was ordered the previous July, he knows the truth. We know, as Gavin does not, that Linda helped Mink get out of the house after the shooting. More and more, Gavin will come to realize his foolish talk of fate and destiny is coming true, that he and Linda are involved in the final act of something that began when Flem first put money before decency and love. Is Gavin an accessory to murder or simply a helpless instrument snatched up willy-nilly by a kind of cyclonic divine retribution? Unable to decide which, Gavin does not turn from the line of conduct he has taken; without reproaches he tells Linda good-by. There he hears what is perhaps as much as any comic hero can expect: "I know now I never needed anybody but you." With Flem buried and Linda gone, there remains, ironically, only one duty for Gavin to perform. Ratliff takes him far out into the country to the ruin of the tenant house Mink lived in forty years ago. Ratliff indicates that Gavin must know that Linda planned the death of Flem. Through his tears, Gavin denies it. Ratliff points out that all of them, Gavin, Mink, Linda, Flem, have only done what they must: "Old Moster don't play jokes." Accessory or not, Gavin gives Mink the money Linda provided to aid his escape. This final action is the removal of the last, the very last, Snopes from Jefferson—that consummation so devoutly wished for so long. Ratliff's comment is the only fitting close to the long career of this quixotic tragi-comic hero who has, in spite of ethics, training, and conviction, helped a man guilty of premeditated murder (or was it an agent of God?) to escape, simply for the love of a woman and of her mother whom he loved even more.

Gentle and tender as a woman, Ratliff opened the car door for Stevens to get in. "You all right now?" he said.

"Yes I tell you, goddammit," Stevens said.

Ratliff closed the door and went around the car and opened his and got in and closed it and turned the switch and snapped on the lights and put the car in gear—two old men themselves, approaching their sixties. "I dont know if she's already got a daughter stashed out somewhere, or if she jest aint got around to one yet. But when she does I jest hope for Old Lang Zyne's sake she dont never bring it back to Jefferson. You done already been through two Eula Varners and I dont think you can stand another one."[1]

The career of the comic hero illustrates that this kind of unswerving idealism is often demanded and must be paid for in anguish and defeat. The outward sign of this idealism is Gavin's romantic readiness—the eagerness of commitment to some area of life, some relationship into which he can project himself with all his energy and emotion—and ultimately his lack of success. This readiness, this unchecked impulsiveness, this romantic fondness for hopeless causes is in one sense a form of weakness. Faced with such romantic idealism, the reader's reaction to Gavin may range from total sympathy to total exasperation. Gavin is defeated because he is human, committed to fighting humanely against inhumanity. The significance of his anguish and defeat, if it is defeat, is that he prefers to be defeated by Snopesism rather than become a Snopes in order to win.

1. William Faulkner, *The Mansion* (New York: Random House, 1959), pp. 433-34.

5.

THE COMIC HERO:
BYRON BUNCH

BYRON BUNCH ILLUSTRATES the perils of two opposite extremes of conduct toward the world. His career shows the strengths and weaknesses of an innocence based on an ignorance of evil, which can remain intact only if the hero can systematically avoid the occasion of sin. On the other hand, Byron also demonstrates the perils of active resistance to evil in life in the world of men. The paradoxical dilemma is the classic one: the good man faces mutually exclusive alternatives. He may either concentrate on saving his own soul by practicing a cloistered virtue in complete withdrawal from the world and deliberately refuse to take up the cudgels in the defense of the helpless, or he may deliberately plunge into the battle with evil and its attendant danger of corruption by that evil.

Byron has adapted the contemplative life to Mississippi conditions and has practiced it. Jefferson, the town, evidently represents to him the temptations and fleshpots of the big city. Therefore he deliberately has as little contact with it as possible, performing the hard physical labor of the planing mill six days a week, volunteering to work Saturday afternoons as well, when everyone else is gone, keeping his own time. When his fellow workers have departed for a week end of family life or of hellraising, as the case may be, Byron rides a mule all night, forty miles into the country, to lead the all-day singing service in a primitive country chapel. Sunday nights he rides the mule back to Jefferson and another six days of hard work. His only diversion during the week is his theological discussions with Hightower on the nature of virtue and goodness, sin and evil. His formula for conduct is simple: idle hands are the devil's workers. A hard and active secular business during the week and an active round of church business at all other times will leave anyone very little time for meanness.

One need not be too far along in *Light in August* to realize that the Lena-Byron relationship is Faulkner's Yoknapatawpha version of the Garden of Eden, if the allegory is translated into reasonably realistic modern terms. Byron Bunch is Adam, who labors in the garden of the world as he knows it and is unfallen not because he is ignorant of the existence of sin but because he is firmly established in his own system for avoiding it. Lena is Eve—in this case, already fallen Eve, who in a few days will give birth to the child whose father she is attempting to locate. Byron is an Adam who will follow his Eve out of his Garden, even though she does not particularly ask him to follow her. The Eden that he has created for himself is austere and spiritual but not unreasonably severe or unpleasant. Without laboring the comparison, we could assert that the graph of Byron's effort at heroism (though comic) traces the Christian paradox of the Fortunate Fall: Byron will leave his cloistered Eden to plunge into the active life—to know sin and run the risk of damnation in order to be the protector of Lena and her child. He is well aware of the ridiculousness of his position and of the sin inherent in his love for Lena, but he continues to suffer that humiliation in his determination to help the two of them. Faulkner presents Byron's quixotic adventures with a mixture of love and irony but, unhappily for the reader, ends the story just when he is about to begin his picaresque journey with Lena and the baby.

In describing Byron as a man who carefully avoids temptation and idleness, it is essential to make clear that he is by no means a prig or a prude, even in the early stages of the book. It is simply that he does not let himself take up the usual forms of dissipation common to young men in his time and place. He is well liked by his fellow workers, who respect and are impressed by his austere way of life even though they would not adopt it for themselves. He displays some ability at ratiocination in his theological discussions with Hightower, but as he will discover ruefully later on, he can never become a very skillful liar. He shows some imagination and even wit in his comments on "Brown" (as Lucas Burch calls himself), when "Brown" first comes to the planing mill to work. As the rest of the novel demonstrates, Lucas Burch is very nearly the epitome of loud-mouthed, half-witted worthlessness. Byron says: " 'He puts me in mind of one of these cars running along the street with a radio in it. You can't make out what it is saying and the car aint going anywhere in particular and when you look at it close you see that there aint even anybody it it.' "[1]

In his estimate of the immorality and meanness of other men, Byron is aware of that immorality but too uninvolved in it to measure it with any accuracy. The other workers at the mill have long known that Christmas and Brown are in partnership, selling whiskey to anyone who can buy it. Christmas has just quit his job at the mill, and the others are discussing how long it will be before Brown will quit as well. Byron is told that Christmas and Brown own a new car, but he cannot imagine how they have paid for it. Only then does he learn about the whiskey. "One or two of the others looked at Byron. They smiled a little. 'They never got that rich out here,' one said. Byron looked at him. 'I reckon Byron stays out of meanness too much himself to keep up with other folks',' the other said."[2]

When the temptation to desert the cloistered life comes to Byron, it comes in the form of the human risk and commitment to human love. He is working away in the empty quiet of the planing mill, loading heavy stacks of planks into a freight car, where he should be safe. He does not slacken his work even for the excitement of the big fire, whose smoke he can see, the burning of what we will later discover is the house of Joanna Burden. "Then Byron fell in love. He fell in love contrary to all the tradition of his austere and jealous country raising which demands in the object physical inviolability . . . when Lena Grove walked into the door behind him, her face already shaped with serene anticipatory smiling, her mouth already shaped upon a name. . . . 'You aint him,' she says behind her fading smile, with the grave astonishment of a child. 'No, Ma'am,' Byron says. He pauses, half turning with the balanced staves. 'I dont reckon I am. Who is it I aint?' "[3]

Again Lena tells her story—how she has come on to find Lucas Burch so that they can be together when the baby is born. She and Byron look at the column of smoke from the burning house on the other side of town, and in an effort to explain to her what Joanna Burden stands for in the community, he begins to tell her about Christmas and Brown and some of the things they are reputed to be involved in.

"What does he look like?" she says. . . .
"Oh. Brown. Yes. Tall, young. Dark complected; women-folks calls him handsome, a right smart do, I hear tell. A big hand for laughing and frolicking and playing jokes on folks. But I . . ." His voice ceases. He cannot look at her, feeling her steady, sober gaze upon his face.
"Joe Brown," she says. "Has he got a little white scar right here by his mouth?"
And he cannot look at her, and he sits there on the stacked lumber when it is too late, and he could have bitten his tongue in two.[4]

ii.

Later that night, Byron recounts the afternoon's events to Hightower, unburdening in a kind of confession the guilt that he feels for two things. One is the fact that he has, even unwittingly, revealed that "Brown" is Lucas Burch, the man Lena is looking for, the father of her child. The other is the guilt he feels for the lie he has told her about Lucas' occupation, what he has been involved in this same day, how he has been making his money, where he can be found at that moment—in a jail cell. He told Lena the lie to conceal the news that her putative husband is a bootlegger and general no-good, involved in some way in the murder of Joanna Burden. He hopes also to protect Lena from the prying questions of the townspeople. At this point, Byron is already in love with Lena, even though it seems certain that he does not realize it yet. He is explaining, rationalizing everything to Hightower. He gives reasons for what he has done, reasons that seem to him to be good and charitable ones but that to Hightower seem to contain a certain element of evasion, even if an unconscious one. Hightower begins to feel some concern for Byron.

But this concern is swallowed up in a greater concern for the terrible facts of murder and pursuit in the case of Christmas, and little mention is made of Lena that night.

Byron's knowledge of the world's sin and malice seems to have grown since the day he met Lena. He not only seems now to have the full details of Lucas' extra-legal activities; he is even able to comment on them with irony: "Because I reckon he does call it work, carrying all them cold little bottles nekkid against his chest. . . . Brown . . . went with them. . . . He may have helped Christmas do it. But I dont reckon so. I reckon that setting fire to the house was about his limit. . . . I reckon he figured that what Christmas committed was not so much a sin as a mistake."[5]

It is almost as if Faulkner were arranging Byron's growing knowledge of sin and crime against the loss of Byron's innocence as he slides into the sin of loving Lena. For the moment, at least, Byron continues to be unaware of being in the condition that Hightower calls sin. He continues to inform Hightower (and the reader) of what is happening, and the importance of Lucas' meanness is swallowed up in the graveness of the murder of Miss Burden, the revelation of her relation to Christmas, and the fact that Lucas says Christmas has Negro blood. Byron regrets that he must bring all this turmoil and trouble into Hightower's life. Hightower, of course, would have preferred not to know of any of it. But life will press in on Hightower, whether he wishes it to or not. Three nights later, Byron comes to Hightower again, ostensibly to ask for counsel, advice, but actually to tell Hightower what he has already decided to do: to move Lena out of the boardinghouse and to the cabin where Lucas and Christmas had been living. Byron says that Lena knows that Lucas is utterly worthless and a fool but that she is determined that she and Lucas be together when the child is born. " 'Nonsense,' Hightower says. He looks across the desk at the other's still, stubborn, ascetic face: the face of a hermit who has lived a long time in an empty place where sand blows. 'The thing, the only thing, for her to do is to go back to Alabama. To her people.' 'I reckon not,' Byron says."[6]

Byron goes on to say that he will move Lena out to the cabin, no matter how it may appear to the townspeople. There he will protect and foster her as best he can: "I reckon I am trying to do the right thing by my lights"—"And that," Hightower thinks, "is the first lie he ever told me. Ever told anyone, man or woman. . . ." Byron reminds Hightower that Lena and Lucas are not man and wife yet, and he brazenly but honestly admits that when he tells Lucas that Lena has caught up with him, it may be that Lucas will run again, perhaps, only perhaps, leaving the field to Byron. Hightower is disturbed by all this; he cannot believe that Byron is right in deed or thought.

"Then what do you think we—I ought to do? What do you advise?"

"Go away. Leave Jefferson." They look at one another. "No," Hightower says. . . . "You are already being helped by someone stronger than I am."

For a moment Byron does not speak. They look at one another, steadily. "Helped by who?"

"By the devil," Hightower says.[7]

There the matter rests until the following night, when Byron comes by Hightower's house to say simply that he has moved Lena out to the cabin and has moved himself into a tent nearby. He will be there in case she needs anything. Hightower warns him that the road he is taking can lead to only two possibilities: sin or marriage. In the light of Lena's history, she is not apt to marry Byron; even if she did, Byron would be coming between Lena and the father of her child. He once again urges Byron to go away, to leave Jefferson completely. Byron refuses, and as Hightower watches him walk away with his load of groceries, he is thinking: "God bless him. God help him. . . . *To be young. To be young. There is nothing else like it: there is nothing else in the world. . . .*" He does not know what Byron will ask of him next; it will not be necessary to ask it until Christmas has been captured.

When Byron comes to Hightower's house on the following Sunday afternoon, he reminds Hightower that Hightower is a man of God, even if the people of Jefferson have unfrocked him. He tells Hightower about Old Doc Hines and Mrs. Hines, the grandparents of Christmas. Later that night, the Hines's unfold their incredible story and even more incredible present relationship and attitudes toward their grandson. It will be Byron's self-imposed task to do what he can, in the only way he can devise, to try to save Christmas from the lynch mob. He will compel the unwilling Hightower—that unhappy, cloistered, withdrawn man who always insists that he has "already paid"—to listen to the horrible story of Christmas' begetting and birth; the present fact that Old Doc Hines, Christmas' own grandfather who is sitting there in the room with them, is determined to have Christmas lynched. Old Mrs. Hines will plead with Hightower to save Christmas' ("Joey's") life:

"I thought . . . I know it aint right to bother a stranger. But you are lucky. A bachelor, a single man that could grow old without the despair of love. . . . I never saw him when he could walk and talk. Not for thirty years I never saw him. I am not saying he never did what they say he did. . . . But if folks could maybe just let him for one day. Like it hadn't happened yet."

"Oh," Hightower says, in a shrill, high voice. . . . "Simple. Simple. . . . What is it they want me to do? What must I do now? Byron! Byron?"[8]

Byron reminds Hightower that there is a price for being good the same as for being bad, and that good men cannot deny the bill when it comes around. He points out to Hightower that there is really no evidence against Christmas except the word of Lucas, whose word is worthless. If Hightower will provide Christmas with an alibi for the nights he was with Joanna Burden, then his life can be saved. Byron shows the extent to which he has learned how the world is. "Folks would believe you. . . . They would rather believe that about you than to believe that he lived with her like a husband and then killed her. . . . They wouldn't do anything to you about it that would hurt you now. And I reckon you are used to everything else they can do."

"Oh," Hightower says. "Ah. Yes. . . . That would be very simple, very good. Good for all." He then accuses Byron of self-interest again, of wishing Lucas to miss the reward, to be scared enough to marry Lena, and then so scared as to run away and leave Lena for Byron to have. He refuses absolutely to tell the lie that would save Christmas. " 'It's not because I cant, dont dare to,' he says; 'it's because I wont! I wont! do you hear? . . .

It's because I wont do it!' . . . Suddenly his voice rises higher yet. 'Get out!' he screams. 'Get out of my house! Get out of my house!' "[9]

Within six hours Byron is back again: Lena's baby is about to be born. Once again, as with the Negro baby years before, it will be Hightower who has to be called from his self-imposed withdrawal from the human community to officiate at the beginning of a new human life. Bringing his razor and medical book, riding Byron's mule, he arrives in time to deliver the baby. Hightower will for a short time be vividly and happily brought back to life by the birth, but for Byron the shock will be a shattering one. He begins to realize why he had not arranged for a doctor, why he had made no preparation for Lena's lying-in. By the usual human process of wish-fulfillment and rationalization, he has managed to let himself ignore the fact that Lena is pregnant at all; his subconscious has decided to ignore the fact as long as possible. Returning with the old doctor, trying to sort out the chaos in his mind, he hears the baby cry. "Then he knew. . . . He stood quietly in the chill peace, the waking quiet—small, nondescript, whom no man or woman had ever turned to look at twice anywhere. . . . With stern and austere astonishment he thought *It was like it was not until Mrs Hines called me and I heard her and saw her face and knew that Byron Bunch was nothing in this world to her right then, that I found out that she is not a virgin.* . . . but that was not all. There was something else. . . . *I'll have to tell him now. I'll have to tell Lucas Burch.*"[10]

Byron has no possible alternative. He must bring Lena and the father of her child together again. He arranges to have Lucas brought out to the cabin by a deputy. Byron believes that he has no choice but to leave Jefferson and his shattered reputation behind. He gathers all his worldly goods into his old cheap suitcase and lashes it behind the saddle of his mule. He watches the deputy bring Lucas to the cabin, where Lena is lying in bed with the baby, and sees him pushed into the cabin. Byron mounts the mule and begins to ride away from Jefferson. He does not, of course, witness the interview between Lena and the frantic Lucas, who wants only to get away, especially when he sees the baby and knows that Lena is determined that they marry at once. Byron

turns in the saddle when he reaches the top of the ridge, to take
his last look at Jefferson spread out below him. He sees the tiny
cabin like a toy and the deputy like a tinier toy on the step; he is
just in time to see the tiny figure of Lucas spring out the rear
window and vanish swiftly into the woods. Without conscious
volition, Byron turns his mule off the road and gallops to inter-
cept Lucas. All the time, something like a clean cold wind is
blowing all the desire and despair out of him. " 'I took care of
his woman for him and I borned his child for him. And now
there is one thing more I can do for him. I cant marry them, because I aint a minister. And I may not can catch him, because
he's got a start on me. And I may not can whip him if I do,
because he is bigger than me. But I can try it. I can try to do
it.' "[11]

He does not witness Lucas' frantic interview with the old
Negro woman or his exasperation with the Negro boy he hires
to take the note to the sheriff, claiming his reward for having
betrayed Christmas. Byron finds Lucas waiting beside the railroad track to hop the northbound freight. Lucas does not know
anyone has found him until Byron speaks: "Get up onto your
feet." The exuberance, the passionate joy Byron feels has more
than one source, probably. There is the anger and disgust with
Lucas and the renewal of hope, but most of all Byron is at this
moment the joyful defender of goodness returning to the fight
he had thought was lost and done with. "It does not last long.
Byron knew that it was not going to. But he did not hesitate.
He just crept up until he could see the other. . . . 'You're bigger
than me,' Byron thought. 'But I dont care. You've had every
other advantage of me. And I dont care about that neither.
You've done throwed away twice inside of nine months what I
aint had in thirty five years. And now I'm going to get the hell
beat out of me and I dont care about that, neither.' "[12]

Byron lies bleeding and quiet until he is able to sit up, just in
time to see Lucas run out and hop the freight train as it comes
by: "Great God in the mountain," he says, with quiet astonishment, "he sho knows how to jump a train. He's sho done that
before." When the last car passes, the world and time and hope
rush down on him like a tidal wave. Byron had committed the

unpardonable sin of the comic hero—he had given up hope. Now hope is bountifully renewed. He gets on his mule and starts back toward the cabin and Lena. *"And then I will stand there and I will. . . . Then I will stand there and I will. . . ."* Perhaps he does hope too far, assume too much too quickly, but at least he does not attempt to project his wish-fulfillment beyond the moment of meeting.

iii.

The structure of *Light in August* is such that at this point the scene is shifted abruptly to the frenzied action of the last day of Christmas' life. The reader discovers that at the moment when the comic hero Byron is fighting with Lucas Burch and emerging battered but temporarily victorious, Christmas is enduring the moment of his death and mutilation. It is in the next-to-last two chapters that the individuals and situations and events are held together in a kind of tension that makes meaningful patterns— the deaths of Miss Burden and Christmas and the birth of Lena's baby, Hightower's "return to life" by his participation in that birth followed by his return home just in time to see Christmas killed in his own kitchen, for whom he now, too late, shouts the lie he would not tell earlier.

Many critics consider *Light in August* Mr. Faulkner's finest novel. But this same majority would be almost unanimous in dispraising the last chapter, or in ignoring it, or in attempting to explain it as a not-too-happy afterthought. They have noticed the abrupt shift in point-of-view and in tone from the agonized in- terior consciousness of tension, flight, and violence to the quite relaxed, easy, casual, and even bawdy narrative of the furniture dealer, a character completely new to the novel and foreign to its action.

But that chapter is artistically necessary, and art forces the necessity for doing it in the manner in which it is done. The chapter and its technique are necessary also for any realistic presentation of life itself. If *Light in August* were structually a formal tragedy in the classic or Elizabethan manner, the comic relief would be excluded altogether or disposed of well before the final act. But while this novel is as deeply infused with tragic emotion as any literary work of the present century, it is neverthe-less a novel and not a formal tragedy in structure.) The critics might be correct in stating that the story ends with the tragic death of Christmas and the tragic self-knowledge achieved by Hightower—if, of course, the stories of Hightower and Christmas were the only stories in the novel. But they are not; there remains the Lena-Byron story to be completed.

Lena and Byron are the first two characters of any importance to appear in the novel. Christmas is shown as early as the second chapter but is presented through the consciousness of Byron, who offers to share food with him—a fact which is not, I think, with-out importance. In the sense of merely formal structural com-pleteness, then, a final chapter to round out the Lena-Byron story is called for. The chapter is written exactly in keeping with the ultimate meaning of the book. As noted earlier in the present study, tragic heroes climb very high and then fall precipitately and forever. But by any comic theory and aesthetic that we know of, the function of comedy is to laugh away whatever is excessive or ridiculous. The comic hero is defined, for the present study, as a man of good will who does what he can to redress the exces-sive imbalance between the powerful forces of ill will and the helpless victims of that ill will. His rise will not be very spec-tacular or consistent, and his success will not be very great. Comedy is, above all, realistic and stays firmly within the realm of the possible. Any account of Lena and Byron will have to conclude with a glimpse of what their future life (if any) together may be like. Honesty demands that this view be presented honestly.

One sin against the comic spirit is a romantic excess of feeling, of hope or trust or optimism. The spectator seeing Byron's hope-less love may become too closely identified with the little man's struggle to win Lena's love—too closely identified to remain objec-tive. Reality demands that his prospects be seen as they really are. For these reasons, a totally fresh observer is needed—one, that is, who knows nothing of what has gone before: Byron's austerity, sacrifice, struggle, and above all, the essential purity of his devo-tion. Therefore, the furniture dealer is introduced to tell what he sees *now,* at the moment it happens, unclouded by any event in the past. The reader may have become too much involved in Byron's hopes, fears, and sacrifices. The comic perspective of such a reader is in need of sharp adjustment. What the dealer sees is a little pathetic, and would be distasteful, even, if it were not for Byron's indomitable determination:

". . . I saw this kind of young, pleasantfaced gal standing on the corner, like she was waiting for somebody to come along and offer her a ride . . . and I didn't see the fellow that was with her at all until he come up and spoke to me. I thought at first that I didn't see him before because he wasn't standing where she was. Then I saw that he was the kind of fellow you wouldn't see the first glance if he was alone by himself in the bottom of a empty concrete swimming pool. . . . I just never thought anything about it, except to wonder how a young, strapping gal like her ever come to take up with him."[13]

The Lena-Byron relationship is revealed to the dealer as he observes it. He learns who they are searching for and overhears Lena refuse Byron's second offer of marriage. He is also feigning sleep when Byron climbs into the truck to attempt to force matters and witnesses Byron's humiliation in being picked up bodily and set outside like a child:

". . . then I heard one kind of astonished sound she made when she woke up, like she was just surprised and then a little put out without being scared at all, and she says, not loud neither: 'Why, Mr. Bunch. Aint you ashamed. You might have woke the baby, too. . . .' I be dog if I dont believe she picked him up and set him back outside on the ground like she would that baby if it had been about six years old, say, and she says, 'You go and lay down now, and get some sleep. We got another fur piece to go tomorrow.'

"Well, I was downright ashamed to look at him, to let him know that any human man had seen and heard what happened. I be dog if I didn't want to find the hole and crawl into it with him. I did for a fact. . . . I knew about how I would have been standing and feeling if I was him. And that would have been with my head bowed, waiting for the Judge to say, 'Take him out of here and hang him quick.' "[14]

The dealer hears Byron thrashing off blindly through the bushes. In the morning, Byron has not returned. The dealer gets his gear loaded and Lena into the truck and is not surprised to find Byron waiting around the first curve.

Sho. He was standing at the side of the road when we come around the curve. Standing there, face and no face, hangdog and

determined and calm too, like he had done desperated himself up for
the last time, to take the last chance, and that now he knew he wouldn't
ever have to desperate himself again He continues: "He never looked
at me at all. I just stopped the truck and him already running back
to go around to the door where she was sitting. And he come around
the back of it and he stood there, and her not even surprised. 'I done
come too far now,' he says. 'I be dog if I'm going to quit now.' And
her looking at him like she had known all the time what he was
going to do before he even knew himself that he was going to, and
that whatever he done, he wasn't going to mean it.

" 'Aint nobody never said for you to quit,' she says."[15]

The furniture dealer's account seems realistic and anti-senti-
mental enough, but at the end of it he predicts that someday Lena
will settle down. Perhaps the insidious germ of romanticism has
begun to infect him too. He tells his wife: "I was pulling for the
little cuss." So are we all.

1. William Faulkner, *Light in August* (New York: Modern Library, 1950),
p. 32.
2. *Ibid.*, p. 37.
3. *Ibid.*, pp. 42, 43, 44.
4. *Ibid.*, p. 48.
5. *Ibid.*, pp. 71, 87.
6. *Ibid.*, p. 264.
7. *Ibid.*, p. 269.
8. *Ibid.*, pp. 339, 340.
9. *Ibid.*, p. 342.
10. *Ibid.*, p. 352.
11. *Ibid.*, p. 373.
12. *Ibid.*, p. 384.
13. *Ibid.*, pp. 433-34.
14. *Ibid.*, p. 441.
15. *Ibid.*, p. 443.

6.

THE COMIC HERO:
V. K. RATLIFF

V. K. RATLIFF TURNS UP in almost as many places as his friend
and fellow Snopes-watcher, Gavin Stevens. He has an added
distinction: he is the man who first discovered the Snopeses and
invented Snopes-watching as a full-time occupation. He is the
shrewdest, the most intelligent, of all the Faulkner comic heroes;
if we can believe the testimony of Gavin Stevens, "Too damned
shrewd, too damn intelligent." His occupation, like Gavin's,
takes him to all parts of the county and requires for success a
practical insight into human personality and motive.

It is a point of pride with Ratliff to have the inside story on
everything that happens in Yoknapatawpha County and to be able
to supply the real motive for any action by any person. His native
intelligence and shrewdness, coupled with his wide acquaintance
among all kinds and classes of people, produce a dual effect in his
own conduct. The sharpness of his insight makes him far better
able to act the comic hero, simply because he almost always knows
what really is happening. But this same intelligence and worldly
practicality, especially after his major entanglement with Flem
Snopes, make him unlikely to plunge headlong into the struggle
against Snopesism.

There is a seventeen-year gap between the publication of *The
Hamlet* in 1940 and *The Town* in 1957. It is to be expected that
some changes will be evident not only in individuals and incidents
but in Faulkner's attitude toward them as well. But Ratliff is a
remarkably consistent individual, both in fictional existence as a

living human being and in his creator's estimate of him. There
are passages in *The Hamlet* in which the tone is one of savage
and almost unrelieved pessimism, but at no point is Ratliff over-
whelmed by the events as such, nor is his own spirit infected by
the pessimism these events seem to produce in others. Thus,
even though Ratliff has reduced the scale and emphasis of his
action from one book to another, his character and personality
have changed very little.

Ratliff had appeared here and there as a minor figure in various stories in the Yoknapatawpha series, sometimes under the
name of Sutliff, but his appearance in *The Hamlet* is the first
one of any importance. It is appropriate that he should be the
commentator on the rise of the Snopeses, because he will be among
the first to try to check Flem and the only one who will have any
degree of success at it. He will, too, be defeated by Flem, trapped
by his hope of getting something for nothing, taken in by one of
the oldest tricks in the history of human chicanery. In *The Town*
his actions will be tempered a good deal, in part by the experience
of having his fingers burned once but more because Flem himself
becomes more temperate in his actions. In *The Mansion,* Ratliff's
activity is largely devoted to observation and analysis, simply
because there is no need for active combat. If, as we are reminded
so often now, the final goal of any civilization is adjustment, then
Ratliff and Flem become somewhat adjusted to each other in *The
Town,* or perhaps it is only that they become adjusted to what
civilization demands of them. Ratliff often implies that he alone
knows what Flem really wants within his new-found responsibility
and finds that often Flem wants for Jefferson what he too wants.
Amazing and embarrassing as it is, he finds himself abetting Flem
to save the good name of Jefferson.

By a curious inversion of the Manichaean heresy, it seems
that goodness per se exists in Yoknapatawpha but that comic
heroism can function only in response to evil and evil action. It
could be asserted with some truth that Ratliff's entire existence
as a comic hero (as distinct from those passages where he functions primarily as a raconteur or historian) consists of his relation to Flem Snopes and Snopesism in general. In the present
study, the major analysis of Flem's callous rapacity and his run-

ning contest with Ratliff is given in the chapter devoted to Flem as villain, since in the important encounters Flem is always the victor. The major effort of the present chapter will be to show Ratliff's essential character as a good man and above all a man of good will; as one who is willing to actively commit himself against evil, but more important, to perform actions of positive good.

ii.

At one point in *The Town*, Ratliff defines the totality of what it means to be involved with a Snopes. "The relationship . . . was like that one between a feller out in a big open field and a storm of rain: there aint no being give nor accepting to it: he's already got it."[1] If, in *The Town*, Ratliff seems to mellow toward Flem and what Flem stands for, it should be remembered that Flem has begun to reform toward outward respectability. Actually, Ratliff has not "mellowed" toward anything, least of all anything he would consider intolerable. Far more important, for the reader's purpose, his behavior at this stage provides the unique, essential insight into his character and his mode of procedure as a comic hero throughout the length of his career. To begin with, Ratliff may not be a conventional Christian, but he is Christian enough to adopt and maintain one essential Christian attitude: to hate sin but not the sinner; Snopes-*ism*, but not Flem himself. There is never any indication that Ratliff wants personal revenge on Flem. No doubt he often wishes to see some nefarious scheme of Flem's backfire or blow up, but this is only to wish a lack of success to conduct that is evil to begin with. Like the true knight of faith, he desires only to stand between the weak and helpless and all cynical, brutal, exploitation. Like the true evangelist, he wishes not to punish but to amend; not to banish and cast out, but to redeem.

Very near the beginning of *The Hamlet*, the first volume of the Snopes trilogy, there is an account of Ratliff's relation to Ab Snopes, Flem's father. The location of this episode, so early in the trilogy, is a clue to its importance. It is told retrospectively by Ratliff as taking place when Ratliff was eight years old. This is the same Ab Snopes who was involved with Miss Rosa Millard in the mule and commissary operations against the Federal army and who was held in part responsible for her death at the time. According to Ratliff, there was a different breed of Snopes in those days: almost human, in fact. Once Ab had lived down the notoriety and humiliation of being a known horse-thief who stole indiscriminately from both sides during the war, he was a reasonable and even likable fellow,* until horse-trading, the great passion of his life, played out on him and left him just a farmer, and a dirt-poor tenant farmer at that. This misfortune occurred when he tangled with Pat Stamper—that legendary horse-trader and make-up artist—and was lucky to get home with as much as the bridle. After this episode, says Ratliff, Ab soured on life altogether.

In the historical present of *The Hamlet,* then, Ratliff is a man who has known old Ab for a long time and who knows of the family's subsequent history as barn-burners. He is not alarmed, therefore, only interested and amused, when he learns that Jody Varner is signing up Ab and Ab's son Flem to crop on shares. Jody crudely plans to get a full season's work out of the Snopes family and then threaten to expose their sordid reputation to the community. He naïvely expects Ab to be so sensitive to community disapproval that he will move on, abandoning his equity in the crop that will have been made. It will be Ratliff's exquisite privilege to play the generous, helpful informant who lets Jody know just what kind of firebugs he has contracted with. The reader laughs with Ratliff as he observes Jody's panic-stricken realization that he has caught tigers in a trap set for rabbits. Jody's distress is the direct result of his own attempt to commit unmitigated fraud and blackmail; both parties to the encounter are equally unscrupulous, and Ratliff feels no particular urge to do more than look on and laugh quietly to himself. The moral initiative that he does take is illustrated in a quiet scene of a page or so, when he seeks out the field where old Ab is plowing. Rat-

* This account occurs in pp. 32-53 of *The Hamlet* (New York: Random House, 1940). What Ab has become by the period of the events which take place in *The Hamlet* itself is shown in pp. 8-24 and in the beautiful short story "Barn Burning." Ab is by this period harsh, vindictive, and treacherous. He is hostile to everyone and burns barns in retaliation for real or imaginary slights or injuries.

liff gives Ab a pint of whiskey, and they talk briefly of nothing
in particular, except for a passing reminder of the adventure
together with Pat Stamper. Ratliff observes that the farm Ab
has now is a good one and that Ab could settle down. Both
understand that Ratliff is offering the friendship he has never
repudiated and indicating that Ab could now relax his savagery
a little, since the need to burn barns has passed. Ab's only indication that he may consider the suggestions is the gruff injunc-
tion: "Go on to the house and tell them to give you some dinner."
And then, "Much obliged for the bottle." Ratliff notices that
he does not say, "Come back again."

This will continue to be Ratliff's attitude for the time being.
He is of course busy as usual with his own activities: the sewing-
machine business and his various swaps and trades. He also
goes through a major illness which takes him out of circulation
for most of the winter. He does not interfere directly in Snopes's
business until he is ready to feel out Flem in a fairly important
test of skill. This is the affair of the goats, which turns into a
matter of Mink Snopes and Flem, and their idiot cousin, Isaac.
In its early stages, this collision with Flem is not purely a disinterested act of corporeal charity. Ratliff deliberately plants
the information that he must have fifty goats in such a way that
Flem must overhear it and then delays two days, giving Flem
time to corner the market. Meanwhile, Ratliff has obtained the
promissory note from Mink Snopes; he wants to see if Flem will
dare to refuse to honor the signature of a murderous and incen-
diary first cousin. When he shows the note, Ratliff has the satisfaction of seeing Flem stop chewing for a moment, at least. In
order to be able to burn Mink's note, Flem has to surrender the
bill of sale for the fifty goats. Ratliff then presents the note
signed with the X of Isaac Snopes. Flem then produces Isaac
Snopes; Ratliff is sickened to discover that Isaac is the helpless
idiot he saw the day before and that Flem is his legal guardian,
using the idiot's money over and over again for his own profit.
Ratliff's only recourse is to burn the note to take it out of Flem's
hands. Ratliff turns over the remaining profit of the goat business to Mrs. Littlejohn to keep for Isaac Snopes in case he should
ever have any need for money, thinking meanwhile: "Only thank

God men have done learned how to forget quick what they aint
brave enough to try to cure."

iii.

Sickened by the realization of what one Snopes is willing to
do even to another Snopes, Ratliff is now prepared to take the
Snopes menace with absolute seriousness and begins to observe
Flem's continued rise in the world with all the analytical insight
he has. When Flem's new station in life demands that he not
spend his days clerking in a store, his clerkship is taken by another
Snopes, named Launcelot—"Lump" in local usage. Lump looks
exactly like Flem, except that he is smaller. Ratliff says of him:
"That Snopes encore—Launcelot. . . . What I was trying to say
was echo. Only what I meant was forgery." Lump works in
the major Snopes tradition that anything and everything in the
world exists solely for his own profit. When the idiot Isaac
Snopes is carrying on his bucolic love affair with the cow, Lump
soon finds a way to turn his cousin's amours into a sideshow.
He has stationed a small boy at the cow-shed and the boy comes
running to alert Lump when each encounter between idiot and
cow is about to begin. Ratliff gradually realizes that the show
has been going on for some time. He goes with the others, to see
and know for himself the worst:

He knew not only what he was going to see but that, like Bookwright,
he did not want to see it, yet, unlike Bookwright, he was going to
look. He did look, leaning his face in between two other heads; and
it was as though it were himself inside the stall with the cow, himself
looking out of the blasted tongueless face at the row of faces watching
him who had been given the wordless passions but not the specious
words. When they looked around at him, he already held the loose
plank, holding it as if he were on the point of striking at them with
it. But his voice was merely sardonic, mild even, familiar, cursing
as Houston had: not in rage and not even in outraged righteousness.
"I notice you come to have your look too," one said.
"Sholy," Ratliff said. "I aint cussing you folks. I'm cussing all
of us," lifting the plank and fitting it back into the orifice. "Does
he—What's his name? that new one? Lump. —does he make you
pay again each time, or is it a general club ticket good for every
performance?" There was a half-brick on the ground beside the wall.
With it he drove the nails back while they watched him. . . . "That's
all," he said. "It's over. This here engagement is completed."[2]

Ratliff takes the initiative at once. He forces the Snopes clan to buy the cow so that she can be killed and part of the beef fed to the idiot to cure him of his affliction. Ratliff takes this overt and public action, as he explains to Mrs. Littlejohn, not because he is any purer or better than the idiot but simply because he is stronger and can put a stop to such things. He takes the step himself because Flem is not there to stop it or be compelled to stop it. Ratliff muses on the ironic fact that this is probably the first time since man drew breath that anyone had ever wished that Flem Snopes were here instead of anywhere else, for any reason, at any price.

As the power and brazenness of the Snopes clan continues to grow, Ratliff will be more and more pressed to do what he can. When Mink Snopes shoots Zack Houston dead from ambush, Flem then allows his cousin to draw a life sentence for the killing. It should be noted that "allows" is precisely the verb to apply in this case. Law and custom at this time and place are such that even a moderately competent lawyer could have got Mink off on a plea of self-defense. It seems clear (both here and in *The Mansion*) that Faulkner wishes us to understand that Flem could have got his cousin off if he had chosen—and he does not choose. It is not even possible to find bail for Mink, so that he may help feed his wife and children.

It is left, as usual, for Ratliff to do what he can. In this particular case, "what he can" is to bring Mink's wife—a backwoods ex-prostitute—and her two small children into his own house, which is kept for him by his widowed sister and her children. He does this over his sister's scandalized protests. Mink's wife finds a job as soon as she can, as chambermaid and general drudge at a disreputable backstreet hotel. She is able to earn some extra money; as one town wit puts it: ". . . her heels blistered running barefooted in and out of them horse-traders' and petty jurys' and agents for nigger insurances' rooms all night long." Mink spends the entire winter in jail; even after spring comes there is still no sign of Flem. Ratliff declares that Flem is determined not to help Mink. " 'Shucks,' Bookwright said. 'Even Flem Snopes aint going to let his own blood cousin be hung just to save money.' " But Ratliff does not agree. " 'He aint coming back here where Mink's wife can worry him or folks can talk about him for leaving his cousin in jail. There's some things even a Snopes wont do. I dont know just exactly what they are, but they's some somewhere.' " Thus the seed is planted which will not be harvested until the close of *The Mansion* and the end of the Snopes trilogy.

iv.

The "Spotted Horses" section of *The Hamlet* has often been printed separately, sometimes in the earlier, shorter version which was published in the old *Scribner's* and which has several interesting technical differences from the version in *The Hamlet*. But in either version, it is by turns improbable, outrageous, and very, very funny. Malcolm Cowley has called it the funniest American short story since the work of Mark Twain. As in Twain's work, there is an underlying stratum of blackness—the blackness of the despair which comes with the awareness of what man is willing to do to man.

When Flem Snopes returns from Texas, he is accompanied by a tall horse-wrangler named Buck Hipps and a herd of small, vicious, unbroken, savage western range-ponies, so vicious they must be lashed to the tailgate of a wagon with halters made of barbed-wire. Flem has found something else to sell his neighbors. Almost as soon as the horses appear, Ratliff tries to joke the impoverished farmers into not throwing away their money on animals that not only are worthless but may kill them. "You folks aint going to buy them things sho enough, are you? . . . giving Flem Snopes and that Texas man your money. . . ." None of the men, even those who are Ratliff's friends, will say that they won't buy, and all of them are on hand for the auction the next day. "All right. You folks can buy them critters if you want to. But me, I'd just as soon buy a tiger or a rattlesnake. And if Flem Snopes offered me either one of them, I would be afraid to touch it for fear it would turn out to be a painted dog or a piece of garden hose when I went up to take possession of it."[3]

To telescope the scenes that follow, the men of Frenchman's Bend bid on the horses in a mixture of shame, defiance, and frustration. The half-crazy Henry Armstid arrives just in time to see the first horse given outright to Eck Snopes and demands his right to bid also. He takes from his wife the last five dollars they have in the world and bids with it, offering to fight anyone who outbids him. The other men try to be oblivious to the scene of domestic humiliation that follows.

Ratliff has seen that he cannot turn any of them from this folly and does not attend the auction. All day long the bidding continues; at dusk the men attempt to catch the horses they have paid for. When someone leaves the gate open, the horses stampede wildly, leaving confusion and destruction behind them. The only serious injury is sustained by Henry Armstid, who not only cannot now make his crop for the year but will have to have his room and board paid for. The next morning Ratliff reports the dialogue between Mrs. Armstid and Mrs. Littlejohn to the loafers around the store. Mrs. Armstid has the wistful hope that Flem may return the five dollars Henry paid for the pony which broke his leg. Ratliff has no fatuous hope that Flem can be shamed into returning the money; all he can do is demonstrate Flem's niggardly meanness to the people of Frenchman's Bend. They all watch as Mrs. Armstid asks for the money and hear Flem affirm that the Texan took all the money with him when he went. Then, in a spirit of pure charity, Flem gives Mrs. Armstid a nickel's worth of candy for the children he has robbed. "By God," says Lump, "you cant beat him." Lump is correct: Flem cannot be beaten in court; he cannot even be subpoenaed there. The lawsuits over the damage caused by the horses are dismissed because there is no case; Flem will not even answer the summons, saying only: "They wasn't none of my horses." Ratliff does not attend these hearings; he is present instead at the final disposition of the case of Mink Snopes and predicts accurately that Flem has seen to it that Mink will not be acquitted.

"Oh," Bookwright said. "Hah," he said, with no mirth. I reckon you gave Henry Armstid back his five dollars too." Then Ratliff looked away. His face changed—something fleeting, quizzical, but not smiling, his eyes did not smile; it was gone.

"I could have," he said. "But I didn't. I might have if I could just been sho he would buy something this time that would sho enough kill him, like Mrs. Littlejohn said. Besides . . . I wasn't even protecting a people from a Snopes. I was protecting something that wasn't even a people, that wasn't nothing but something that dont want nothing but to walk and feel the sun and wouldn't know how to hurt no man even if it would and wouldn't want to even if it could, just like I wouldn't stand by and see you steal a meatbone from a dog. I never made them Snopeses and I never made the folks that cant wait to bare their backsides to them. I could do more, but I wont. I wont, I tell you!"[4]

Flem has just performed what will come to be recognized as the classic Flem Snopes maneuver: removing two antagonists who are or might become a threat to Flem, by causing them to destroy each other. Houston was such a threat because he was a fearless, forceful, strong-willed man, free enough from financial worries to avoid capture by Flem. Mink is proud and fierce: treacherous enough and Snopes enough to kill from ambush, but dangerous because he kills for pride and manhood, rather than calculating profit and loss. With Houston dead and Mink in jail for life, Ratliff is the sole remaining threat to Flem—the only person who possesses the intelligence and means sufficient to fight back. The stage has been cleared for a major encounter.

v.

The final section of *The Hamlet* is not very long, but it presents a major crisis: one of those explosive moral collisions in which something of real importance is changed in a way that can never be undone. In this case the collision is the climactic encounter between Ratliff and Flem, and it leaves no ambiguity in its outcome. The atmosphere is tragic, for in spite of the fact that he is on the side of the angels, Ratliff is seduced by the forces of evil and roundly defeated. He is defeated because he is offered a temptation and succumbs to it. The tragedy lies in the fact that if he had not succumbed to the temptation the defeat would not have occurred.

Perhaps even the comic hero may be allowed his *hubris*. One of Ratliff's most consistent points of pride is his belief that he can "risk fooling with" Flem Snopes. He hints as much to Will Varner early in the novel. Encounters occur, but the question of who is the sharper man remains undecided until the end of *The Hamlet*. On the level of simple realism, the reader may wonder what all the fuss is about. Ratliff, himself a businessman of experience and ability, is foolish enough to be taken in by Flem Snopes' trick of planting treasure in the garden of the Old Frenchman Place. He buys the property at a considerable price, only to discover that he has been fooled. Of course, Odom Bookwright loses on the deal also and Henry Armstid, the third partner, now permanently crippled by the horse he bought with his wife's last five dollars, is driven irrevocably insane by the impact of this final experience. But even this is not the point, any more than the fact that Ratliff is beaten in a business deal. The point is this: not only have the powers of darkness prevailed, they have done so in a way which validates the Snopes view of Mankind.

As George Marion O'Donnell pointed out years ago, there can be found two views of Mankind in Faulkner's work, diametrically opposed and often in conflict with each other. One is the Snopes view, which is this: man is a simple economic object, to be exploited or robbed for the benefit of any Snopes who can get at him. The other view O'Donnell called "traditional": man is a creature infinitely precious, who has an individual importance endowed by God. Flem represents the first view; Ratliff, even as a businessman, vehemently represents and upholds the opposing view. Ratliff is shrewd and clever and intensely enjoys the experience of swapping and trading, but he never uses his cleverness to cheat or defraud the people of the countryside. This truth is demonstrated by Faulkner's statement: "He could have passed from table to table in that country for six months without once putting his hand into his pocket"—he is that much genuinely liked. Flem's victory consists not merely in the fact that he takes Ratliff in but in the fact that Ratliff by his conduct—greed, secrecy, and the desire to get something for nothing—seems to demonstrate resoundingly that the Snopes view of humankind and human conduct is the correct one. This is not to say that Flem enjoys or is even aware of the moral nuances of the situation. No doubt he may receive an extra twist of satisfaction when he discovers that the fish in his trap is Ratliff, but primarily he is performing once more the classic Flem Snopes maneuver of killing two birds with one stone: he has disposed of an unwanted white elephant and disarmed a potent opponent. In point of fact Flem has not set his trap for Ratliff particularly; probably he merely notes that

Ratliff has bitten and moves on to wipe him out as thoroughly as possible. The major irony of the Frenchman Place episode is that it precisely repeats the pattern of the spotted horses, with exactly the same kind of temptation. But where Ratliff was able to "see through" the hokum of the spotted horses, he is completely trapped by the bait of buried treasure.

In the case of the horses, the bait, the glamour, is produced by the appeal to the small boy that lurks in every American male—the aura generated by the Wild West ponies and the presence of Buck Hipps, an authentic cowboy. The same appeal to the small-boy element surrounds the Old Frenchman Place—the persistent myth of treasure hastily hidden just before Grant's advance toward Vicksburg. There is also the more immediate motive: the eternal human hope of getting something for nothing. To be blunt, Ratliff and the others want to defraud Flem, to buy his land before he learns there is money there. If it were not for the elements of deliberate fraud, the heavy loss of tangible goods by Bookwright and Ratliff, and the complete bankruptcy and insanity of Armstid, the entire episode could easily be construed as comic. The plotting, the going without sleep, the chasing about the countryside after dark—all this has a little of the atmosphere of Tom Sawyer organizing a raid on a Sunday-school picnic. But the humor is blocked by the constant, sibilant madness of Armstid's savage whispers, and later on by Ratliff's own shocked awareness of what the lust for money is doing to him.

It is Armstid who makes the initial discovery that Flem Snopes is secretly digging in the garden of the Old Frenchman Place at night. We are not told how Ratliff becomes involved, but we watch step by step Ratliff's logic and shrewdness, his competence in estimating the economic motivation of the people, Will Varner and Flem Snopes in particular, overwhelming bit by bit his native skepticism and awareness of human gullibility and folly. Bit by bit he rationalizes himself to the point of knowing beyond question that Will Varner's and Flem's retention of the ruined plantation can only be governed by a direct knowledge that the treasure is there. He wills himself to believe that Flem Snopes would not otherwise spend his nights in furtive digging. Bookwright is convinced when he sees Flem actually on the scene.

The entire final section of *The Hamlet* is a small masterpiece depicting the effects of frantic greed on otherwise decent men, somewhat reminiscent of that fine novel, *The Treasure of Sierra Madre*. In its original magazine publication as a self-contained short story, the section was entitled "Lizards in Jamshyd's Courtyard." Every effect in the story is bent toward contrasting the frantic and furtive scurrying of the treasure hunters against the vast timelessness and indifference of the *mise en scène*. There is the constant reference, not only here but throughout the book, to the Ozymandias-like grandiosity of the ruined plantation house and its overgrown gardens. ("The slope had probably been a rose-garden. None of them knew or cared, just as they . . . did not know that the fallen pediment in the middle of the slope had once been a sundial.") Over, above and beyond the ruins of house and garden, broods the timelessness and indifference of Nature itself. This is seen in the rank overgrowth of briers which is gradually blurring the patterns of the garden and in the August stars seen through the remnants of the great mansion's roof. This timeless indifference is seen even more readily in the person of Uncle Dick Bolivar, the old hermit who douses for water and buried treasure with a forked twig. To a degree, Uncle Dick represents the occult, with his diet of frogs and lizards and his charms and nostrums, but it is made clear that his powers and abilities derive from white magic and may indeed consist of nothing more than a complete and loving affinity with the natural rhythms of the earth itself. When Ratliff has fetched Uncle Dick at midnight to the garden, Henry Armstid has already begun his furious digging. Uncle Dick will not begin his work until Henry stops "bruising the yearth." He tells them: "There air anger in the yearth. . . . Ye kin dig and ye kin dig, young man. . . . For what's rendered to the yearth, the yearth will keep until hit's ready to reveal hit."

Once Uncle Dick has located the sacks of treasure, there follows the depraved comedy of Ratliff's lying in wait for Flem and buying the Old Frenchman Place at Flem's price—a price that severely strains the resources of Ratliff and Bookwright and that deprives Armstid of the last thing he has in the world: his small farm, along with its pitiful stock of tools, animals, and equipment.

Even at the height of his treasure-madness, when he is scrambling in the dark as frantically as the others, those attitudes of character and personality which make Ratliff the admirable creature he is do not entirely desert him. At one point he is struggling violently with his good friend Bookwright for possession of a shovel; both of them are hissing threats at each other. Suddenly, Ratliff lets go his grip on the handle. He whispers, mostly to himself: "God. . . . Just look at what even the money a man aint got yet will do to him." After several nights of fruitless digging, the old qualities of skepticism and analysis reassert themselves. Ratliff and Bookwright soon establish beyond all question that they have been taken. It is easy and painful to imagine what might follow this realization in the hands of a less gifted writer: despair, rage, cries of anguish. In Faulkner's hands the reaction is reduced to simple comment, as Ratliff and Bookwright very quietly put down their tools to go and at last take a careful look at the coins they have dug up: "Bet you one of them I beat you."

They go into the empty, ruined, magnificence of the mansion they have been sleeping in. Here, under the skeleton of the crystal chandelier and the empty sweep of what had been the curving staircase, they light the lantern and examine the dates on the coins. Without exception, the dollars are all post-1865. "1871," says Ratliff. Bookwright replies "1879. . . . I even got one that was made last year. You beat me."

These quiet remarks sum up the reaction to the discovery that they have been defrauded and put under real and severe financial strain. For Ratliff at least, it means much more—it is the awareness of the degree to which he has acquiesced in his own corruption. Perhaps the quietness and restraint are caused only by the lack of proper food and sleep during the past week. But a contrast to this conduct is provided by Henry Armstid, whom they can see through the ruined window under a blue-saffron sky growing lighter, still digging away, waist-deep in the hole ". . . as if he had been cut in two at the hips, the dead torso, not even knowing it was dead, laboring on in measured stoop and recover like a metronome as Armstid dug himself back into that earth which had produced him to be its born and fated thrall forever until he died." In the half-dozen pages which conclude *The Hamlet,* there is presented the final tableau of Henry Armstid's public madness, his monomaniacal determination, and the crowds of people who come to watch him frenziedly digging for treasure that is not there.

Ratliff and Bookwright, of course, do not go on digging. Whatever else they have lost, they have retained sanity, balance, a sense of reality. In something more than a figurative sense, these nights of frenzied, futile digging and his own lapse into rapacious hostility represent Ratliff's dark night of the soul. His soul and spirit have been severely bruised, but in this minor version of the Fortunate Fall, he is the stronger for it. It is his vanity which is most severely chastised, and he knows better now what his strengths and weaknesses are. He enlists newer and younger allies and begins to share the delights of Snopes-watching with Gavin, Gowan, and Chick Mallison. As noted earlier, Ratliff's tactics change in *The Town* and *The Mansion* as the nature of Snopesism changes. With a mixture of amusement and embarrassment, Ratliff will see more and more of the actual business of Snopes-blocking carried out by Flem himself. While never for a moment forgetting Flem's basic rapacity and heartlessness, Ratliff sees easily what no one else realizes: that in his own untutored but unerring way, the one thing Flem really wants is to become a great and powerful financier. As bankers always must, Flem must become more conventional, more indubitably "legitimate" than anyone. And, whatever his motives, so long as Flem is clearly operating within the framework of law and convention, Ratliff can find no reason to thwart him.

If it were not such a ridiculous term for a man so alert, quizzical, and—in the final sense—so much more sophisticated than his friend Gavin, we could say that in the later books Ratliff is becoming the elder statesman, the senior philosopher, of Snopes-watching. Throughout *The Town* and *The Mansion,* we learn to look to Ratliff for the final insight on any matter. Faulkner still has his moments of high comedy with Ratliff's native rural caution in the matter of New York and the Allanovna neckties, but it is Ratliff, not Gavin, who is presented with the Barton Kohl sculpture. On the rare occasions when overt action is needed, the old Snopes-fighter comes forward to show how it is done.

He snaps off the career of Senator Clarence Eggletone Snopes
(whom we first learned to despise in *Sanctuary*) just at the
moment when Clarence is preparing to become a successful combination of Bilbo, Huey Long, and Joe McCarthy. Ratliff does
it with the aid of nothing more than two small boys and a dog-
thicket, but the results are enough to cause Uncle Billy Varner to
blow the whistle on Clarence's political career forever. He can
dismiss such a menace as "jest another Snopes."

To use the words of a major American poet, Ratliff is firmly
established on that high level where wit, occupation, and virtue
are one and the same, where "work is play for the highest
stakes"—he can say again and again, "Mankind aint really evil,
he jest aint got any sense." In the long, retrospective view, the
Snopeses have been like an invasion of Goths or Vandals. One
by one, the commonwealth has subdued, converted, or exiled them
all. Ratliff's comment at the end of *The Town,* when Flem is
sending the half-Apache children of Byron Snopes back to Texas,
may serve as an epigraph to all of the Snopes lore. ". . . they're
down at the dee-po now. Would . . . you gentlemen like to go
down with me and watch what they call the end of a erea, if that's
what they call what I'm trying to say? The last and final end of
Snopes out-and-out unvarnished behavior in Jefferson, that's what
I'm trying to say." It is more than fitting that this should be
said by Ratliff, who like Dilsey, has seen the beginning and the
end.

1. William Faulkner, *The Town* (New York: Random House, 1957), pp. 348-
49.
2. William Faulkner, *The Hamlet* (New York: Random House, 1940),
pp. 224-25.
3. *Ibid.,* p. 318.
4. *Ibid.,* p. 367.

7.

THE COMIC HERO: McCASLIN

V. K. RATLIFF IS, of all Faulkner's men of good will, the most worldly, the most practical. He is a sharp trader and in his own words an admitted philistine. In contrast, some of the McCaslins—most particularly Isaac (Uncle Ike) McCaslin—in their commitment to ideals and their rejection of materialism, most nearly approach the condition of sainthood. R. W. B. Lewis has recently published a book in which he labels Ike McCaslin a "picaresque saint."[1] This designation is very illuminating, although I should reserve the adjective picaresque for Isaac's father and brother, Uncle Buck and Uncle Buddy. There are in the life and career of Ike McCaslin deeper paradoxes than that implied in the picaro-saint opposition. Ike is saintly, more so perhaps than any character in the Faulkner canon; yet he is of all the comic heroes the one who most nearly approaches the condition of tragedy. This is paradox indeed, for admittedly a hero on the side of the angels is not tragic; yet in Isaac's case both sides of the paradox are precisely so. Perhaps this duality is possible because his tragedy grows not out of the saintliness of his personal rectitude but out of the failure of his lonely and lifelong passion to make that saintliness and rectitude operate dynamically and forcefully to do good in the lives of others.

Isaac McCaslin's life, and his struggle to achieve worthiness, is a very long one, even though we are shown only selected portions of it. Reduced to its simplest paraphrase, his progress can be assessed as follows: very early in life he aspired to and was found worthy of acceptance into a communion of secular initiates who practiced their dedicated vocation in the romantic, other-worldly demesne of the Wilderness. There he learned well how to live by a code right and fitting for that condition of life. By a constant process of self-examination and the exercise of humility, he managed to live up to the requirements of the code and thus came to be accepted by the Wilderness as one worthy to be part of itself. This way of life is whole and perfect, and Ike never discovers another code or condition to which he can feel so perfectly attuned. Yet, the brooding, elegiac awareness quietly grows on him, as it does on the reader, that none of it can last. The state of being which is the Wilderness is too pure, too otherworldly, too remote from the hurly-burly of human affairs to be lived in, even by a saint such as Isaac McCaslin.

The Bear illustrates many themes which are predominant in great American literature. One of the most persistent is the theme of pristine innocence being destroyed by the march of progress and the disappearance of the frontier. Another is the great moral truth that Huck and Jim must learn: that life on the raft is perfect and self-sufficient but that even the Mississippi finally comes to an end. Put another way, this realization is the same discovery made at Walden Pond. Thoreau had, after all, more than one life to live and other duties to perform, and the time came for him to return to the world of men.

Another illustration of this same necessity can be drawn from Plato. In the great allegory of the cave, the prisoner is forced, against his will, to engage in the slow and extremely painful process of giving up his comfortable delusions and struggling toward a union with the ultimate light. Yet, as Plato assures us, the achievement of this final state of being is meaningless, selfish, and irresponsible—unless the now enlightened prisoner returns to the darkness of the cave and attempts with whatever discouraging results to bring enlightenment and release to the other prisoners.

In precisely this same fashion, as part of his discovery of the meaning of his relationship to the Wilderness, Ike realizes that the Wilderness and its code are not suitable for the whole life of Man, because Man, including Ike McCaslin, must live in the world as it is. The Wilderness life—no matter how primitive or open or free—is in essence a life of morality based on an interior and private awareness and belonging. It is highly specialized, not suitable outside the rather special world which is the Wilderness.[2] The boy Ike realizes very soon that what he must have is a code of life that will function outside the Wilderness. As part of this same realization, Ike comes to know intuitively (along with Sam Fathers and Old Ben) that the Wilderness is doomed to go down before the onset of men and the mechanization of the world. Those who are most purely a part of the Wilderness, Old Ben the primal manifestation and Sam Fathers the high priest, will not be content to live after it is gone. Those who are less purely a part of it, Boon Hogganbeck for instance, will survive as a pitiful shadow of what they once were. Ike McCaslin, because he is man as well as saint, will spend the rest of his long life attempting to live the code of the Wilderness, with whatever success, in the world as it is, the world of materialism and mendacity.

ii.

Much goes into the making of a saint. Ike McCaslin is, as any man is, the unique result of the forces that have operated upon him. These are his time, his place, the social pattern in which he lives, as well as his growing self-awareness and the decisions he makes in the light of this awareness. Ike is the sum of his ancestry, and his life pattern is shaped by his discovery of what his heritage, both personal and social, has been. The first McCaslin in Yoknapatawpha was old Lucius Quintus Carothers McCaslin, that "evil and unregenerate old man" who was Ike's grandfather, who ". . . bought the land, took the land, got the land no matter how, held it to bequeath, no matter how, out of the old grant, the first patent, when it was a wilderness of wild beasts and wilder men. . . ."[3]

Convinced that the entire system is as cursed as the heritage of miscegenation and incest which their father has left them, his sons, Buck and Buddy, begin the process of removing themselves from any participation in the system of exploitation that has brought about the evil. As soon as their father is buried, they move out of the great unfinished shell of a plantation-house into a two-room log cabin they have built with their own hands. From there, they direct the operation of the plantation, because some competent person must do so, but they do not profit from it.

Like many things in the Faulkner canon, the "system" the McCaslin twins put into operation is never presented directly but must be pieced together from hints and fragments of the conversations of others. The system is shown twice indirectly in *Go Down, Moses*, once comically in the story "Was" and once with some critical assessment in the long dialogue between Ike and McCaslin (Cass) Edmonds in Part 4 of *The Bear*. The most complete account occurs in another book entirely, *The Unvanquished*, and is given third-hand by the boy Bayard Sartoris in explaining the eccentric actions of Uncle Buck. Part of this description gives the full flavor of the comic side; evidently all Yoknapatawpha takes part in the enjoyment of it, since Buck and Buddy are universally respected and admired in the community. All the countryside knows how Uncle Buck herds the Negroes into the big house and makes a great show of locking them in for the night while they are running out the back to dodge the patterollers and reveling in the forbidden pleasures of visiting on other plantations. By the unspoken gentlemen's agreement between the McCaslins and the slaves, Uncle Buck and Uncle Buddy will not peek around the house and the Negroes will be back by work time the following morning. It should be kept in mind that Bayard is quoting the assessment of the McCaslin "system" made by his father, Colonel John Sartoris, who, whatever else, was a man of some learning and executive ability. Behind the comic aspects, there is a great deal of serious purpose.

There was more to Uncle Buck and Uncle Buddy than just that. Father said they were ahead of their time; he said they not only possessed, but put into practice, ideas about social relationship that maybe fifty years after they were both dead people would have a name for. These ideas were about land. They believed that land did not belong to people but that people belonged to land and that the earth would permit them to live on it and out of it and use it only so long as they behaved and if they did not behave right, it would shake them off just like a dog getting rid of fleas. They had some kind of a system of bookkeeping which must have been even more involved than their betting score against one another, by which all their niggers were to be freed, not given freedom, but earning it, buying it not in money from Uncle Buck and Buddy, but in work from the plantation.[4]

According to the Sartoris account, there was even more to it than that. The system also embraces and helps the poor whites from the surrounding areas, as well as the McCaslin Negroes, ". . . promising them in return nobody knew exactly what, except that their women and children did have shoes, which not all of them had had before, and a lot of them even went to school."[5]

Uncle Buck and Buddy are men who seem in every way to be successful. They are able to make a realistic appraisal of the legacy of evil their father left them and to make their own effective adjustment to it. Their system of operating the plantation for the benefit of the slaves who live on it is dynamic and effective in human terms as well as economic and even leaves them to a large degree free to enjoy their fox-hunting, poker, and generally happy bachelor existence. The war and the subsequent Reconstruction put an end to the simplicity of this system, and Ike would have been compelled in any case to devise his own. Even though his father and uncle die when he is very young, he has them for precept and example and is able to pattern his morality after theirs to some extent.

Within Ike McCaslin's own lifetime, there are the two forces, the two lines of development, which will shape him toward the man he will become. One of them is his relation to the Wilderness and the Wilderness code as a way of life; the other is his discovery of the hidden and more shameful aspects of the heritage which old Carothers McCaslin has left him. These two forces are interdependent and by no means separable from each other, but they can be to some extent divided on the basis of chronology, since Ike reaches a definite assessment of his relationship to the Wilderness by age eighteen, and although he becomes aware of his heritage earlier, he cannot make the formal renunciation until he is twenty-one. At that time the final synthesis emerges, and Ike McCaslin will attempt for the remainder of his long life to live by a version of the Wilderness code which will be operative, dynamic, and effective in the world of men and affairs.

iii.

Structurally, *Go Down, Moses* is a loosely compacted chain
of episodes, some of which are concerned with groups of people
only distantly related to the McCaslin-Beauchamp dynasty. The-
matically, the book is all of a piece, because in one way or another
each section is a story of the relatedness or non-relatedness of
black people and white people to the world which they share.
Loose and episodic as the book is in parts, it does contain *The
Bear,* which page for page is unquestionably Faulkner's most
densely packed achievement and may easily be his greatest work.
As in any great work of literature, there are in *The Bear* neces-
sarily deeper levels of meaning which connect with and success-
fully reinforce each other. But also, as in any work that is truly
great, the story can be read with coherence and significance even
if the deeper meanings are missed at first reading.

Precisely because of this highly numinous quality, *The Bear*
has presented the critic with a variety of approaches: archetypal,
historical, sociological, theological, all of which are richly reward-
ing in the insights which they present. Obviously, *The Bear* is
concerned with dynastic and regional history, and this history is
one factor in Isaac McCaslin's final assessment of his heritage
and his developing pattern of life. Certainly, much of the novel
is concerned with magic, totemism, myth of all kinds, and rites of
passage. There is, in Ike's long and demanding process of training, preparation, and purification to gain acceptance by the Wilderness, more than a hint of the matter of chivalry and the Grail
legends. There is an obviously intended theological atmosphere
in the relation of Sam Fathers ("the priest") to the Wilderness;
the way in which Old Ben is made manifest to Ike once Ike has
performed the necessary purification; and the various blood cere-
monies, sacrifices, and deaths.

The book is consciously filled with symbols, but these symbols
are so organic and the fusion between object and significance so
perfect that the symbols never appear overtly, simply because they
are seldom so imperfectly chosen as to jar upon the consciousness
of the reader. Often symbols and significance are identical. For
instance the gun, watch, and compass which Ike must discard in
the process of purification do not merely "stand for" the gadgets

of mechanized civilization, they *are* such gadgets, and typical ones. Old Ben is a bear; he does not stand for the numen of the Wilderness, he contains that numen and so is the most significant part of the Wilderness. One continuing symbol is the silver-mounted, deerskin-covered hunting horn which belonged to General Compson, who used it all his life and willed it to Ike as the only suitable inheritor. Many, many years later, Ike gives it to the mother of Roth Edmonds' illegitimate son to keep until the boy comes of age. In the time of the great Wilderness hunters, it was a hunting horn and as such stirs the memory of the reader, at whatever subconscious level, with echoes of other sagas and heroes— Beowolf or Roland or Siegfried. When Uncle Ike gives it away, it has become one of the pitifully few possessions of a broken old man, and as such it is appropriate for the child who is the last of the tragic McCaslin-Beauchamp-Edmonds line. All these avenues to understanding *The Bear,* fascinating as they are, must be relinquished in favor of the examination of Isaac McCaslin as a man of good will, comic hero, and secular saint.

iv.

If Ike McCaslin's life can be summarized as a constant and consistent attempt to achieve worthiness, then his earliest efforts at virtue are expressed in his boyish longing to be allowed to go into the Wilderness with the men who are already confirmed in the status of hunters and to become like them, so that he may gain acceptance by them and by it. In his long period of apprenticeship he has the best of masters: Sam Fathers, the great hunter, the chief priest of the Wilderness. Gradually the realization begins to grow on Ike, as it does on the reader, that Sam is preparing him for much more than the simple role of the hunter. Sam has found in Ike an acolyte who is worthy of great trust by reason of his more sensitive awareness, his response to the mystique which Sam offers him, and his inherent willingness to take upon himself the responsibility and stewardship which Sam has held so long. In the process of preparation, Ike must learn what the heritage of the past has been in order that he may know what use to make of it.

And as he talked about those old times and those dead and vanished men of another race from either that the boy knew, gradually to the boy those old times would cease to be old times and would become a part of the boy's present, not only as if they had happened yesterday but as if they were still happening, the men who walked through them actually walking in breath and air and casting an actual shadow on the earth they had not quitted. And more: as if some of them had not happened yet but would occur tomorrow, until at last it would seem to the boy that he himself had not come into existence yet, that none of his race nor the other subject race which his people had brought with them into the land had come here yet. . . .[6]

When at last Ike can "write his age in two ciphers" he is allowed by his cousin McCaslin Edmonds to go into the Wilderness with the other hunters. He is trained in technique by Sam, taught "when to shoot and not to shoot." But he is not yet worthy; it will be two more years before Sam will allow him to kill a deer and have his face marked with the symbolic blood. But there is much else to do; there is the last day of the trip which is always set aside for the hunting of Old Ben. Like many Faulkner characters who seem to absorb their cultural and mythic heritage almost by the process of osmosis, Ike cannot remember a time when he had not heard of Old Ben. At first, he knows of the legendary bear only as most people who have not seen him know of him: as a legend, a creature of incredible size, supernatural strength, and cunning, and a charmed life, but indubitably a corporeal bear and nothing more. Ike's one great concern at this age is to be permitted to take part—to be found worthy to take part—in the "yearly pageant-rite of the old bear's furious immortality." He is afraid that the bear may be killed before he can have even the opportunity to see it. This concern, to "see the bear," becomes the central hope of his life at this age.

On his first hunt, the year he is ten, he hears the hounds when they strike Old Ben's scent by accident. Later he sees the little hound bitch who has been raked by Old Ben's claws, and he knows it was "no living creature but only the wilderness which, leaning for a moment, had patted lightly once her temerity." Then Sam takes him far into the woods and shows him the actual pawprint of Old Ben. Standing in the gloom of the dying November afternoon, he knows what it was that he heard in the abject sound of the hound's voices: the sense of fragility and impotence against the immensity and timelessness of the Wilderness. Sam tells him that if tomorrow the dogs should find desperation and courage enough actually to press the great bear, then it would be Ike, the youngest and least experienced of the hunters, that he would run over to escape.

Ike waits throughout the short winter daylight for the hunt to come near him, but it never does. The only noise is the loud and steady clatter of a giant woodpecker. More and more he feels the immensity and loneliness of the Wilderness he is in; he seems to share the awe and terror of other, more ancient men who also crept through this vastness. Suddenly he realizes the woodpecker is silent, and he knows that Old Ben is somewhere close, looking at him. Transfixed in awe but not in fear he waits, holding the gun which he now knows he will never fire at this bear. Then the woodpecker starts again, and he knows the bear has gone. Sam later says that they do not yet have the dog which can bay and hold Old Ben, "But maybe someday."

Ike's distinct status as a novice is indicated by the ease of his assumption that none of it—the bear, the hunters, the Wilderness—can ever change. "Because there would be a next time, after and after." He is learning; Old Ben has emerged from the limbo of legend into the actuality of time, and however casually, has acknowledged the existence, at least, of Isaac McCaslin. Ike is growing to realize that it will be his destiny to inherit all of it; he could not avoid it even if he wished. To "see the bear" he has only to go through the necessary preparation and ritual purifications, if he can discover what they are. Now, like the young knight in the Grail legends, he must actively search on his own. When the hunters go back on the following June for their holiday, Ike pretends to be hunting squirrels. In reality, he is attempting to track the bear down to get a glimpse of him. Finally Sam tells him: "You ain't looked right yet. . . . It's the gun. . . . You will have to choose." Long before daylight of the next day, Ike sets out, leaving the gun behind.

Using only the sun and his compass, he ranges very far into the Wilderness but discovers no sign of Old Ben. He realizes he is still tainted by the devices of mechanistic civilization, his compass and watch. Without hesitation, he makes the final gesture: he removes his watch and compass and hangs them on a bush, then pushes on. Almost at once he is lost. On the second back-cast he sits on a log to rest. He sees the first fresh prints of the maimed, two-toed foot, and beyond it the series of fresher ones.

. . . and the wilderness coalesced. It rushed, soundless, and solidi-fied—the tree, the bush, the compass and the watch glinting where a ray of sunlight touched them. Then he saw the bear. It did not emerge, appear; it was there, immobile, fixed in the green and windless noon's hot dappling, not as big as he had dreamed it but as big as he had expected, bigger, dimensionless against the dappled obscurity, looking at him. Then it moved. It crossed the glade without haste, walking for an instant into the sun's full glare and out of it, and stopped again and looked back at him across one shoulder. Then it was gone. It didn't walk into the woods. It faded, sank back into the wilderness without motion as he had watched a fish, a huge old bass, sink back into the dark depths of its pool and vanish without even any movement of its fins.[7]

In the fullest sense, the numen of the Wilderness has been made manifest, and the godhead become flesh has shown itself to Isaac McCaslin. This is only the first of many such glimpses. At the moment, Ike has a vocation that is sufficient to inform him that the bear's manifestation is not a final achievement, only a beginning of what is to come. It seems to him that he alone realizes what the actual significance of the old bear is. Sam Fathers knows Old Ben as coeval and a fellow spirit, but even now Ike sees the bear in what might be called a historical perspective.

It was as if the boy had already divined what his senses and intellect had not encompassed yet: that doomed wilderness whose edges were being constantly and punily gnawed at by men with plows and axes who feared it because it was wilderness . . . through which ran not even a mortal beast but an anachronism indomitable and invincible out of an old dead time, a phantom, epitome and apotheosis of the old wild life which the puny little humans swarmed and hacked at in a fury of abhorrence and fear. . . .[8]

With such knowledge comes responsibility. He is an expert woodsman by the time he is twelve and within a short time knows game trails that not even Sam has seen. He finds himself becom-ing so skillful so fast that he is afraid he will never become worthy, simply because he has not found a way to learn humility or the appropriate forms of pride. These qualities will be taught him by Sam Fathers and a small mongrel fyce. On one occasion between the regular hunting seasons, Ike and Sam take a brace of hounds and Ike's fyce and set up an ambush for the bear. Their reason for the ambush is not clear even to them; perhaps it is merely part of Ike's intense desire to know more and more, to gain a closer look at Old Ben. The ambush is successful. The fyce's yapping is so frantic and hysterical that the bear stops short and rises on his hind legs, bigger and bigger, while the transfixed Ike clutches his gun, unable to move. "Then he realized that the fyce was actually not going to stop. He flung the gun down and ran. When he overtook and grasped the shrill, frantically pinwheeling little dog, it seemed to him that he was directly under the bear. He could smell it, strong and hot and rank. Sprawling, he looked up where it loomed and towered over him like a thunderclap. It was quite familiar, until he remembered: this was the way he had used to dream about it."[9] When he looks up again, Old Ben is gone and Sam is standing over him with the gun. " 'You've done seed him twice now, with a gun in your hands,' he said. 'This time you couldn't have missed him.' The boy rose. He still held the fyce. Even in his arms it continued to yap frantically, surging and straining toward the fading sound of the hounds like a collection of livewire springs. The boy was panting a little. 'Neither could you,' he said. 'You had the gun. Why didn't you shoot him?' "[10]

Sam does not answer; he takes the still frantically yapping fyce in his hands and calms it with words. " 'You's almost the one we wants,' he said. 'You just aint big enough. We aint got that one yet. He will need to be just a little bigger than smart, and a little braver than either.' He withdrew his hand from the fyce's head and stood looking into the woods where the bear and the hounds had vanished. 'Somebody is going to, some day.' 'I know it,' the boy said. 'That's why it must be one of us. So it wont be until the last day. When even he dont want it to last any longer.' "[11]

v.

In Lion, the hunters have found the dog who may be powerful and fearless enough to bay and hold Old Ben. In all the circumstances surrounding the discovery, capture, and training of Lion there is more than a hint of the mysterious but not the fortuitous. No one knows where the dog came from, and there is no explanation of how a creature given to killing and eating things as big as foals and calves has gone so long undetected. When the dead colt is found only Sam knows that the killer is a dog and is *the* dog. With unerring skill he traps the animal and begins to train him—not to break his spirit, savagery, and strength, but simply to render him subject to control, to focus that cold, implacable violence toward the one end of matching him against Old Ben. Lion is as yet only a potential. The first year there is hardly a contest; the bear eludes both dog and hunters easily. The second year, he is bayed and held for a few moments; the hunters draw blood. "Never mind," says Major de Spain, with calm confidence. "Next year . . . we'll get him." No one disagrees. Even the rankest outsiders, the totally uninitiated, can sense the implication of portent, the atmosphere of foreboding. More perhaps even than Sam, the fifteen-year-old Ike realizes the portentousness: "So he should have hated and feared Lion. Yet he did not. . . . It seemed to him that something, he didn't know what, was beginning; had already begun. It was like the last act on a set stage. It was the beginning of the end of something, he didn't know what except that he would not grieve. He would be humble and proud that he had been found worthy to be a part of it too or even just to see it. . . ."[12]

The death of Old Ben in Part 3 is in one sense the climactic point of *The Bear*. This climax is also a major turning point in the life of Ike McCaslin as it is in that of every other character in the story. The death of the great bear is the end of something, for some of the men involved the end of a great deal. Only for Ike McCaslin is it the beginning of something new. Structurally, there is at the beginning of Part 3 a long digression in the form of the trip which Ike and Boon Hogganbeck make to Memphis. As narrative, the interruption is explained by a long, hard spell of freezing weather, during which the ground is too cold and dry to hold a scent and the dogs cannot trail. Boon is sent to Memphis for more whiskey, and Ike is sent to see that Boon gets back to camp with at least part of it. Aesthetically, this episode interrupts the flow of the story, but in terms of meaning and significance, the Memphis trip is inserted to demonstrate that Boon cannot function outside the Wilderness. This significance is underlined in the impact of his wildly uncouth appearance on the city people, his inability to stay out of saloons, his unrestrained drunkenness, and his quarrelsome tirades on the magnificence of Lion delivered to total strangers too terrified to ignore him. By diplomacy and force, Ike gets him back to Hoke's and eventually to the camp. The weather is overcast and thawing. "Lion will get him tomorrow," says Boon.

Never has the chase gone so well. Old Ben follows his custom of plunging into the river; Ike, Sam, and Boon swim the December-cold stream to find the bear bayed erect against the trunk of a great tree. Lion has Ben by the throat, and the bear is raking Lion's belly with his forepaws. Boon throws down his gun and leaps astride the bear's back, knife in hand. Once, twice, the knife falls, and Old Ben crashes to the ground, incredibly dead. Gently, ignoring the blood from his own wounds, Boon pries Lion's jaws loose from the dead bear and gives orders to Tennie's Jim to go for the doctor. Only then does anyone notice that Sam Fathers is lying face-downward in the mud. Neither Major nor Edmonds nor even Boon guesses what Ike already knows: that Sam will not live. He alone understands why Sam dropped, stunned and paralyzed, at the moment of Old Ben's death. On the level of realism, Sam's "stroke" is simply the result of swimming rivers in December. Symbolically, Sam and old Ben are both so deeply a part of the Wilderness that the death of one all but kills the other. Old Ben has willed to die because he knows the Wilderness is doomed. Sam also has no wish to live after the Wilderness is gone.

After Lion is buried, the hunters begin breaking camp to return to civilization. Ike's near-hysterical insistence that he be allowed to stay with Sam causes General Compson to intercede with Edmonds. When Edmonds and Major return three days later they find Sam buried Chickasaw fashion in a tree-platform, Ike and Boon keeping vigil below. " 'Did you kill him, Boon?' asks McCaslin. 'Tell the truth . . . I would have done it if he had asked me to.' " Boon is the appropriate instrument when

Sam asks to die, just as he is the appropriate instrument for the death of Old Ben. Throughout, Faulkner has concentrated on Boon's non-human or half-human characteristics. He responds to the death of Lion by drunken talk and singing. Once Boon and Ike have performed the death rites of Sam and stood vigil over his Chickasaw tree burial, there is nothing for Boon to do, since the Wilderness and hunting are all he knows. He has spent most of his life in the woods, but he is not one of the true initiates. This is shown with finality in the episode of the gum tree and the squirrels. Each of the hunters responds in his own way to the death of Old Ben and the passing of the Wilderness. From *The Sound and the Fury* we know that old General Compson leaves his house in Jefferson and moves out to a fishing camp in the river bottom to spend his last days. Major de Spain, embroiled in his bank, sells the Wilderness to the timber company without telling the others. Edmonds, especially after Ike has formally repudiated his inheritance, is more and more taken up with running the McCaslin plantation and gradually drifts away from the attitudes and mystique of the hunter. Of all the hunters, only Ike McCaslin finds a way to take the morality of this special world on to the end of his life.

vi.

Part 5 of *The Bear* begins with a deliberately low-key recollection of two episodes involving half-grown bears. One is used to underscore the sickened response of Ike to the sprawling stockpiles of equipment being readied for the destruction of the Wilderness—twenty years ago it was possible to hold up the log train for two days while a frightened cub gained enough courage to come out of a tree. The other memory is a comic one in which a grumbling Old Ash is taken to hunt in the snow and is prevented from killing a cub. The recollection of this winter scene is used for the subtle shift into that sonorously orchestrated celebration of "——; summer, and fall, and snow, and wet and saprife spring in their ordered immortal sequence . . . ," which in turn is the affirmation that there is no death. Here ". . . where dissolution itself was a seething turmoil of ejaculation tumescence conception and birth . . ." corruption has put on incorruptibility. Ike places the libation of tobacco and peppermint he has brought, setting it in the axle-grease tin nailed to a tree near Sam's grave, knowing it will soon be dissolved back into the seething life that fills the wilderness. Perhaps he has stepped on the grave itself, but this does not matter, since what does matter of Sam and Lion has been transmuted: ". . . myriad yet undiffused of every myriad part, leaf and twig and particle, air and sun and rain and dew and night, acorn oak and leaf and acorn again, dark and dawn and dark and dawn again in their immutable progression and, being myriad, one: and Old Ben too, Old Ben too; they would give him his paw back even, certainly they would give him his paw back: then the long challenge and the long chase, no heart to be driven and outraged, no flesh to be mauled and bled. . . ."[13]

Sam, Lion, and Old Ben were each true enough to himself to know when to die. It should be remembered that Sam and Ike agreed that Old Ben would be killed only when he himself no longer wished to live. That time comes with the beginning of the end of the Wilderness. In his own mysterious way, Sam knows also. Only then does the great mongrel Lion appear, full-grown, powerful, and ruthless, for Sam to train and use as the appropriate instrument to bring the lives of all three and a certain segment of history to a close. Lion, who cares for no person and no thing, is destructive, unfeeling, and completely alien to the Wilderness. As directed and used by Sam, and by his partici-pation in the rites and his death, Lion becomes a part of that which will never die. In the dappled, springtime green when Ike is walk-ing, all this is possible. His meditation is broken with a chilling shock; almost under his foot there is an enormous rattlesnake:

. . . the old one, the ancient and accursed about the earth, fatal and solitary and he could smell it now: the thin sick smell of rotting cu-cumbers and something else which had no name, evocative of all knowledge and an old weariness and of pariah-hood and of death. . . . even now he could not quite believe that all that shift and flow of shadow behind that walking head could have been one snake: going and then gone; he put the other foot down at last and didn't know it, standing with one hand raised as Sam had stood that afternoon six years ago when Sam led him into the wilderness and showed him and he ceased to be a child, speaking the old tongue which Sam had

spoken that day without premeditation either: "Chief . . . Grandfather."[14]

For all the multi-leveled symbolism, the significance of these
closing pages should be clear. Everything that has happened
previously in *The Bear* has prepared for this moment, even the
content of Part 4, which covers a period three years after Part 5.
Ike moves from subjective vision to rattlesnake to Boon under
the gum tree. These closely juxtaposed tableaux may be taken to
represent three conditions of life or modes of being. Ike's rhap-
sodic vision of a life beyond death for Sam, Lion, and Old Ben
("no flesh to be mauled and bled") echoes the mythology of the
American Indian. A life in which hunter and hunted live in
amiable immortality would be a final purification of that state of
purity which the boy Ike wanted for himself, the Wilderness code
lived in the Wilderness, which cannot be lived in the world of
men. Within this same mythology, the rattlesnake, like the bear,
was regarded with special reverence. The sacramental significance
is deepened when the snake is moved to wider frames of reference,
particularly the Judaeo-Christian. The serpent, symbol of pariah-
hood and death and instigator of Man's fall from grace ("the old
one, ancient and accursed about the earth") must appear at this
moment because the Wilderness, Eden-like as it is, is not Eden
but part of the fallen world. Evil is in the world, even in the
Eden of the Wilderness. Concurrently, the snake is a sacred,
totemic animal and entitled to its place there. Like Old Ben, it
is powerful, self-sufficient, ruthless, and indifferent. Only after
the snake is gone does Ike realize that he has been standing with
his hand raised in the ritual gesture and has spoken the words in
the old tongue he learned from Sam: "Chief . . . Grandfather."
He is saved from death by the same inexplicable rapport that
caused Old Ben to spare him; he is recognized as one of the initiate
Wilderness creatures and is safe from harm. On his part, Ike
acknowledges the snake, who is simultaneously sacred and a dis-
inherited outcast, like Oedipus or Philoctetes. Thus Ike accepts
the reality of evil in the world.

Throughout *The Bear*, Boon Hogganbeck is shown as half-
savage, half-child ("the mind of a child, the heart of a horse").
The hunters tolerate him easily, though with a tinge of condescen-

sion. All the evidence shows Boon lacking the true hunter's dispensation; he cannot move quietly in the woods and has never hit anything with his gun. His symbolic status as inferior to Sam is constant, and for this reason he is the instrument that kills Old Ben, the sacred object which is death to touch. It is this action which can never be undone, even though Boon had no choice. With the end of the Wilderness, the cup of Boon's life is truly broken. Being only half-human, he is still not absolved from the responsibilities of his humanity or his actions. (Lion, being animal, is blameless.) Hysterical and helpless under the gum tree, he is torn between two worlds. One is the real world of progress, machines, and technology, in which he cannot master so simple a thing as an archaic pump-gun; the other is the vanished world he helped to kill, now gone forever.

vii.

Part 4 is easily the most "difficult" part of the novel, the one which is by far the most demanding of the reader's attention. The difficulty is partly the result of style; large portions of the section are subjective dialogue and interior monologue, as opposed to the objective, narrated action of the other sections. A greater difficulty grows out of the content. Part 4 is a grabbag of miscellaneous parts of apparently unrelated ideas which seem to have little connection with one another. But this apparent welter of bits and pieces contains the necessary parts of the puzzle; taken together with the other parts, it makes *The Bear* the wonderful entity it is. Like other works in the canon, it is part of the larger time-space continuum which is the Yoknapatawpha Chronicle. It contains the long debate between Ike and McCaslin Edmonds which finally resolves itself into the classic dichotomy between the claims of the active and the contemplative life. These are the patterns the lives of the cousins will take. Aside from the Wilderness, its creatures, and hunting, the major focus of Isaac McCaslin's moral concern is people and land. The concern for people primarily implies good will toward humanity but applies most immediately to the white and near-white descendants of old Carothers and how best to help them. The McCaslin theories about land apply most immediately to the plantation which Ike

is to inherit. It is from the old ledgers in the office of the plantation commissary that Ike learns the whole truth about his family
heritage. These ledgers record the outlay of clothing and supplies
against each tenant's credit for his share of the crop, the income
and outgo. Historically, the plantation system is summed up this
way: ". . . that slow trickle of molasses and meal and meat, of
shoes and straw hats and overalls, of plowlines and collars and
heel-bolts and buckheads and clevises, which returned each fall
as cotton—the two threads frail as truth and impalpable as equa-
tors yet cablestrong to bind for life them who made the cotton to
the land their sweat fell on. . . ."[15]

Ike discovers in the ledgers that series of personal memoranda
which Uncle Buck and Uncle Buddy wrote to each other. These
are concerned with the routine of the plantation, but one notation
unlocks a record of human outrage and heartbreak. *"Turl Son
of Thucydus @ Eunice Tomy born Jun 1833 yr stars fell Fathers
will"*[16]

Fitting the jig-saw puzzle together, Ike finds that old Carothers
bought Eunice in the New Orleans slave market in 1807 and
married her to Thucydus in 1809. Tomey was born shortly
thereafter. In 1832, when Tomey was twenty-two, her mother
drowned herself. Tomey's child was born the following June,
Tomey dying in childbirth. In 1837, old Carothers died, leaving
the legacy to be paid to Tomey's Turl. There seems little doubt:
Carothers McCaslin fathered Turl on Tomey, his own near-white
daughter. Like Orestes, or Oedipus in his old age, Ike's problem
is not so much to assess and assign blame but to find a way to
cancel the past evil and expiate what has been done. He is not
blind to the indifferent cynicism which the legacy demonstrates.
Carothers knew he would never live until Turl became twenty-one;
he cynically left the bequest to be paid by his sons. There is more
than simple depravity in such actions; a deeper philosophy is implied. To summon his own daughter to the house and get a child
on her and dismiss them both with cynical indifference indicates
that Carothers did not regard them as human at all. The black
men, women, and children in his care do not have souls infinitely
precious to God but are chattels like mules or cotton, to be used or
sold as the owner sees fit.

Throughout the present study, the definition of evil has been limited to human terms—the evil that man does to man. In the long debate between Ike and McCaslin Edmonds, Ike says that he is trying to explain the reason for the drastic step he is taking. He is certain there is a connection between the earth, the land, the soil, and the accursed things which have happened on it. He can only conclude that the land itself is accursed. Groping for an explanation, he attempts to trace out the process by which it happened. Perhaps the logical starting place is the myth of the New Eden. With the discovery of the New World, the notion arose that the new hemisphere offered a new hope, a second chance at Eden. Here in this fresh, unspoiled wilderness, it might be possible to establish a way of life that would be free of the Old World's turmoil, strife, injustice, and oppression. Here, free men might be able to live in dignity, peace, and integrity before God. It seems unlikely such a happy state could exist on this continent or any other, but the impact of the possibility, the potential, left the early observers of the continent awe-stricken with the dream, which did not entirely die until the end of the nineteenth century.

The dream of human dignity and individual liberty (which reached its final crystallization perhaps in Jefferson's draft of the Declaration of Independence) already contained the seeds of its own destruction in the institution of human slavery, the denial of dignity and individual liberty to human beings, primarily for the purpose of exploiting the land. With the invention of the cotton gin, more and more ways were found to justify slavery. As Ike explains it, God sent the Civil War and Reconstruction not merely to destroy the institution of slavery but also to compel the North and Middle West ("the drawers of bills and the shavers of notes and the schoolmasters and the self-ordained to teach and lead and all that horde of the semi-literate with a white shirt but no change for it") to stand together for a decent cause. Reconstruction demonstrated that there is no morality of movements or wars or institutions; there is only the morality of individual men. Therefore, Ike must get completely outside the pattern his ancestors have followed, so that he may be free to carry out his self-appointed task. He intuits the connection between land and people and the interchange of cause and effect from one to the other. All the evil, he tells Edmonds, grows out of the violation of stewardship—the Christian idea that all things in the Universe are God's, not Man's. Things, objects—land, for instance—are simply entrusted, subject to proper use, and are never owned outright, however much the individual man may think so. Ike can repudiate ownership of the plantation because it was never his father's or grandfather's to begin with. In this way he can remove himself from further effects of his accursed heritage and free himself to help others who have been damaged by the chain of evil which was set in motion at the time of the New World's discovery. With all the humility Sam Fathers taught him, Ike tells his cousin McCaslin of his conviction that he is following God's will in repudiating the plantation, that God gave Man a second chance in the New World, and Man despoiled that. The war accomplished very little that was permanent, so that now God has used an old man, a little dog, and a fierce old bear to teach a boy a lesson and set his Will working again. In the light of this conviction it is not surprising that Edmonds cannot dissuade him, either at the moment or in the future. The life of Isaac McCaslin illustrates that most Christian of all paradoxes: he who loses his life shall gain it. By giving up his material inheritance, Ike has gained the most precious of all freedoms: freedom to choose and execute courses of moral action. At the end of his long life it appears that the paradox may cut both ways; he who saves himself cannot save others.

viii.

Many other threads in Part 4 radiate outward. We learn how Ike became a carpenter, married, and lost his wife when he refused to claim the plantation, thus becoming "father to no one." There is the recital of the slow disintegration of Hubert Beauchamp, that "bluff burly roaring childlike man." In the story "Was," Mr. Hubert's aimless way of life is innocent social comedy. In Part 4 of *The Bear* (without his sister Sophonsiba to hold him down, as McCaslin said, or to raise him up, as Uncle Buddy said), he brings his yellow wenches into the house to live and sells the priceless family possessions one by one. When Ike was born, his Uncle Hubert had filled a silver loving cup with gold coins, packaged it in burlap, and sealed it in wax, as a tangible legacy. When he is destitute, living on the McCaslin plantation, he steals the coins one by one from the cup, leaving scribbled notes of hand. At last he steals the cup itself, substituting a bright, new tin coffeepot. It is this pot that Ike uses on his hunting trips for the next sixty years. What has been sophisticated comedy in "Was" becomes a parody of the Grail legends. The decay of roaring Hubert slides over into a Chekhovian tragedy of a life wasted in the drift of a purposeless existence.

The Bear ends just as Ike sets out into his mature life. A concluding chapter of his career is found in the story "Delta Autumn," also a part of *Go Down, Moses*. There is a lapse of almost sixty years. Uncle Ike has staked a lifelong struggle for integrity on his principle of renunciation; in this story he faces a crisis that seems to question even the sacrifice itself. He is almost eighty years old. By that time, the hunters must drive two hundred miles in automobiles to find a wilderness where there is game. From the conversation in the car, Ike learns that Roth Edmonds, grandson of McCaslin Edmonds, has had an affair with a woman living somewhere nearby. In camp, the bantering conversation of the other hunters leads Ike to reaffirm his belief in the dignity of Man, the need to protect "fawns and does"—children and childbearers—and a trust in a God who has given both the right to hunt game and the responsibility this right entails. In reply to another question, there is implied everything his brief marriage must have held for him, all he wanted in the son and the family life he did not have: "I think that every man and woman, at the instant when it dont even matter whether they marry or not, I think that whether they marry then or afterward or dont never, at that instant the two of them together were God."

Imagery and tone are used skillfully here to underline the singleness of purpose in the life of Isaac McCaslin, to show how past and present are a single entity. Even the sound of the November rain is just as it always was. Lying sleepless in his cot, Isaac McCaslin reviews the events of his life so long ago; Major de Spain and McCaslin, and how Sam Fathers taught him all he knew; how into all the magnificence and humility which was the wilderness came the knowledge of the "wrong and shame" which is his heritage from old Carothers, embodied and contained in the "tamed land" which is the McCaslin plantation. ". . . even if he couldn't cure the wrong and eradicate shame . . . at least he could repudiate the wrong and shame . . . and at least the land itself in fact, for his son at least . . . and, saving and freeing his son, lost him."[17]

Before dawn, as the others are leaving to hunt, Roth brings a bundle of money to Uncle Ike's cot and says "Tell her No." When the woman arrives with the baby, Ike is impressed by her quiet dignity and her obvious moral superiority to the spineless father of her child. He is shattered when she tells him who she is. "You're a nigger!" he cries. "Yes," she says, "James Beauchamp—you called him Tennie's Jim though he had a name—was my grandfather. I said you were Uncle Isaac." Tennie's Jim was Ike's near-white first cousin, helper and participant in all the hunts, particularly at the death of Old Ben. Through whatever distance, the blood that flows in this poised and undaunted young woman and her child is the blood that flows in Isaac McCaslin. The child is the only male in whom the McCaslin blood is carried on. Uncle Ike makes his gesture of positive recognition; even though he angrily orders the young woman to take the money out of his tent, he tells her to take also the silver-mounted hunting horn to keep for her son. This child is the latest fruit of the tragic pattern of miscegenation and incest—a repetition of everything Ike had tried to repudiate and atone for. Untried and uncertain in his future, the child is nevertheless given the horn, the legacy of old General Compson, the symbolic object from the old times, since he is the only deserving inheritor.

Shock, grief, and the helplessness of old age play a part in what follows. Realizing the fatuity of what he is saying but unable to stop, Isaac tells this educated and cultured young woman her only hope is to go back North and "marry a man of your own race. Then you will forget all this." Her reply is calm but merciless. "Old man . . . have you lived so long and forgotten so much that you dont remember anything you ever knew or felt or even heard about love?" After she is gone he lies on the old cot, listening to the November rain, shaking with cold and the shock of what his life has come to. The tragic pattern is classic and clear.

He has chosen a line of moral conduct, of austerity and renunciation, and has persisted in it. He has freed the son he never had,
but in freeing him, he has lost him. The wrong and shame
has settled on Roth Edmonds. "I would have made a man of
him . . . ," the young woman had said. "You spoiled him . . .
when you gave to his grandfather that land which didn't belong
to him. . . ." Isaac McCaslin's long life has accomplished nothing.
The pattern of shame and wrong has come full circle. "No wonder the ruined woods I used to know dont cry for retribution . . . ,"
he thinks. "The people who have destroyed it will accomplish
its revenge." All his grief and anguish are brought to a focus as
the loud and bustling Will Legate stumbles into the tent.

"Looking for Roth's knife," Legate said. . . . "We got a deer on
the ground."
"Who killed it?" McCaslin said. "Was it Roth?"
"Yes," Legate said, raising the flap.
"Wait," McCaslin said. . . . "What was it?"
"Just a deer, Uncle Ike," he said impatiently. "Nothing extra."
He was gone; again the flap fell behind him, wafting out of the tent
again the faint light and the constant and grieving rain. McCaslin lay
back down, the blanket once more drawn to his chin, his crossed hands
once more weightless on his breast in the empty tent.
"It was a doe," he said.[13]

1. *The Picaresque Saint* (Philadephia: Lippincott, 1958). One chapter is
devoted to Faulkner.
2. See, for instance, the short story "Race at Morning" in the volume *Big
Woods*, a collection published in 1955 by Random House, containing this new
story and several previously published selections of Faulkner's work, all on the
subject of hunting and the Wilderness.
3. William Faulkner, *Go Down, Moses* (New York: Random House, 1942),
p. 256.
4. William Faulkner, *The Unvanquished* (New York: Random House, 1938),
p. 54.
5. *Ibid.*, p. 55.
6. Faulkner, *Go Down, Moses*, p. 171.
7. *Ibid.*, p. 209.
8. *Ibid.*, p. 193.
9. *Ibid.*, p. 211.
10. *Ibid.*, p. 212.
11. *Ibid.*, p. 212.
12. *Ibid.*, p. 226.
13. *Ibid.*, pp. 328-29.
14. *Ibid.*, pp. 329-30.
15. *Ibid.*, pp. 293-94.
16. *Ibid.*, p. 269.
17. *Ibid.*, p. 351.
18. *Ibid.*, pp. 364-65.

8.

FAULKNER'S SOCIAL COMEDY

THE SIGNIFICANCE of humor and comedy in the work of William Faulkner is still ambiguous. The various commentators on the subject have usually assigned such work as "Spotted Horses" to the broad and blatant half-horse, half-alligator school of the frontier ("it was the biggest drove of just one horse I ever seen"). Once in a long while, an isolated critic may sense that gradual fusing of comedy and tragedy at the outer limits of human experience that was adumbrated by Socrates at the close of the *Symposium* and that is a part of the essential awareness of every great comic artist from Aristophanes to the present time. What most estimates of Faulkner's significance seem to ignore is the very wide diversity of his comic creation, which extends over the entire spectrum of comic possibility. At one end of the spectrum there are such existential dirty jokes as *Sanctuary* and *Pylon,* whose inhabitants are damned and are not at all interested in redemption; at the other end there is the fragile, spun-glass sophistication of the comedy of manners. Perhaps this aspect of Faulkner's comic talent had been ignored largely because it does not often occur in the formal isolation of a separate major work, distinct from any other qualities or elements. This lack of a major example was remedied to some degree by the publication of *The Town,* which may yet turn out to be a better book than many reviewers have realized. Anyone contemplating the Great Rouncewell Panic will see it for what it is.

The comedy of savage extremity, such as that found in *Sanc-*

tuary and *Pylon* or in the work of Swift or Kafka, is usually the violent response of an intelligent man who has just discovered some of the abysses which humanity finds opening at its feet and who cares, and cares intensely, about what Man has done to himself and to his fellow creatures. The drubbings and thumpings which a Quixote or a Joseph K. must endure are richly deserved for the crime of not knowing what the universe is like and what his place in it really is. This spewing-out of spleen by the artist is healthy and cathartic and in rare instances may even shock the great public into a temporary awareness, as did "A Modest Proposal." This phase usually, though not always, belongs to that period in the life of the artist when he is losing his illusions but has not yet lost them all. It is the amputation itself that is most violently painful, not the life afterward. If the artist is able to survive and keep most of his sanity (as Swift was not), he comes at last to that final awareness so evident in Cervantes and Shakespeare, which for lack of a better term I should call perspective: the realization that the human condition has always been like this and that, if nothing can permanently be improved, then at least the extremity he has depicted is really the extreme. It is the attainment of this awareness in the comic hero (and by the comic artist) which most nearly matches the tragic acceptance of the tragic hero and consists primarily in realizing that the great bulk of Mankind will not merely endure but prevail.

ii.

If it is true that the comedy of Aristophanes could take place only in an Athens that had begun to question its national assumptions, then I should like to suggest that the reception accorded *Sanctuary* and *Pylon* took place in an America no more ready to have its assumptions questioned then than now. Unfortunately, the major function of the comic artist is to question somebody's assumptions, even at times his own. The basic premises of social comedy are well known; it is perhaps adequate to generalize and say its major function is to chastise and correct the folly, the affectation, or even the sins of a representative individual or group by exhibiting a laughable example of extravagances that an audience can easily recognize as typical. To accomplish this effect, the comic artist must be able first of all to recognize affectation when he sees it.

Faulkner has shown this ability from the beginning. In *Soldiers' Pay* there is already the comic awareness in the portrait of Jones and in the painfully precise estimate which the returned servicemen have of their own importance to society now that the shooting is over. *Mosquitoes* is probably Faulkner's worst novel, and within itself it is worst when it most obviously is not another *Point Counter Point*. Yet, the comic sensibility is definitely there, and the comic contrast between illusion and fact is remarkably well worked out, from the flat abstraction of Pete and his hat to the raddled Mrs. Maurier who believes she can buy acceptance as an equal from the arty set by taking them on her yacht (which never goes anywhere) and feeding them largely on grapefruit. Even the "glamorous fatality" of *Sartoris* is occasionally punctured, usually by the incisive and acid comments of Miss Jenny Du Pre. The grim absurdity of *Sanctuary* is relieved somewhat by such elements as the delicately *social* response of Horace Benbow to the letter in which Gowan Stevens bids a romantically fatal farewell to Narcissa. We need hardly be reminded that the episode Gowan is speaking of is the one in which he takes Temple Drake to the moonshiners' hideout, wrecks his car, drinks himself insensible for the third time that day, and then abandons Temple after he has at last become sober enough to realize all that has happened. His greatest point of pride is, of course, that he did not have to attend the local state university with the clodhoppers but went instead to Virginia where, he affirms with the utmost seriousness, they taught him to drink like a gentleman. His farewell letter to Narcissa runs, in part, ". . . if my heart were as blank as this page, this would not be necessary at all. I will not see you again. I cannot write it, for I have gone through with an experience which I cannot face. I have but one rift in the darkness, that is that I have injured no one save myself with my folly, and that the extent of that folly you will never learn. . . ."[1]

This is the purest kind of burlesque and nothing more. But Horace's comment, "Good Lord, someone mistook him for a Mississippi man on the dance floor," is the purest comedy. In light of what Gowan has actually done it is not funny at all, and Horace's reaction when he discovers the truth is very different.

One of the most comic spectacles in the world is provided by a man who is horribly in love. But even more comic are the antics of a man attempting to evade the stratagems of a woman intent on trapping him into marriage. Many of the perennial occasions of comedy are found in the overthrow of a determined and foolish ascetic ideal by an all-too-human impulse or carnal appetite. Gluttony, avarice, or simple ego-gratification provide their share of comic matter, but the most fertile field for it is the relation of man to woman. At one end of the range of possibility is courtship; at the other is the never-ending war between the sexes.

One of Faulkner's richest sources of comic matter is the frivolity of empty assertion of aristocratic status, especially when the pretension consists simply of demands without a corresponding dynamic of leadership and responsibility. Often this attitude is treated with savage irony, as when Mrs. Compson whines, "I'm a lady," or Temple Drake insists, "My father's a judge." But a gentler, more sophisticated comedy is obtained when Faulkner merges this theme of status assertion with the tensions of the sex relationship to create his comedy of manners. Two clearly realized examples of this fusion are the story "Was," from *Go Down, Moses,* and the short story "My Grandmother Millard and General Bedford Forrest and The Battle of Harrykin Creek," which is found in *Collected Stories.*

As everybody knows, *Go Down, Moses* relates the McCaslin saga, that epic of renunciation and austere heroism. But "Was" is the opening section of it, set in an older, happier time before the war and Reconstruction. It is almost as if Faulkner were creating his own version of the Garden of Eden, containing only those two wise innocents, Uncle Buck and Uncle Buddy, and the nine-year-old McCaslin Edmonds. Uncle Buck and Uncle Buddy may not know how to avoid the serpent, but they do know enough from Adam's example to avoid Eve. In fact, the whole movement of the comedy is about just that: the avoiding of Eve, who exists in the person of two women: Mr. Hubert Beauchamp's slave girl, Tennie, whom Tomey's Turl is after, and Mr. Hubert's sister, Miss Sophonsiba, who desperately desires to marry Uncle Buck, who is just as desperately anxious to preserve his freedom and save the Eden that is the McCaslin plantation from invasion. It is almost as if Faulkner had set aside for the moment the tragic heritage of exploitation and miscegenation which the McCaslins have to expiate, to tell this happy (if temporary) triumph of masculine virtue (and poker-playing) over the wiles of a scheming woman.

Uncle Buck and Uncle Buddy are well aware of the threat Miss Sophonsiba poses to the very existence of their idyllic, fox-hunting, bachelor way of life.

Tomey's Turl . . . was heading for Mr. Hubert Beauchamp's place just over the edge of the next county . . . to hang around Mr. Hubert's girl, Tennie, until somebody came and got him. . . . And if somebody didn't go and get Tomey's Turl right away, Mr. Hubert would fetch him back himself, bringing Miss Sophonsiba, and they would stay for a week or longer, Miss Sophonsiba living in Uncle Buddy's room and Uncle Buddy moved clean out of the house. . . . And one midnight last summer Uncle Buddy just happened by accident to be awake and hear Mr. Hubert drive out of the lot and by the time he waked them and they got Miss Sophonsiba up and dressed and the team put to the wagon and caught Mr. Hubert, it was almost daylight. . . . Uncle Buddy didn't own a necktie at all; Uncle Buck said Uncle Buddy wouldn't take that chance even in a section like theirs, where ladies were so damn seldom thank God that a man could ride for days in a straight line without having to dodge a single one.[2]

It is bad enough that Miss Sophonsiba is a woman and automatically carries the ever-present threat of matrimony, but even worse is her dreadful affectation and silliness:

. . . presently there was a jangling and a swishing noise and they began to smell the perfume, and Miss Sophonsiba came down the stairs. Her hair was roached under a lace cap; she had on her Sunday dress and beads and a red ribbon around her throat and a little nigger girl carrying her fan and he stood quietly a little behind Uncle Buck, watching her lips until they opened and he could see the roan tooth. He had never known anyone before with a roan tooth and he remembered how one time his grandmother and his father were talking about Uncle Buddy and Uncle Buck and his grandmother said that Miss Sophonsiba had matured into a fine-looking woman once. Maybe she had. He didn't know. He wasn't but nine.

"Why, Mister Theophilus," she said. "And McCaslin," she said. She had never looked at him and she wasn't talking to him and he knew it, although he was prepared and balanced to drag his foot when Uncle Buck did. "Welcome to Warwick."

He and Uncle Buck dragged their foot. "I just come to get my nigger," Uncle Buck said. "Then we got to get on back home."

Then Miss Sophonsiba said something about a bumblebee, but he couldn't remember that. It was too fast and there was too much of it, the earrings and the beads clashing and jingling like little trace chains on a toy mule trotting and the perfume stronger too, like the earrings and beads sprayed it out each time they moved and he watched the roan-colored tooth flick and glint between her lips; something about Uncle Buck was a bee sipping from flower to flower and not staying long anywhere and all that stored sweetness to be wasted on Uncle Buddy's desert air, calling Uncle Buddy Mister Amodeus like she called Uncle Buck Mister Theophilus, or maybe the honey was being stored up against the advent of a queen and who was the lucky queen and when? "Ma'am?" Uncle Buck said.[3]

This affectation is found not only in her overt vulgarity but in her attitudes toward family and land as well. The Beauchamp plantation is not a very good one to begin with and is badly looked after to boot, but after many years it is the one that "Miss Sophonsiba . . . was still trying to make people call Warwick after the place in England that she said Mr. Hubert was probably the true earl of only he never even had enough pride, not to mention energy, to take the trouble to establish his just rights."[4]

Miss Sophonsiba and Mr. Hubert are able between them to throw up enough obstructions to delay the hunt until late in the afternoon. Then follows the hilarious sequence of the hunt itself: when the dogs discover they are chasing an old friend, both dogs and Tomey's Turl stroll amiably into the woods together. (Several hours later, the mighty hunters find the dogs shut up in a cotton-house.) It is at this point that Uncle Buck is goaded into the rash bet that he will have Tomey's Turl and be away by dark. Mr. Hubert sends one of the Negroes for more whiskey and a fyce that can trail the dogs and Tomey's Turl.

. . . in about a half an hour the nigger came back with a little bob-tail black fyce and a new bottle of whiskey. Then he rode up to Uncle Buck and held something out to him wrapped in a piece of paper. "What?" Uncle Buck said.

"It's for you," the nigger said. Then Uncle Buck took it and unwrapped it. It was the piece of red ribbon that had been on Miss

Sophonsiba's neck and Uncle Buck sat there on Black John, holding the ribbon like it was a little water moccasin only he wasn't going to let anybody see he was afraid of it, batting his eyes fast at the nigger. Then he stopped batting his eyes.

"What for?" he said.

"She just sont hit to you," the nigger said. "She say to tell you 'success.' "

"She said what?" Uncle Buck said.

"I dont know, sir," the nigger said. "She just say 'success.' "

"Oh," Uncle Buck said.[5]

After Uncle Buck and Mr. Hubert have reiterated the terms of the bet, Mr. Hubert goes back to supper, and Buck and Cass continue the hunt. Many hours later they do find Tomey's Turl exactly where Mr. Hubert predicted he would be: in Tennie's cabin. But Uncle Buck makes the mistake of startling Turl, and he runs right over Uncle Buck, knocking Buck down and breaking the whiskey bottle in his hip pocket. Buck refuses to move "until he knew for certain if it was just whiskey and not blood." The terrified fyce is still yelping and running ahead of Tomey's Turl, who is well away. Young Cass is optimistic. " 'We'll catch him tomorrow,' he said. 'Tomorrow, hell,' Uncle Buck said. 'We'll be at home tomorrow. And the first time Hubert Beauchamp or that nigger either one set foot on my land, I'm going to have them arrested for trespass and vagrancy.' "[6]

There is nothing to do but cut their losses and go back to the big house. They creep into the house cautiously, looking for an empty bedroom to sleep in.

The house was dark. They could hear Mr. Hubert snoring good now, as if he had settled down to road-gaiting at it. But they couldn't hear anything from upstairs, even when they were inside the dark hall, at the foot of the stairs. "Likely hers will be at the back," Uncle Buck said. "Where she can holler down to the kitchen without having to get up. Besides, an unmarried lady will sholy have her door locked with strangers in the house." So Uncle Buck eased himself down on the bottom step, and he knelt and drew Uncle Buck's boots off. Then he removed his own and set them against the wall, and he and Uncle Buck mounted the stairs, feeling their way up and into the upper hall. It was dark too, and still there was no sound anywhere except Mr. Hubert snoring below, so they felt their way along the hall toward the front of the house, until they felt a door. They could hear nothing beyond the door, and when Uncle Buck tried the knob, it opened.

"All right," Uncle Buck whispered. "Be quiet." They could see a little now, enough to see the shape of the bed and the mosquito-bar. Uncle Buck threw down his suspenders and unbuttoned his trousers and went to the bed and eased himself carefully down onto the edge of it, and he knelt again and drew Uncle Buck's trousers off and he was just removing his own when Uncle Buck lifted the mosquito-bar and raised his feet and rolled into the bed. That was when Miss Sophonsiba sat up on the other side of Uncle Buck and gave the first scream.[7]

Uncle Buck pleads his innocence with some eloquence:

"It was an accident. . . . Be reasonable. Say I did walk into a lady's bedroom, even Miss Sophonsiba's; say, just for the sake of the argument, there wasn't no other lady in the world but her and so I walked into hers and tried to get in bed with her, would I have took a nine-year-old boy with me?"[8]

Mr. Hubert's judgment is merciless but fair:

"Reasonable is just what I'm being. . . . You come into bear-country of your own free will and accord. All right; you were a grown man and you knew it was bear-country and you knew the way back out like you knew the way in and you had your chance to take it. But no. You had to crawl into the den and lay down by the bear. And whether you did or didn't know the bear was in it dont make any difference. So if you got back out of that den without even a claw-mark on you, I would not only be unreasonable, I'd be a damned fool. After all, I'd like a little peace and quiet and freedom myself, now I got a chance for it. Yes, sir. She's got you, 'Filus, and you know it. You run a hard race and you run a good one, but you skun the hen-house one time too many."[9]

They decide to settle the question by playing poker, the lowest hand to "win" Sophonsiba and buy the other half of the Tomey's-Turl–Tennie romance, so that this source of trouble can be ended also. Uncle Buck loses, and Cass slips out to go fetch Uncle Buddy, the greatest poker player in the Mississippi valley. With a much more complicated package of Sophonsiba, slaves, dowry, and cash involved in the pot, Uncle Buddy demands that someone other than the innocent Cass deal the cards. Mr. Hubert sends for the nearest person, and this turns out to be Tomey's Turl. Uncle Buddy shuffles, Mr. Hubert cuts, and Tomey's Turl deals. The game is stud, and as the cards are dealt in turn the stakes

mount. Mr. Hubert has three threes in his hand, but if Uncle
Buddy's hole card is the other three, then Buddy has a straight.
If Uncle Buddy does have the straight and Mr. Hubert calls him,
Mr. Hubert will not only lose Miss Sophonsiba's bridegroom but
will have to buy the worthless Tomey's Turl as well, who wants
nothing better than to live with Tennie for the rest of his life. If
Mr. Hubert does not call, then the McCaslins will have to buy Tennie. " 'Who dealt these cards, Amodeus?' Only he didn't wait to
be answered. He reached out and tilted the lamp-shade, the light
moving up Tomey's Turl's arms that were supposed to be black
but were not quite white, up his Sunday shirt that was supposed
to be white but wasn't quite either. . . . Then he tilted the shade
back down and took up his cards and turned them face-down and
pushed them toward the middle of the table. 'I pass, Amodeus,'
he said."[10]

Happy and festive, the heroes return to their unviolated Eden.
Even though we know from the rest of the McCaslin saga that
Miss Sophonsiba will finally catch Uncle Buck (and it is somewhat
ungallant to speak in this fashion of the lady who will become
Isaac McCaslin's mother), still for the moment at least Uncle
Buck has his freedom, Tomey's Turl has his Tennie, and Uncle
Buddy has once more demonstrated his power and cunning at the
art of playing poker.

"My Grandmother Millard" deals with some of the same conditions which are found in "Was," but they are seen from a different perspective. It could be argued, of course, that what Cousin
Melisandre is suffering from is not aristocratic pretension but
an exaggerated theory of courtly love absorbed by way of the
lady novelists, operating within an extravagant case of Victorian
prudery. Which is exactly what Cousin Melisandre is: a Victorian pretending to be an aristocrat, with all of Victorian morality's morbid horror of the body and its physical functions but
little else. Yet the poor girl is only a part of the times, and much
of the exquisitely subtle comedy comes out of the way Faulkner
is able to tell the story without ever saying *precisely,* in words,
what the dreadful position was in which Cousin Melisandre found
herself and which she thinks has so irrevocably disgraced her that

she keeps not only the Sartoris household but General Forrest's army in an uproar for several days.

The time is toward the middle of the war. Memphis has already fallen, and Yankee troops are expected in Jefferson at any time. Granny has been wearing out Bayard and Ringo and the rest of the servants in trunk-drill: the fatiguing routine of gathering the family silver and other valuables, loading them into the trunk, carrying the trunk out, burying it in the ground, covering the evidence under piles of brush, and then reversing the entire process. And all to no avail, because when the Yankees do come, there isn't time to bury the trunk. Granny hastily falls back on an expedient that was used the year before, even as Ab Snopes is trying to tell her that it won't work again. The trunk full of valuables is placed inside the privy, and Cousin Melisandre, complete with bonnet and parasol, is placed on top of the trunk. The door is slammed to, and Louvinia takes her stand in front.

. . . they swept around the house in a kind of straggling clump—six men in blue, riding fast. . . . the men leaped down and unslung the pole and jerked the horses aside and picked up the pole, three to a side, and began to run across the yard with it as the last rider came around the house, in grey. . . . the sabre lifted and not only standing in the stirrups but almost lying down along the horse's neck. . . . the whole mass of them . . . rushing on across the yard until the end of the pole struck the outhouse door. It didn't just overturn, it exploded. One second it stood there, tall and narrow and flimsy; the next second it was gone and there was a boil of yelling men in blue coats darting and dodging around under Cousin Philip's horse and flashing sabre until they could find a chance to turn and run. There was a scatter of planks and shingles and Cousin Melisandre sitting beside the trunk in the middle of it, in the spread of her hoops, her eyes shut and her mouth open, still screaming, and after a while a feeble popping of pistol-shots from down along the creek that didn't sound any more like war than a boy with firecrackers.

"I tried to tell you to wait!" Ab Snopes said behind us, "I tried to tell you them Yankees had done caught on!"[11]

After Bayard and the others have finished burying the trunk, he and Ringo find the lone Confederate soldier in the summerhouse. His name will eventually turn out to be Cousin Philip, we discover. He has a dazed look on his face, and about all he can say is "That beautiful girl. . . . That beautiful, tender girl."

He will not consent to meet the family until he has been brought a comb, wash basin, and clothesbrush and has had Ringo polish his boots. There is a further delay while his trousers are sent in to Granny to have a rip repaired. Also, he instructs Bayard to bring him some flowers which he can make into a nosegay. Only after Bayard has repeated three times what is to be said will Cousin Philip consent to be announced.

"Announce me," he said. He said his name again. "Of Tennessee. Lieutenant, Savage's Battalion, Forrest's Command, Provisional Army, Department of the West."

So I did. . . . I know he couldn't even see Cousin Melisandre for a minute, even though he never had looked at anything else but her. "Lieutenant Philip St-Just Backhouse," I said. I said it loud. . . .

While you could count maybe five, there wasn't anything at all. Then Cousin Melisandre screamed. She sat bolt upright on the chair like she had sat beside the trunk in the litter of planks and shingles in the back yard this morning, with her eyes shut and her mouth open again, screaming.[12]

At last, even without Cousin Melisandre, they sit down to dinner. Cousin Philip sits there, halfway between the "beautiful girl" look and suspended hysteria. Finally Bayard says:

"Why don't you change your name . . . ?"

He laughed some more. That is, his face did the same way and he made the same sound again. "My grandfather was at King's Mountain, with Marion all through Carolina. My uncle was defeated for Governor of Tennessee by a corrupt and traitorous cabal of tavern-keepers and Republican Abolitionists, and my father died at Chapultepec. After that, the name they bore is not mine to change. Even my life is not mine so long as my country lies bleeding and ravished beneath an invader's iron heel." Then he stopped laughing. . . . "Unless I lose it in battle," he said.[13]

The next morning, Cousin Philip is back with fifty cavalry-men, mooning under the window to say good-by before he gallops his men across Granny's flowerbeds to go tend to the enemy. At this point Granny announces she has had enough and sends word to General Forrest, ordering him to stop fighting the war and come take care of "that boy." It soon develops that Lt. P. Backhouse has been doing his best to lose his life in battle by leading suicidal charges against the enemy, contrary to orders. This behavior plays hob with General Forrest's well-known tactics for decoying the Federal armies where he wishes.

The nature of this comic impasse is quite clear: Philip Backhouse is trying to get himself killed because Cousin Melisandre will not have anything to do with him; Cousin Melisandre, in view of the circumstances of their first meeting, cannot allow herself to converse with a man named Backhouse. General Forrest cannot fight the war so long as Cousin Philip continues his mad tricks. Granny provides the solution: Cousin Philip will lose his name in battle. She writes out the dispatch and General Forrest signs it.

Lieutenant P. S. Backhouse, Company D, Tennessee Cavalry, was this day raised to the honorary rank of Brevet Major General and killed while engaging the enemy. Vice whom Philip St-Just Backus is hereby appointed Lieutenant, Company D, Tennessee Cavalry.

N. B. Forrest Genl[14]

But General Forrest must have a battle to keep the record correct. Bayard tells him that the stream that runs through the Sartoris pasture is called Harrykin Creek. The second battle order is written.

A unit of my command on detached duty engaged a body of the enemy and drove him from the field and dispersed him this day 28th ult. April 1862 at Harrykin Creek. With the loss of one man.

N. B. Forrest Genl[15]

The next day Melisandre and Philip are married; General Forrest can go back to chasing Yankees in confidence, and Granny's flowerbeds will be secure.

This extensive display of quotation is designed to illustrate Faulkner's construction of the comedy of manners. These stories seem to meet the requirements of that level of sophistication: the situations are delicious if improbable; the actions of the comic figures grow out of some image of the self which is carried to the point of affectation, but in the end common sense and reality prevail. The humor is delicate, without grossness: a good bit of the subtlety surrounding Cousin Melisandre's predicament is in the way in which everyone talks around the subject: like Horner's pretended affliction, no one ever quite puts it into blunt, hard words. Violence, vice, and hatred are banished firmly: Philip's Graustarkian heroics at the battle of the privy and Uncle Buck's terror of a shotgun marriage take place in the arena of comic limitation; anything offensive is dispatched to another place. There is nothing very funny in a slave being pursued by horses and dogs, but that violence is rendered harmless and amusing when the slave and the dogs are friends of long standing and walk off amiably together into the woods. In fact, Tomey's Turl has been running the whole show all along: it may have been Uncle Buddy who was playing the poker, but Tomey's Turl dealt the cards.

iii.

A major problem that confronts the artist who wishes to write authentic tragedy today is, bluntly put, the problem of "nobility." Once the archaic denotations of the term are stripped away, the dynamics of the problem resolve themselves quite simply into the difficulty of creating a protagonist who is at the same time "modern," "typical," and "special." If the works that are accepted by most critics as the most nearly perfect examples of the comedy of manners (Molière, *The Way of the World, The Importance of Being Earnest*) allow us to make any generalization at all that will stand, it is probably that this most refined and delicate form of comedy makes its effect when it achieves "correction" solely by the pressure of sanity, reason, and morality upon the consciousness of the comic figure. The change must be made, and believably made, by the use of no form of force other than the force of wit. Sticks, stones, and broken bones may be part and parcel of the comedy of Aristophanes and Cervantes, but once the noise of physical contact sounds in the comedy of manners, that comedy has already collapsed into the burlesque of slapstick. The problem of creating the comedy of manners involves the same difficulty of "nobility" as does tragedy. The comic figure must come to realize, and to correct, his own extravagance, and he must be depicted as having, for the duration of the comedy at least, a sufficiently large scope of action to guarantee that he will not be reformed by such crude measures as, for instance, the threat of police action or discharge from his position by his employer. No doubt our appreciation comes from the very keenly felt moral and intellectual superiority that the artist allows us to enjoy.

The comedy of manners by definition will reflect the manners and mores of a given time and place. These are of course subject to change. Even so protean a genius as Shakespeare seemed able to get little more than a low comedy out of his "base mechanicals." (Bottom's "Ille roar you as gently as any sucking dove" is the quintessence of delicacy, but the implied rebuke is to the silly and affected Athenian ladies; the major preoccupation of the dramatic aspiration of Bottom's crew is to avoid being whipped.) When the attempt to create comedy at the peasant level is made, a wonderfully vital comedy sometimes results, as in Brueghel's scenes of peasant life, but the result is not usually a comedy of manners. Occasionally a national or regional social group at this level, such as the Spanish peasants who have a word like "aburrimiento" in constant use, will have developed a system of social rituals and forms of behavior elaborate and stylized enough, and well enough established, to provide the raw material for a comedy of manners. Fairly often, Faulkner has been able to create an authentic comedy of manners on the level of the Mississippi tenant farmer or even the backwoodsman. This achievement is possible only because the social rituals of these groups are elaborate and highly formalized. The subtler nuances of this behavior are perhaps most accessible to those who are familiar with Southern protocol, but in at least two of his short stories, Faulkner has presented a flawlessly realized capsule comedy of manners that can be apprehended by anyone. One of these stories is "A Courtship," that Eden-like account of the epic contest between the young Ikkemotubbe and David Hogganbeck for the hand of Herman Basket's sister. The other is the contemporary "Shingles for the Lord," which creates every nuance of the cross-currents of rivalry and self-assertion that swirl against the ideals implied by the dedication to the task at hand. All these implications of comic comment are made beautifully clear even to the reader who has never been nearer to Mississippi than the pages of the *New York Post*.

Sometimes even an earlier, cruder story is infused with the

comic spirit. In the short story "A Bear Hunt" (not to be confused with the magnificent short novel *The Bear*), a character named Lucius Provine makes his first appearance. Certain commentators on comedy in the nineteenth century remarked that the comedy of manners requires a certain moral neutrality. So it does, unless stupidity, greed, excess, affectation, folly, and hypocrisy are sinful (which they should be) and common sense, moderation, tolerance, and wit are moral qualities (as they no doubt are). Lucius Provine is guilty of the gravest offenses against the morality of comedy: gluttony, dim-wittedness, and pointless, stupid, cruelty. Ratliff is telling the story, and it is an earlier, far cruder, Ratliff than the shrewd, humane, more perfectly realized Ratliff we meet in *The Hamlet, The Town,* and *The Mansion.*

The occasion is Major de Spain's annual hunting trip to the great wilderness. Lucius, uninvited, has attached himself to the camp and for two days and nights has crammed himself with bear meat and whiskey. Now he has a severe case of spasmodic hiccups, seemingly incurable. He is a nuisance to everyone and a guarantee against getting near any game.

. . . walking along behind Major, saying "Hic-ah! Hic-oh! Hic—oh, Lord!" until Major turns on him and says:
"Get to hell over yonder with them shotgun fellows on the deer stands. How do you expect me to walk up on a bear or even hear the dogs when they strike? I might as well be riding a motorcycle."
. . . So Luke gets up and kind of staggers away again, kind of dying away again like he was run by one of these hyer one-cylinder gasoline engines, only a durn sight more often and regular.[16]

This is the period in Ratliff's life before he has learned to resist the temptation to play a practical joke. He suggests that Lucius go to be cured by old John Basket, the chief of what remains of the Chickasaws. Lucius goes, followed shortly by Old Ash, Major de Spain's body servant. Ratliff sees Ash go, but thinks nothing of it. In the beatific silence of Lucius' absence, the nightly poker game can begin in peace:

. . . when we hyeared the sound. Hit sounded like a drove of wild horses coming up that road, and we hadn't no more than turned toward the door, a-asking one another what in tarnation hit could be, with Major just saying, "What is the name of—" when hit come across the porch like a harrycane and down the hall, and the door busted open and there Luke was. He never had no gun and lantrun then, and his clothes was nigh torn clean offen him, and his face looked wild as ere a man in the Jackson a-sylum. But the main thing I noticed was that he wasn't hiccuping now. And this time, too, he was nigh crying.

"They was fixing to kill me!" he says. "They was going to burn me to death! They had done tried me and tied me onto the pile of wood, and one of them was coming with the fahr when I managed to bust loose and run!"

"Who was?" Major says. "What in tarnation hell are you talking about?"

"Them Indians!" Luke says. "They was fixing to—"

"What?" Major hollers. "Damn to blue blazes, what?"

And that was where I had to put my foot in hit. He hadn't never seen me until then. "At least they cured your hiccups," I says.[17]

After some four or five others have subdued Lucius and pulled him off the badly beaten Ratliff ("I be dog if for a minute I didn't think the roof had done fell in"), Ratliff attempts to discover what really happened. Recalling that Old Ash was gone at the same time, he forces Ash to admit that he told the Indians that Lucius was a revenue agent. The Indians captured Lucius and put him through a mock trial: "'Never much happened,' he says, 'Dey jest went down de road a piece en atter a while hyer he come a-hickin' en a-blumpin' up de road wid de lant'un en de gun. They took de lant'un en de gun away frum him en took him up pon topper de mound en talked de Injun language at him fer a while. Den dey piled up some wood en fixed him on hit so he could git loose in a minute, en den one of dem come up de hill wid de fire, en he done de rest.' "[18]

Outwardly, this crude and obvious story seems as far removed from the delicate criteria of the comedy of manners as possible. All three of the central figures are depicted as no better than before, unchanged, apparently, by the experience they have gone through: Lucius certainly shows no amendment; Ratliff hams up the account of his own discomfiture for the benefit of whatever town loafers are listening; and Old Ash is shown in further accounts from the McCaslin–de-Spain–Sam-Fathers narratives as one of those old Negroes who have grown sour and sullen and unco-operative in the importance of their position and are as jealous of their privileges and prerogatives as the chief eunuch of any oriental harem. Yet, paradoxically, if there is no amendment in the characters, the atmosphere of the story is permeated with the comic spirit. To quote another fragment of the story, the third-person narrator who is repeating Ratliff's version says:

Five miles farther down the river from Major de Spain's camp, and in an even wilder part of the river's jungle of cane and gum and pin oak, there is an Indian mound. Aboriginal, it rises profoundly and darkly enigmatic, the only elevation of any kind in the wild, flat jungle of river bottom. Even to some of us—children though we were, yet we were descended of literate, town-bred, people—it possessed inferences of secret and violent blood, of savage and sudden destruction, as though the yells and hatchets which we associated with Indians through the hidden and secret dime novels which we passed among ourselves were but trivial and momentary manifestations of what dark power still dwelled or lurked there, sinister, a little sardonic, like a dark and nameless beast. . . .[19]

Lucius—the clodhopper sport who neglects his wife and children and whose idea of humor in his daredevil youth was galloping his horse through crowds of Sunday school children or shooting up Negro revivals—is getting about what he deserves for his gluttony in cramming himself with bear meat and whiskey. But there is an even more comic irony in the fact that he is being punished for his cruelty to Ash twenty years ago without knowing it and is even wrong completely about who actually instigated his terrifying experience with the Indians. But the values of the story in terms of social comedy are deepened when we realize that Lucius' terror is generated not by reason and probability but by the arrogance of his own ignorance and xenophobia. Within the folklore of his personal intellectual patterns, it is not only possible but probable that these Original Americans burn people at the stake whenever they can.

In the case of Ratliff there is a slight degree of comic amendment. He is fully aware that he has been caught by the backfire of his own trick. "I be dog if hit don't look like sometimes that when a fellow sets out to play a joke, hit ain't another fellow he's playing that joke on; hit's a kind of a big power laying still somewhere in the dark that he sets out to prank with without knowing hit, and hit all depends on whether that ere power is in the notion to take a joke or not, whether or not hit blows up right in his face like this one did in mine."[20]

As for Old Ash, the comic instinct easily tends to see the beautiful appropriateness of the pattern: Lucius' being scared out of his hiccups not by anything which Ratliff instigated but rather scaring himself out of his hiccups by means of his own ignorance and cowardice, within the pattern of something actually set in motion by Old Ash, who after all has all the weight of his color against him where Lucius has all the advantage. Ash is able to engineer a pattern of retribution which even the shrewdness of Ratliff is not able to see into, and he still emerges not merely without physical injury but without being suspected of anything by Lucius. But here a caveat must be inserted. Just as our identification with the defender of the underdog and the agent of comic retribution and our approval of him are about to settle on Ash, Ratliff uses the rather mean pressures of a white man being harsh to a Negro, and we learn the final truth about Ash's motives:

"I ain't skeered for him to know. One time dey was a picnic. Hit was a long time back, nigh twenty years ago. He was a young man den, en in de middle of de picnic, him en he brudder en nudder white man—I fergit he name—dey rid up wid dey pistols out en cotch us niggers one at a time en burned our collars off. Hit was him dat burnt mine."

"And you waited all this time and went to all this trouble, just to get even with him?" I says.

"Hit warn't dat," he says. . . . "Hit wuz de collar. Back in dem days a top nigger hand made two dollars a week. I paid fo' bits fer dat collar. Hit was blue, wid a red picture of de race betwixt de Natchez en de Robert E. Lee running around hit. He burnt hit up. I makes ten dollars a week now. En I jest wish I knowed where I could buy another collar like dat un fer half of hit. I wish I did."[21]

And there it is. The story is completely infused with the comic spirit, but Ratliff is not the only one who has been tricked. Cruelty, stupidity, and gluttony have been chastised by means of cleverness and a kind of moral judo in which the very grossness of appetite in the excessive one is used to topple him. But our quixotic underdog champion is revealed as being motivated not by comic intelligence but only by the memory of a celluloid collar.

Sentimental idealism is likewise a sin against the morality of comedy.

iv.

If "A Bear Hunt" shows a certain degree of boorishness in the characters and certain elements of slapstick in its action, then "Shingles for the Lord" and "A Courtship" hang suspended in the purest essence of social comedy. The people involved are a far cry from the court circles of Molière, but the atmosphere in "Shingles" is one in which all real hostility and violence are kept carefully at arm's length and all comic denouements are obtained by the cross-currents of human self-assertion within a group of people who really do have a common, commendable, purpose— however much they may succeed in getting in each other's way.

In "A Courtship," hostility and violence are a hovering threat which is kept in check only by the essential nobility and decency of the two rivals for the hand of Herman Basket's sister. The seriousness of the rivalry between Ikkemotubbe and David Hogganbeck is in every sense deadly, and it is their mutual realization that to resort to any mean or underhanded advantage would be to lose that keeps that rivalry on the high-hearted level of heroic comedy.

In "Shingles for the Lord," a group of neighbors have agreed to give their time and labor for one day to re-roof the small wooden country church which has been the spiritual and religious center of their rural neighborhood for more than fifty years. The story is told by an unnamed narrator who is a boy of ten or twelve, and the story's comic impact centers largely in his father. Res Grier ("Pap") is much like his neighbors, except that he seems to consider himself a bit worse off in material goods than they are. This attitude has certain results: he never uses his own tools when he can borrow tools from a neighbor; he is apt to be over-possessive where his own property is concerned; and he is quick to detect a slighting reference to himself, even when none is intended. For all these reasons, he tends to be somewhat more self-defensive and self-assertive than the others.

The trouble begins when Pap is two hours late on the day work begins at the church because he has been delayed in borrowing the necessary tools. This leaves him "owing" six man-hours ("work units") of work to the church—two for himself and two each for Quick and Bookwright. Throughout the day he smarts under Preacher Whitfield's accusation of irresponsibility in being late and carries out his shingle-splitting as though he were killing snakes. His co-workers are very skillful not so much in needling him as in helping him to needle himself. He comes finally to feel that his manhood or his self-respect or something demands that he somehow redress the balance of things and, if possible, come out ahead of the others in some dramatic and startling fashion.

The plot which he devises is a dark and Machiavellian one, involving his half-ownership of a mongrel squirrel dog that Quick covets. Pap openly sells his half of the dog to Quick. He plans to corner the other half-ownership of the dog from his co-owner, Tull, in exchange for performing Tull's share of the work of tearing the old shingles off the church, which was to be Tull's contribution to church repair. After dark, and after some difficulty in borrowing the necessary crowbar, Pap returns to the church with his young son (the narrator), intending to remove all the shingles under cover of darkness and face all the others with the *fait accompli* of the completed job and a continued half-ownership of the dog. He hangs the lantern inside the peak of the roof, and begins work at the same furious pace he has held all day. Only one thing spoils the scheme: in violently ripping off the old shingles he dislodges the lantern, which smashes on the floor of the church, filling the whole interior with flame. The church is an old wooden building and burns fiercely. Armstid is quickly on the scene, but Pap insists violently on carrying the water-barrel to put out the fire by himself. He stumbles, falls, is knocked unconscious by the barrel. This is the only water nearby. By this time Tull, Bookwright, Quick, and the Reverend Whitfield have arrived to watch the church burn down. Preacher Whitfield has striven against sin and human frivolity and weakness for so long that he seemingly is not dismayed even by the magnitude of what has now to be done. He calmly makes the arrangements for beginning the construction of the new church the following morning. Pap offers to do his part.

"Not you," Whitfield said. "Arsonist."

"Arsonist?" Pap said.

"Yes," Whitfield said. "If there is any pursuit in which you can engage without carrying flood and fire and destruction and death behind you, do it. But not one hand shall you lay to this new house until you have proved to us that you are to be trusted again with the powers and capacities of a man."[22]

Pap is taken home by his son and wife to have his slashed-open head dressed and his even more lacerated feelings attended to. Maw dresses his head and finally gets him into bed, as all the while he offers defiance to the absent Whitfield and the others as well. He says to Maw and his son:

"Hand me my snuff; then you get out of here and stay out too. . . ."

But before I could do that maw come back. She had a glass of hot toddy, and she went to the bed and stood there with it, and pap turned his head and looked at it.

"What's that?" he said.

But maw never answered, and then he set up in bed and drawed a long, shuddering, breath—we could hear it—and after a minute he put out his hand for the toddy and set there holding it and drawing his breath, and then he taken a sip of it.

"I Godfrey, if him and all of them put together think they can keep me from working on my own church like ary other man, he better be a good man to try it." He taken another sip of the toddy. Then he taken a long one. "Arsonist," he said. "Work units. Dog units. And now arsonist. I Godfrey, what a day!"[23]

What Faulkner has done in "A Courtship" even better, I think, than in "Red Leaves" is to render the *impression* of life among the Chickasaws, rather than any carefully documented historical version of it. Hemingway is one of the modern masters of rendering rather than translating the essence of the colloquial speech of a people, specifically the colloquial Spanish of *For Whom the Bell Tolls* or the old fisherman's meditations in *The Old Man and the Sea*. But most of us have no knowledge of Chickasaw, so that we cannot compare our enjoyment of the rendition of the cultural matrix against an actual, literal rendition of the tongue and the cultural pattern. But this is of course not the point. The point is that Faulkner has succeeded in doing in his own way and in his chosen milieu the same thing that Gilbert and Sullivan did in such comic masterpieces as *The Mikado*—while getting as much comic effect as possible from the exotic and absurd antics which are attributed to, for instance, the Japanese, the comic artist who uses this technique will skillfully and subtly draw on those universal human responses which make the whole world kin: Ko-Ko's explanations of why beheading himself would be so difficult, or the response of Ikkemotubbe and David Hogganbeck to the sight of Herman Basket's sister, and the *emotion* of their competition with each other, however extravagant and barbarously exotic the techniques of that competition may be.

I have already called this jewel of a story "Eden-like," and it is the cruelest kind of arrogance to attempt to convey its structural and emotional perfection by the cold process of analytical dissection. Part of the beautifully sustained tone—that austere blending of high, almost chivalric comedy with a gently elegiac but not lamentational regret for the days when men were simply and more nobly men—is established by the characters of Ikkemotubbe and David themselves. The contest is a deadly serious one in spite of the chivalric way in which it is conducted:

"We could fight for her," Ikkemotubbe said. "But white men and the People fight differently. We fight with knives, to hurt good and to hurt quickly. That would be all right, if I were to lose. Because I would wish to be hurt good. But if I am to win, I do not wish you to be hurt good. If I am to truly win, it will be necessary for you to be there to see it. On the day of the wedding, I wish you to be present, or at least present somewhere, not lying wrapped in a blanket on a platform in the woods, waiting to enter the earth." Then my father said how Ikkemotubbe put his hand on David Hogganbeck's shoulder and smiled at him. "If that could satisfy me, we would not be squatting here discussing what to do. I think you see that."

"I think I do," David Hogganbeck said.[24]

Thus, neither of the two ever descends to meanness, trickery, or subterfuge. They compete in ways which are scrupulously fair to each of them, simply because both (and all the spectators) know that a victory achieved by trickery would be meaningless. David Hogganbeck is twice as large as most of the young men of the People, which is why he can out-dance, out-drink, and out-fight most of them easily and why a horse race would not be fair, since no horse could carry David and still go fast. In spite of these advantages, Ikkemotubbe tries to out-drink David and is humiliated. In desperation, he challenges him to an eating-contest, and partly because of the state of his emotions, he vomits before he is well begun. But David Hogganbeck proves his right to be in competition with Ikkemotubbe for the beautiful sister of Herman Basket.

. . . and now my father said he [Ikkemotubbe] even smiled again, as at the end of the long hard running when the young men knew that he would go on, not because he was still alive but because he was Ikkemotubbe; "—you see, although I have lost, I still cannot reconcile."

"I had you beat before we started," David Hogganbeck said. . . . And now my father said how they loved David Hogganbeck at that moment as they loved Ikkemotubbe; that they loved them both at that moment while Ikkemotubbe stood before David Hogganbeck with the smile on his face and his right hand flat on David Hogganbeck's chest, because there were men in those days.

"Once more then, and then no more." Ikkemotubbe said. "The Cave." . . . the Cave was a hundred and thirty miles away . . . a black hole in the hill which the spoor of wild creatures merely approached and then turned away and which no dog could even be beaten to enter and where the boys from among all the People would go to lie on their first Night-away-from-Fire to prove if they had the courage to become men, because it had been known among the People from a long time ago that the sound of a whisper or even the disturbed air of a sudden movement would bring parts of the roof down and so all believed that not even a very big movement or sound or maybe none at all at some time would bring the whole mountain into the cave. Then Ikkemotubbe took the two pistols from the trunk and drew the loads and reloaded them. "Whoever reaches the cave first can enter it alone and fire his pistol," he said. "If he comes back out, he has won."

"And if he does not come back out?" David Hogganbeck said.

"Then you have won," Ikkemotubbe said.

"Or you," David Hogganbeck said.[25]

Rubbed with bear-grease and mint, they set out to run the one hundred and thirty miles, Ikkemotubbe faithfully pointing out the route and describing the landmarks to David Hogganbeck, sometimes one of them running ahead and sometimes the other. They even share with each other what food they find, so that the contest may be scrupulously fair. They are both very nearly dead when they reach the cave, both of them at nearly the same moment.

The cave represents, of course, a great deal more than just a cave. Entering the cave, especially with such a deadly purpose, is a descent, a plunge back into the irrational and terrible abyss of the pre-human darkness before man's struggle to create such concepts as justice, chivalry, and reverence for human life. Ikkemotubbe fires his pistol and the roof collapses, but instead of killing each other, the two young men further risk their lives to save each other. They are found, more dead than alive, by the other young men who have followed after them, and the entire issue has already been settled: one of the young men has to report that while they were away, Herman Basket's sister married the worthless Log-in-the-Creek, who cannot dance, cannot drink whiskey, cannot fight, and indeed cannot do anything except lie on his back on the gallery and play his harmonica.

After this, Ikkemotubbe and David cannot stay on the scene of their crushing disappointment. They go away in the steamboat, and as it starts downriver they stand together in the pilothouse, consoling themselves with philosophy, as Ikkemotubbe attempts to control his tears.

"But not for her!" Ikkemotubbe said. "And not even because it was Log-in-the-Creek. Perhaps they are for myself: that such a son as Log-in-the-Cheek could cause them to wish to flow."

"Don't think about her," David Hogganbeck said.

"I don't. I have already stopped. See? . . . There was a wise man of ours who said once how a woman's fancy is like a butterfly which, hovering from flower to flower, pauses at the last as like as not where a horse has stood."

"There was a wise man of ours named Solomon who often said something of that nature too," David Hogganbeck said. "Perhaps there is just one wisdom for all men, no matter who speaks it."

"Aihee. At least, for all men one same heartbreak," Ikkemotubbe said. Then he drew the crying-rope, because the boat was now passing the house where Log-in-the-Creek and his wife lived. . . . Then it crawled again and then it walked again, until at last the People could no longer keep up, and it cried once more beyond the last bend and then there was no longer either the black shapes of the young men leaping to hurl wood into its red stomach or even the sound of its voice in the Plantation or the night.[26]

And that, concludes Mr. Faulkner, is how it was in the old days.

1. William Faulkner, *Sanctuary* (New York: Modern Library, 1931), p. 154.
2. William Faulkner, *Go Down, Moses* (New York: Random House, 1942), pp. 5-7.
3. *Ibid.*, pp. 10-11.
4. *Ibid.*, p. 5.
5. *Ibid.*, pp. 15-16.
6. *Ibid.*, p. 20.
7. *Ibid.*, pp. 20-21.
8. *Ibid.*, p. 22.
9. *Ibid.*, pp. 22-23.
10. *Ibid.*, p. 29.
11. William Faulkner, *The Collected Stories of William Faulkner* (New York: Random House, 1950), pp. 676-77.
12. *Ibid.*, pp. 680-81.
13. *Ibid.*, p. 682.
14. *Ibid.*, p. 696.
15. *Ibid.*, p. 697.
16. *Ibid.*, pp. 68-69.
17. *Ibid.*, pp. 75-76.
18. *Ibid.*, p. 78.
19. *Ibid.*, p. 65.
20. *Ibid.*, p. 70.
21. *Ibid.*, p. 79.
22. *Ibid.*, p. 41.
23. *Ibid.*, p. 43.
24. *Ibid.*, p. 371.
25. *Ibid.*, pp. 373-74.
26. *Ibid.*, pp. 379-80.

9.

FAULKNER AND THE COMEDY OF EXTREMITY

I HAVE SAID THAT the various modes of comedy that Faulkner has constructed span a very wide spectrum. His comic sensibility ranges from the crude slapstick of "A Bear Hunt" to the half-horse, half-alligator frontier tradition in "Spotted Horses" to the gentle laughter of "My Grandmother Millard" and "Shingles for the Lord," even to the tragicomic anguish of such thwarted Quixotes as Gavin Stevens. Beyond these established and conventional modes is sometimes seen another kind of comedy, a comedy of depravity, inhumanity, and horror. Historically, this sense of comic extremity is the response of the artist to that element in human life that our own century labels the Existential Absurd. Awareness of this element is older than Aristophanes and can be found throughout the Old Testament. The mode is comic in the precise sense that the activity of the sinners in the *Inferno* of Dante or the paintings of Hieronymus Bosch are comic; the more frenetically human beings are caught up in sterile rounds of purposeless activity, the more comic they are. In the Faulkner canon, a few such comic figures cannot help themselves, but by far the greater number are as they are for the precise reason the medieval sinners are in Hell—because they wish to be.

Awareness of this aspect of human life is to be found in every novel and many short stories of Faulkner's first two decades of writing and to some extent in the work written since then. What the present chapter proposes to do is to examine the nature of this awareness in Faulkner's work but more particularly to establish his own response to these phenomena and to relate that response to the more general pattern of human existence seen in the Faulkner canon. Here a preliminary generalization may be offered. Faulkner's response to the problem of Man's apparently absurd position in the cosmos is typical of and consistent with his prevailing estimate of Mankind. He was a writer who clung stubbornly to his belief in the integrity of the individual human heart; who could say with Ratliff: "Mankind aint evil, he just aint got any sense." Thus the problem became one of projecting—without falsification and with a reasonable degree of credibility—his vision of human integrity against conditions in human life that often, too often, seem irrational and absurd. After the history of the past half-century, it should be unnecessary to mention that the horror and depravity of these conditions grow not out of anything the author invents for his fiction but rather out of the depraved and absurd actions which Man at times commits against himself and the apparently depraved and absurd universe in which he lives. It is possible to state that such actions and situations are extreme, are for the most part outside general human experience, and are outside the main lines of the Yoknapatawpha Chronicle. This mode of Faulknerian comedy reaches its most overt expression where the characters concerned are most completely involved in the dehumanization and depersonalization of a mechanistic existence.*

I have pointed out that the extremity of this comic realization is not new. We find in the comedy of Molière the definite assumption that individuals or even groups are in need of correction and deserve to be exhibited in their foolishness as an amusement for the sane and healthy majority of humanity. This sane and sophisticated comic theory had its origin in one of Mankind's most whimsically beautiful notions: the delusion that Man himself is a reasonable being. In *Candide* the realization begins to grow on the reader that the compact majority is not commonsensical but rather prefers its own stupidity and folly and lives by the herd instinct. In *Gulliver's Travels* there is the final contrast between the Houyhnhnms and the Yahoos. The comic view of our own

---

* For greater ease of handling, the present chapter will deal with evil which is cosmic and mechanistic. Evil of a more personal nature—what man does to man—is reserved for the more extensive section on "Villains" that follows.

time is much nearer the savage and merciless comedy of Aristophanes, particularly in the amount of authentic violence it contains. In the nightmare dramas of human existence we find in the work of Kafka, for instance, the inescapable conclusion is that anxiety is the dominant condition of human life. In the work of Sartre or the earlier Camus, only occasionally is the individual capable of rising to a gratuitous act of disinterested virtue or even kindness. Once science had established that Mankind could be manipulated with ease, the highly interesting question of manipulation toward what end came into being. It then remained for the writer only to project his own particular vision of reality, and the superficially different but equally horrible versions of Celine, Orwell, and Aldous Huxley were held up to view. In a cosmos so designed, not merely does humanity appear absurd and depraved but the ultimate purposes of the cosmos itself seem inscrutable, if not actually hostile to human aspiration.

Thus, Faulkner's treatment of the comic element in human life is similar to Molière's in theory, even if sometimes it equals Swift's for savagery of treatment. If the comedy of Kafka seems to be devoid of hope for any part of humanity and that of Camus optimistic only about isolated actions of isolated individuals, then Faulkner seems entirely content with Nature as he sees it and is hopeful about humanity in the mass, at least to the extent that it remains uncorrupted by the more poisonous and fatal aspects of modern life. These fatal aspects are among those things that Faulkner is most concerned about, and it is out of the corruption of Mankind by those aspects that his violent and savage comedy of extremity grows. Whatever the occasion or degree may be in a given case, the individual has lost his humanity or has abdicated it in the process of some extra-human or non-human commitment. One thinks at once of those characters in the grip of a mildly comic or tragically fanatic delusion: Rosa Coldfield, Joanna Burden and Hightower, Henry Armstid, Old Doc Hines or Percy Grimm. Or, there are the literally deformed, those who were born or have become pathetically or horribly less than human: Mahon, Isaac Snopes, Popeye, Lonnie Grinnup, Tawmy, and the old blind man in *Sanctuary*. There are those who suffer mildly from the maliciousness of inanimate objects, like Uncle Buck and

Res Grier, and such thwarted altruists as Benbow, Gavin Stevens, and Ratliff. And then there is the degree of tragic frustration (like that of Lear and his button) that dogs the existence of Roger Shumann, Mink Snopes with Houston's hound and the body that keeps coming apart, Boon Hogganbeck with his gun under the gum tree, Quentin Compson with his fist fights and local magistrates on the last day of his life, or Nancy in the Compson kitchen or the Indian in "Red Leaves," caught in the demoralizing terror of certain death. Even the major tragic figures are not exempt from the comic depravity concomitant with existence: Colonel Sartoris, with his deadly quarrels with old friends, his killing of former associates, old men and adolescent boys, his consciousness of his self-destruction but his inability to stop; Joe Christmas' pattern of affirmation and flight counter to a system he never made; or even Sutpen, with his stale candy and cheap ribbons, his colossal dynastic designs crumbled at last into the dust of merely human materials. The early reviews were quick to detect the symbolic exaggeration and horror, the one-ninth of the iceberg that showed on the surface. This concern for the superficial was the basis for the statements that Faulkner was the leader in the new "cult of cruelty," for all the fulminations over "unmitigated cruelties and abnormalities," "lust and disease, brutality and death," and for the ringing affirmation that "There is nothing . . . behind his atrocities, no cosmic echoes. . . ." Another reviewer remarked that the game of *frisson nouveau* required constantly rising stakes and that Faulkner was determined not to become a piker. In a very few years, Dachau and Buchenwald would make a piker out of Faulkner.

ii.

Faulkner's view of the natural world is a serenely traditional one, achieving its fullest statement, perhaps, in the stories about the Wilderness, the Indians, the hunters, and the various McCaslins. The natural world, or at least the wilderness uncorrupted by men, has its own morality, even though that world may appear indifferent or even hostile to human aspirations, particularly when the individual's purpose is the "de-swamping and denuding" of the countryside or the setting of himself against actual natural forces, as does the convict in *The Wild Palms*. In the quieter and more pastoral moments, human life is arranged in harmony and consonance with the rhythms of natural phenomena.

This morality of Nature has its more complicated if less rigorous human counterpart within the human community. This communal morality is approximately if undogmatically Christian, and immorality consists of a single if apparently unlimited area of wrong action: violence or injury to others or to the self, particularly violence which injures the mind and spirit. Often this violence takes the form of denying the individual human even the recognition that he is human by regarding him openly as a thing to be used, having no particular importance or significance. In Yoknapatawpha, this kind of violence often takes the form of keeping human beings in a futile round of degrading and repetitive toil, particularly as in the period before Reconstruction. In the modern world this violence sometimes degrades humanity in the service of the machine. This "machine" may be any mechanism: actual machinery which destroys and denudes the wilderness or over-farms the fields; a mechanistic process, such as banking; or the whole complex structure of finance capitalism which dares not recognize the existence of human hopes and fears.

The point where these two evils meet—where there is the continuing, steady, maximum impingement of mechanistic destruction and Man's violence against men—is of course war. It is not surprising that Faulkner should find in war (or the conditions approximating it) one appropriate locale for his comedy of the Absurd. To distinguish clearly, it should be pointed out that "war" in this context is not the War Between the States but the First War, which was truly a world war and the first in which many millions of men hurled themselves to death against machines. His own response to this particular war begins with *Soldiers' Pay,* is the major concern of *A Fable,* and is reflected in parts of *The Town* and *The Mansion.*

No doubt a Kafkaesque comedy of cosmic emptiness and violence could be centered in what Wylie Sypher has called "the absurd and depraved comedy of the concentration camp." In spite of such fine works as *The Wall* and *The Diary of Anne Frank,* which are germane to the whole subject of totalitarian dictatorship and genocide, the major literature of the concentration camp has yet to be written. Perhaps it never can be. Faulkner did not attempt it, one would suppose, primarily because he had not seen it at first hand. What he had seen at first hand was the incredible life of the combat pilot in war—that other war—when the machines that were flown were wood and fabric held together with glue and spit, with a two-hour fuel supply and no space for parachutes.*

The novels and stories that deal with combat flying can in no way be considered part of Faulkner's major fiction. The short stories are technically adroit, but both *Soldiers' Pay* and *Sartoris* were written in the period of relatively immature apprenticeship and even so deal not with the combat but its aftereffects. What seemed to fascinate Faulkner about this life (and his later barnstorming experiences) was not primarily the combat itself but the response of the individual to the conditions of combat and the infinite variations in that response.

Men still under the stress of daily combat are "legitimately" subject to whatever psychic or spiritual aberrations they may develop. These range from the violently suicidal to the quiet resignation of the already-doomed. A macabre comedy is developed when irrational trivia are driven to the point of monomania, as in Comyn's repetitive "I will fight yez for a shilling" and John Sartoris' feud with Spoomer and his obsession with Spoomer's dog. The absurdity is heightened when men must make do in combat with equipment that is inadequate or that refuses to function, as in "Turnabout." Occasionally, but not often, a certain sentimentality of tone (though certainly not of event or situation) intrudes in the writing, as in Bogard's reaction to the youth and vulnerability of Midshipman Hope or in the "glamorous fatality" of the Sartoris legend. When the danger of combat no longer exists and the aberrations are cultivated as a form of affectation or as a justification of irresponsibility, the attitude of the author is sharply different—self-induced neurosis or sickness usually involves a denial of life. Young Bayard's "troubles" in *Sartoris* are little more than self-indulgence coupled with an intelligence unable or unwilling to see beyond its own self-created myths.

* Faulkner was never in combat, but crashed twice. He was gravely injured in the second crash and was near death for several weeks.

Other war stories, such as "Crevasse" and the beautifully controlled "Victory" also turn upon the same background of combat, disorder, and violence. But the emphasis is always on the human; whatever the reason in the individual case, these men have been unalterably changed by what they have done and seen. The unnamed narrator in "Ad Astra" says of the pilots on the night of the Armistice, ". . . we the flotsam. . . . It had no beginning and no ending. Out of nothing we howled, unwitting the storm which we had escaped and the foreign strand which we could not escape; that in the interval between two surges of the swell we died who had been too young to have ever lived."[1]

Perhaps none of these young men could have explained why they had joined the armed forces of a foreign nation. Consciousness of a métier, of being a part of a glamorous elite, might have been part of it. Perhaps the young men would have stuck it out from choice, if they had had the choice. Fatalism, self-dramatization, the habit of violence—all might have served to keep them going up day after day in their flying death-traps. But they had no choice; the only alternative was a firing squad. Perhaps the ultimate study of a total involvement in a life of mechanized violence would be one in which the sustaining motivations would be wholly personal and interior. A study of such commitment exists in *Pylon,* that curiously uneven but steadily fascinating novel which was written as a relaxation between the two undoubted masterpieces, *Light in August* and *Absalom, Absalom!*

iii.

The métier in *Pylon* is airplane racing as it is no longer done because it is too dangerous: not a contest against an electronic timer to reach Mach 3 and Mach 10 but actual participating competition against other airplanes on a marked course around pylons at a perilously low altitude. There are in such a contest all the normal hazards found in sports-car racing or the Indianapolis 500: collision with each other or some other object, plus the added fillip of the possibility of plowing into the ground and the disconcerting tendency of the plane to simply disintegrate on the turns.

Pylon spans the four days of an air meet staged to coincide with the promotion of Mardi Gras. The locale, so carelessly disguised as to fool no one, is New Orleans. From first to last there is a consistent tone, focused to one effect: the feeling of alienation, disassociation, and dehumanization. The world (including even the sinister Colonel Feinman) is not so much hostile as vastly indifferent, a place of uncaring, unfeeling emptiness. Within this wasteland the inhabitants carry on their sterile, empty, meaningless cycles of futility. The streets are thronged each night with crowds of people dancing and drinking in the dogged effort to enjoy themselves, repeating endlessly the tragicomic absurdity of sin and vice: drunkenness to lechery to hangover to drunkenness. At the airport (built literally on a foundation of garbage) they throng each day into the grandstands in the hope that a pilot or jumper will be killed as an added amusement. These images of dehumanization apply particularly to the major characters in the novel.

In the opening parts of the novel, Shumann and his *cuadrilla* appear as the especially elect among the damned; immobilized in a kind of static non-humanity until that moment each day when it is time to hurl the wasp-like, obsolete, over-souped airplane around the pylons. The chorus to this drama is the group of newsmen who cover the air meet. What astonishes them is not the *ménage-à-trois* (which is hardly unique in their reportorial experience) but the consistent and total fashion in which Shumann and his group seem to have got completely outside what even the reporters would consider normal humanity. It is not merely the extent to which these persons are mechanized extensions of their machines but the way they have divested themselves of nearly every human requirement.

Yair, this day Shumann comes down at whatever town it was in Iowa or Indiana or wherever. . . . And maybe she sent a postcard back from the next cowpasture to the aunt or whoever it was that was expecting her to come home to dinner, granted that they have kinfolks or are descended from human beings, and he taught her to jump parachutes. Because they aint human like us; they couldn't turn those pylons like they do if they had human blood and senses and they wouldn't want to or dare to if they just had human brains. Burn them like this one tonight and they dont even holler in the fire; crash and it aint even blood when you haul him out: it's cylinder oil the

same as in the crankcase. . . . and they went off maybe with a canopener and a blanket to sleep on under the wing of the airplane when
it rained hard; and then the other guy, the parachute guy, dropping
in, falling the couple or three miles with his sack of flour before
pulling the ripcord. They aint human, you see. No ties; no place
where you were born and have to go back to it now and then even if
it's just only to hate the damn place good and comfortable for a day
or two. From coast to coast and Canada in summer and Mexico in
winter, with one suitcase and the same canopener because three can
live on one canopener as easy as one or twelve.[2]

Shumann helps create this impression by his emotionless personality and attitudes, his essential humorlessness and indifference
to good luck or bad. Nearly all human responses seem to have
been drained out of him by his commitment to his métier, his mode
of existence. He is already doomed, in the precise sense that the
combat pilots are doomed: assume the continuation of the mode
of existence and it is only a matter of time and statistics. But he
will not quit; his persistence in his profession and the manner of
his death make him one with that company of battered old pros
which fills the fiction of Hemingway: the aging boxers and mata-
dors who go on even after youth and reflexes are gone and contemplate defeat and even death with the true professional's refusal
to quit.

Even so, *Pylon* is none the less a novel about humanity and
human values. What Faulkner has done, as if by deliberate design, in this careless, almost slovenly novel is to depict human
beings in a state of dehumanization which seems irremediable and
then without apparent effort to restore them to their full status in
humanity without mitigating the comic absurdity of their milieu
at all. This sense of restoration is what rescues *Pylon* from its
third-rate status and infuses it with the unmistakable Faulknerian
authority. The restoration grows out of the death of Roger Shumann, the manner of his death, and the response of those who
knew him. We know that Shumann will be killed by the deadly
and unreliable craft he flies. His profession has made him the
mechanistic distortion he seems to be, yet paradoxically, it is a
professional value which makes him give up his life for the safety
of the thrill-hungry crowd that has come to see him die—to use
what altitude he has to put the disintegrating airplane into the

lake instead of using his parachute and letting the plane go into the grandstand. He has taken the risks he has out of loyalty to the group and to provide for the child Laverne is to have, almost certainly this time the child of Holmes.

Laverne grieves for him in her own way, even if it is a way without hysterics and the self-indulgence of tears. Holmes, the jumper, leaves money with the Reporter so that Shumann's body will not be shipped home collect in case it should be recovered. Jiggs, the half-horse, half-thug alcoholic mechanic cannot see any point in waiting sentimentally for the body to be recovered either; he takes the best offer he can get and joins up with another barnstormer. "But Jesus," Jiggs says, "it wont be like racing."[3]

In *Pylon* the comedy is a harsh and humorless comedy of extremity, and much of the comic effect grows out of the juxtaposition of opposed extremes of behavior. Against the hard, emotionless, extreme dehumanization of the flyers is set the ludicrous excess of the Reporter: the excess of feeling, of concern; the elaborate, awkward, inept attempts to help people who do not particularly want or need help and who will not change their mode of life.

Laverne, Shumann, Holmes, and Jiggs approach the category of the Absurd because of the extremity of their mode of existence, their disjunction from the usual patterns of human behavior. The Reporter manages to inhabit several categories of the Absurd simultaneously. There is first of all his ridiculous appearance: the extreme height and cadaverousness, leading to all the repetitive and unoriginal jokes about the cemetery gates being left open. Ineptness is hardly the term to describe his fantastic awkwardness and inefficiency: he literally cannot do anything well, and there are many things he cannot do at all. Even the relatively simple assignment of phoning in to the re-write men is beyond him. Finally, there is the grotesque disparity between his effort and his success. Here he is truly the Faulknerian comic hero, but the comic hero *manqué*. In part, perhaps a large part, his effort is motivated by his compulsion to get into bed with Laverne. But that is not all: he feeds, houses, and even buys liquor for the entourage and pays for these favors by haggling with his editor for advances against his salary. For all his effort, he accomplishes nothing. He and Jiggs put his last salary advance and Roger's burial money in the toy airplane for Laverne to find, but it is discovered by old Dr. Shumann, who burns it on the assumption that Laverne has earned it in what he believes is the only way she could. The Reporter's feverish round of activity is carried out in a cosmos that seems totally indifferent to his dreams and aspirations and perhaps even to his presence.

It was Kafka who said that he wanted to exaggerate until everything became clear. Shumann and the Reporter often appear as grotesque characters against the backdrop of a hostile and absurd cosmos. But the measure of Shumann's impact on at least one human being is found in the gradually rising tone of savagery in the three different pieces of copy which the drunken Reporter leaves for his editor. There is no expectation that the Reporter will improve himself or reform his life: he will remain forever the grotesque, gangling, adolescent drinker who dreams of being a master seducer. He spends most of the four days of the air meet attempting to cuckold Shumann, but it is he who keeps the lonely vigil beside the lake while the search for Shumann's body goes on, and the solemn bells mark the transition from the orgy of Mardi Gras to the austerity of Lent.

One definition of the comedy of extremity is that it deals with the more violent and exaggerated aspects of human behavior. The use of the term implies also an awareness of Kierkegaard's statement that the comic and tragic touch one another at the absolute point of infinity. The greatest tragedies—the *Oedipus Tyrannus* or *Hamlet* or *King Lear*—arouse the complex emotion of *katharsis,* which is in part a subjective awareness of cleansing and liberation. But another part of that complexity of emotion is the response to the customary conclusion of the plot, which sets right whatever evil has been working or restores justice and harmony to the world. In some final sense, the function of comedy—from the most savage to the most gentle—is in a degree the same as the function of tragedy: to cleanse and to restore.

1. William Faulkner, *The Collected Stories of William Faulkner* (New York: Random House, 1950), p. 408.

2. William Faulkner, *Pylon* (New York: Harrison Smith and Robert Haas, 1935), pp. 44-46.

3. *Ibid.,* p. 264.

10.

FAULKNER VILLAINS

Fathers and teachers, I ponder "What is hell?" I maintain
that it is the suffering of being unable to love.

IN THE TOTAL CORPUS of Faulkner's work and particularly in the
work of his first fifteen years as an author, there is often a terrifyingly pervasive sense of evil. At times, this vision of evil seems
to imply a view of the cosmos that approaches the Manichaean—
in the blacker moments of pessimism, the evil seems not merely
autonomous but triumphant. The previous chapter on the extreme limits of comedy deals with those sometimes almost sentient
forces of mechanistic evil which combine to destroy the hopes and
aspirations of humanity. In that chapter the emphasis is more
or less on impersonal evil—the natural and particularly mechanistic forms of evil—rather than on the evil done by persons. The
present chapter deals with evil done to man by his fellow man.
In general, the Faulkner villain is a person who commits such evil.

As the present study so often reveals, any attempt to sort and
classify all the individuals who inhabit the Faulkner canon, if
extended too far, is ultimately to distort the significance of many
of those individuals. As we all know, great tragic heroes often
commit actions that are monstrous, especially if the heroes are
created against the background of a culture heavy with conflict
and violence. With such a figure as Shakespeare's Richard III or
Macbeth, when does the protagonist escape becoming the villain,
and at just what point does the tragic hero emerge from his own
monstrous actions? To cite a more recent example, how should

Stavrogin be classified? By the simplest of all possible definitions, the tragic hero is an essentially noble person who engages in certain actions that are evil or even despicable but who nevertheless engages the sympathy and loyalty of the beholder. The process by which this emotion is aroused was ultimately inexplicable to Aristotle and remains inexplicable to us. By using a simple criterion we may be able to distinguish between heroes and villains. The hero is one who, however twisted or mistaken or despicable his actions may be, performs those actions in a commitment to something more than simple aggrandizement, something, perhaps, that is bigger and better than he is. The villain, conversely, is one who is full of the sickness of self, who is not committed to anything beyond himself, and who often is unable to apprehend what greatness or magnitude is. Even this simple distinction is sometimes hard to draw, as in the case of a Richard III or Iago or Milton's Satan, who at the beginning, at least, has a certain sulfurous magnificence of his own. Sometimes, in his single-mindedness and devotion to an aim, his self-denial and firmly leashed passions, not more than a hairline of difference will separate a villain from a tragic hero. Between Sutpen and Flem Snopes there is only the final, essential difference in the heart's reason for doing: Flem bloodlessly and blindly accumulating money for no person and no purpose except to sit in a bank-president's chair; Sutpen determined to build something for posterity even bigger than his own ambitions, no matter who or what he has to destroy to complete his grand design. In the Faulkner canon, so simple a distinction will not produce final definitions but may constitute a beginning.

A typical instance of the difficulty is Joe Christmas. An early Faulkner critic who has contributed enormously to an understanding of Faulkner regards Christmas as a villain. I happen to regard Christmas as a tragic hero and as one of the most important archetypes of the twentieth-century hero yet created. Whatever else this difference of opinion may indicate, it does demonstrate the difficulty of sorting great heroes from great villains. Among the minor characters there are those who commit murder or incite mobs. However much these men of ill-will attempt to convince themselves that their aims are pure, they are infected with varying

degrees of the characteristic sickness of our time, which Robert
Penn Warren has described as "a vanity springing from an awareness of the emptiness and unreality of the self which can only attempt to become real and human by the oppression of people who
manage to retain some shreds of reality and humanity."[1]* [A
villain, then, is one who with coldness and calculation carries out
acts of violence and injury, usually more damaging spiritually
than physically, upon the weak, the helpless, children or old
people—in other words, those unable to defend themselves. The
ultimate motives for these actions may be unknown to the villain
himself, but they grow out of some crippling inadequacy of the
soul, which he can compensate for only in the way the evil is
carried out. He is usually otherwise quite moral, even upright.
He has few, if any, of the physical vices, lacking even this re-
deeming touch of humanity.] Doc Hines is a fanatical fundamentalist; Percy Grimm, aside from the horrible kink in his soul,
is as pure and idealistic as any Galahad. Popeye, aside from
chain-smoking and a tendency to shoot people, has no bad habits,
since he cannot commit fornication and knows that a single drink
of whiskey would kill him. Jason Compson has no dissipations
except a kind of decorous, monogomous, common-law relationship
with a professional prostitute from Memphis. Flem Snopes has
no vices at all, except for the occasional chew of tobacco he took
early in life; vices simply have no appeal for him.

Therefore, I exclude from the classification "villains" all the
merely unpleasant, or self-pitying, or morally infantile and irresponsible persons in the Faulkner canon, even when they are
calculating and rapacious, like Lucus Burch, of whom it was said,
". . . he'd be bad soon enough, if only someone would show him
how." Under this classification, such moral half-wits as Cecily
Saunders, Narcissa Benbow,† Temple Drake,† and Gowan
Stevens† are excluded; they fail the test for simple lack of ability.
The actions of these people are essentially infantile. A major
villain must be involved in deeper evil than these creatures are
capable of. As in the major work of Dostoyevsky, evil consists of
acts of insult and injury carried out against human beings. There

* For instance, Charles Starkweather, the "mad-dog" killer from Nebraska,
who killed eleven people because "nobody ever paid any attention to me."
† As seen in *Sanctuary,* not elsewhere.

are many characters in the Faulkner canon who seem, in the words of one French critic, "to have no soul"—that is to say, they have no will or volition of their own. But the villain—the major villain—*chooses* to do evil rather than good. In one or more aspects of his humanity there is either a grotesque excess or a grotesque defect that in its abnormality sets him apart from the rest of humanity. In the case of Popeye this defect is literally a physical deformity. Flem's sexual impotence within itself is merely pitiful; as symbol for his parasitic inability to create anything or to enter into any meaningful human relationship, it becomes terrible. As the evil which is done becomes more monstrous, both the defect itself and the evil done tend to enter the area of the spiritual. As in the work of Hawthorne, the greatest evil is a violation of the individual human heart. Perhaps the greatest possible deformity of spirit is the will to commit such a violation.

To be sure, Popeye commits two cold-blooded murders and carries out the terrible actions on Temple, both in the corn-crib and later on in the upstairs room at Miss Reba's. These are crimes, but the rational mind knows that sooner or later another criminal or the processes of law, however slowly, will remove Popeye permanently from the scene. His sphere of action is outside the law, and retribution may overtake him at any time. Jason Compson and Flem Snopes are very different creatures. They have as their immediate aim material gain, but ultimately Jason seems to be outraging innocent and helpless persons in retaliation for what he thinks the world has done to him. One major strategic error in the case of Flem is the assumption that he wants only money. Only when he unpins his symbolic twenty-dollar gold piece is his ultimate aim revealed.

Minor Villains

Faulkner's most monumental villain, the person who most nearly approaches the Shakespearean and Miltonic scale, never appears in his own person in any novel or story. His evil lives on in the memory of his descendants, white and half-white, and in the legacy of miscegenation and incest which he cynically leaves behind him for others to clean up. He is old Carothers McCaslin, ". . . that evil and unregenerate old man who could summon, because she was his property, a human being because she was old enough and female, to his widower's house and get a child on her and then dismiss her because she was of an inferior race, and then bequeath a thousand dollars to the infant because he would be dead then and wouldn't have to pay it. . . ."[2]

In Faulkner's first novel, there is a sort of sub-embryonic villain named Januarius Jones. Jones likes to imagine he is a satyr and hell with the ladies. He attempts to seduce Mrs. Powers and Cecily Saunders but gets nowhere with either of them. He blackmails Cecily to a point of complete surrender but does not seem to realize his opportunity and lets it slip by. He ends by chasing the servant girl Emmy through the house and garden with rape as his object, until the outraged Joe Gilligan catches him and beats him up. His entire performance is an unbroken process of comic incompetence. Only at the end of the novel does he manage to lead Emmy, who is incoherent and half-irrational with grief over the death of Mahon, away to her bedroom. Yet, in embryo, he is the complete Faulknerian villain. His conversations with Mrs. Powers clearly demonstrate that he considers women, all women, his natural and legitimate prey. His blundering clumsiness and absurdly fat body may be comic, but there is nothing comic in his unflagging willingess to do evil to anyone he happens to encounter. His success may be nil for the moment, but his own intentions are perfectly clear to him. He reveals that he has never imagined sex as a mutually shared experience or even as a thing enjoyable within itself. He is using his brutal and callous sexual aggression as a weapon, a means of self-assertion, of compensation for himself and punishment for others.

Popeye

Sanctuary is Faulkner's most notorious book. In the purely physical sense, Popeye is clearly the most repulsive of all Faulkner's creatures, and his actions certainly involve the most violence. Yet, Popeye is the least credible of the villains, and once the reader survives the shock of reading *Sanctuary* for the first time, the events do not linger in the mind. Popeye is not convincing simply because he is too atypical, too far outside the forms of evil the average reader has experienced. He is a night-

mare but one from which recovery is easy. Faulkner in the
final chapter of *Sanctuary* documents a medical history that would
account for Popeye, but he remains not so much inhuman as non-
human. Obviously, his soul is as warped and crippled as his body
and even more stunted. He kills Tawmy and Red and does what
he does to Temple. Yet, all this, terrible as it is, is purely *physical*
evil. He can murder, but lacks the power to corrupt souls. He
cannot corrupt an entire community as Flem does; he can only
corrupt Temple, who is, as the text makes plain, already ripe for
corruption.

The author's emphasis is always on Popeye's physical absurdity and deformity; the bloodless pallor of his skin, the meager
body, the face without a chin, "like the face of a wax doll set too
near a hot fire and forgotten." Even more consistent is the efflu-
vium of sterile, back-alley, urbanized gangsterism: the dangling
cigarette and slanted straw hat, the tight black suit, the pistol—all
in all, "that vicious depthless quality of stamped tin." He has a
hatred of anything natural, animal, and alive. He has killed
Tawmy's dog for no reason and is afraid of the woods in the dark:

Then something, a shadow shaped with speed, stooped at them and
on, leaving a rush of air upon their very faces, on a soundless feather-
ing of taut wings, and Benbow felt Popeye's whole body spring against
him and his hand clawing at his coat. "It's just an owl," Benbow
said. "It's nothing but an owl," . . . with Popeye crouching against
him, clawing at his pocket and hissing through his teeth like a cat.
He smells black, Benbow thought; he smells like that black stuff that
ran out of Bovary's mouth and down upon her bridal veil when they
raised her head.[3]

This description, with all its implication of poison and death
and evil is nasty enough and convincing enough. It images perfectly the deadliness of Popeye; how he can and will kill anything
which is an affront to him. But in a fashion that is almost medieval, Popeye illustrates the ultimate futility and helplessness of evil.
Evil can exist only by feeding on good. Crippled by his inability
to love, Popeye cannot win any positive emotional response from
other human beings, not even respect. The only emotional grati-
fication he can experience is the sadistic satisfaction derived from
observing fear or pain in others. Normal human gratifications in

particular seem to enrage him. He kills Tawmy because of
Tawmy's fumbling attempt to shield Temple, his openness, his
simple-minded, hedonistic enjoyment of the whiskey that would
kill Popeye. Red is killed when he and Temple begin to enjoy
themselves too much. Popeye is then trapped in the small-town
Alabama jail by the irony of being unable to defend himself from
one charge of murder because he killed Red somewhere else the
same night. His pistol is both agent and symbol of his power, and
once it is taken from him he becomes powerless. Still, being the
nihilist he is, living outside the law, he remains true to his own
self-definition and does not accept any of the legal expedients his
lawyer holds out to him.

They came for him at six. The minister went with him, his hand
under Popeye's elbow, and he stood beneath the scaffold praying,
while they adjusted the rope, dragging it over Popeye's sleek, oiled
head, breaking his hair loose. His hands were tied, so he began to
jerk his head, flipping his hair back each time it fell forward again,
while the minister prayed, the others motionless at their posts with
bowed heads.
Popeye began to jerk his neck forward in little jerks. "Pssst!"
he said, the sound cutting sharp into the drone of the minister's voice;
"psssst!" The sheriff looked at him; he quit jerking his neck and
stood rigid, as though he had an egg balanced on his head. "Fix my
hair, Jack," he said.
"Sure," the sheriff said. "I'll fix it for you"; springing the trap.[4]

Having killed so often, the creature who was terrified of an
owl is not afraid of hanging. Once the trap is sprung, Popeye
vanishes from our consciousness like something filthy flushed
down the drain.

Jason Compson

Compared to Popeye, Jason Compson is a far more convincing,
more disturbing villain. Jason is "normal," is a recognizable
human being that we have seen many times. He is disturbing
because we all know he lurks in us. Jason embodies the instinctive, irrational love of self, the monstrous, incestuous self-concern
that leaves no room for love of others. Since we dare not admit
the fear of imperfection in the self that is loved, we seek out and
punish others in retaliation for any frustration or thwarting that
the self encounters. Thus far Jason seems to be in the standard

pattern of the sadist who injures others in the half-conscious, irrational hope of deflecting harm from himself. In the "Compson appendix" published in 1945, Mr. Faulkner called Jason the first sane Compson since Culloden and "rational contained and even a philosopher in the old stoic tradition." Jason believes all the human race except himself to be predictable if essentially inexplicable, hence not to be trusted. The rest of humanity operates on the basis of emotion (pity, love, generosity, even pride), which is why they are insane and Jason is not.

Occasionally a critic will pull the leg of the credulous public and pretend to see Jason with Jason's own paranoid vision: a long-suffering, put-upon man, whose fate it is to live as the only sane human being in a world of irrational, incompetent fools. Usually such commentary has an axe to grind; Jason must be made to appear the innocent victim of bad sociology. Some have gone so far as to endorse Jason's own justification of his embezzlement and perjury in the filing of false statements in the expenditure of money as the legal guardian of his niece: he has the right to steal this money because of the "job he lost." The joke seems to be to see how much the scholarly public can be made to swallow. Jason does have some real troubles and burdens, it is true: a ruined patrimony, a neurotic and constantly whining hypochondriac mother, a worthless uncle who sometimes sponges on his mother's bank account, an idiot brother who bellows loudly at times, and an illegitimate niece who under his constant torturing is slowly turning into the slut he always knew she was.

Gradually the reader begins to realize the extent to which Jason's insane vision has fractionized the world and reconstituted the fragments to conform to his needs. Without his delusions, Jason could not live, since there would be no one to blame and hence no one to punish. He sees nothing illogical in blaming his dead or banished kinfolk for his misfortune but discharging his frustration and hatred on his illegitimate niece, his defective brother, or the Negroes. His sadism is usually verbal: the cutting remark, the groundless accusation, the ruining of some small, harmless pleasure for anyone too powerless to be worth the effort.*

* This is shown when he lets Luster watch the burning of the two tickets to the carnival show that Luster is wild to see.

Jason's sadism is thus more refined than Popeye's, more nearly in the area of the spiritual than the physical. Jason may construct elaborate and violent fantasies in which he strangles his niece or beats someone to a pulp, but he actually strikes only Ben and Luster. His extreme selfishness was manifested in childhood, in the kite business with a younger boy and in the pointless destruction of Benjy's paper dolls.

The cripplingly traumatic relation to his family is seen in his habit of satisfied reflection on the number of times he has tortured his mother and Caddy by lying to each about the other. These memories are genuinely savored, as the lies are a deliberate and cunning procedure, rather than the shabby human expedient that lying usually is. Useless and pointless also (except as the creation of an artist in sadism) is the episode after their father's funeral when he takes a hundred dollars from Caddy to allow her to see her infant daughter "just for a minute." Jason keeps his bargain by galloping the hired hack past his sister while holding the infant aloft in the cold and rain.

Jason's most complex, most deeply sensuous wound is his relation to his niece, Quentin. To Jason, Quentin is both the outward proof of Caddy's shame and the living reminder of the "lost job." Thus she is both the constant focus of his hatred and the most gratifying target for his retaliation and cruelty. In all truth, Jason probably does not recognize the source of his constant neurotic anxiety over Quentin's chastity or what Jason is sure is a complete lack of it. In the monologues of his incessant interior fantasies, he can at once believe she is beyond redemption and still complain of the effort he is making to save her. He can assert that he does not care what she does, even when running up and down back alleys to spy on her. He leaves work in the middle of the afternoon to chase her through ditches and poison oak in an attempt to catch her in the act. He mentally abandons her at one moment ("Like I say, let her lay out all day and all night with everything in town that wears pants, what do I care?"), while mentally threatening violence to the carnival man ("I'll make him think that damn red tie is the latch string to hell, if he thinks he can run the woods with my neice"). While still in the middle of his spying, he will say piously: "I dont mind trying to help her but I know when I've had enough."

When Jason bothers to analyze this constant expenditure of effort at all, he usually tells himself that it is simply one more of his burdens, done to "protect my mother's good name." Part of his hatred is transference of his deeply repressed incestuous attraction toward Quentin. This helps explain the continual fantasies in which he vividly pictures her in the act with the carnival hand or one of the local "damn slick-headed jelly-beans." He can use moral outrage as his conscious reaction to Quentin's "nakedness," which he constantly harps on: ". . . if a woman had come out doors even on Gayoso or Beale street when I was a young fellow with no more than that to cover her legs and behind, she'd been thrown in jail. I'll be damned if they dont dress like they were trying to make every man they passed on the street want to reach out and clap his hand on it."

The entire pattern of Jason's life, both inward and outward, is perfectly adjusted to his needs and desires. His mother, Quentin, Benjy, and "six worthless niggers" to feed are essential to the pattern of self-justification and outraged martyrdom which is Jason's image of himself. In point of fact, Jason is not contributing anything to the support of any of them, since he is stealing each month the money sent by Caddy for Quentin's support, which is greater than his salary. A further irony is that without Quentin, for whom it is sent, and his mother, whom he puts through the shabby farce of burning the check each month, this money would not come at all. Jason will never be the financial wizard he thinks he is; in his ignorance and arrogance he makes many business errors. The first and most damaging of these is in needlessly driving Quentin away with his profitless cruelty. She is the cause if not the source of the golden eggs. When she runs away, she not only takes the seven thousand dollars with her; she stops the golden flow of Caddy's checks each month. Jason's day of reckoning dawns on Easter Sunday.

Many teasing possibilities are suggested by the choice of an Easter for the climax of *The Sound and the Fury*. Keeping firm grasp on the many ironic contrasts already established—the tensions between past and present, Dilsey's nobility and Jason's meanness, the Resurrection in the Negro church and Jason's insane pursuit of money that is already gone—one generalization can be drawn. For Jason, as for Quentin, Easter is in a powerfully ironic sense a day of awakening and flight. Quentin has fled with her bigamous lover to what shabby future can be readily imagined. For Jason the day will be an awakening from a life of easy money and sadistic idleness to an unbearable nightmare of reality in which both bitch and money are gone and there is no longer anyone physically present to blame for his troubles.

Jason is sitting at Sunday breakfast, calm and decorous, savoring his latest theft and anticipating the entire day in which to torment his family. He has the additional raw material of the broken window in his bedroom to work from, not yet realizing its significance. He begins the ritual of refusing to eat until Quentin is up and at the table. Only when he realizes that Quentin is not in her room does the edge of an apprehension, too terrible to be thought of, intrude itself. ". . . he stood . . . as if he were listening to something much further away. . . . His attitude was that of one who goes through the motions of listening in order to deceive himself." For a time he seems unable to believe that both money and niece are gone. There follows the frustrating interview with the sheriff who will not join in Jason's headlong pursuit of the fugitives. Jason's sense of outrage and injury is so great and his self-justification so violent because there is no immediate, physical object on which to discharge them. He must retreat again into fantasy. As he drives furiously toward Mottson [sic] he visualizes himself with a file of soldiers, entering the courthouse and dragging the sheriff out. Certain that the weather is against him, he imagines his car stuck in the muddy road, himself forcibly taking a team from in front of a church to pull it out, striking down the owner if he protests. "I'm Jason Compson. See if you can stop me. See if you can elect a man to office who can stop me." When the weather brightens, it seems this is one more evidence that even Omnipotence is against him. " 'And damn You, too,' he said, 'See if You can stop me,' thinking of himself, his file of soldiers with the manacled sheriff in the rear, dragging Omnipotence down from His throne, if necessary; of the embattled legions of both hell and heaven through which he tore his way and put his hands at last on his fleeing niece."[5]

The great sensuous wound of Jason's complex relation to his niece is far too precious to relinquish. He still wishes, hopes, wants to believe that he will be able to slip stealthily up to Quentin and the man with the red tie, beat them both severely, and regain every cent of the money. He is not yet ready to accept what his common sense might have told him long before. The agonizing headache that strikes him at this point does not deter him. Still full of the fictitious role he has constructed for himself, he roughs up the elderly carnival cook, who retaliates by almost splitting Jason's head with a hatchet. Rescued by the carnival owner, Jason sits in his car, blind with pain, haggling futilely with a series of Negro youths to drive him back to Jefferson. People who pass in their Easter clothes look at him, "the man sitting quietly behind the wheel of a small car, with his invisible life raveled out about him like a worn-out sock." Eventually he pays the price one of the youths is asking.

Meanwhile, Benjy's hopeless moaning has caused Dilsey, against her judgment, to allow Luster to drive Benjy in the surry for his Sunday visit to the cemetery. In his self-importance, Luster drives to the wrong side of the statue of the Confederate soldier. Instantly terrified by the dislocation of tangible objects, Benjy begins his loud terrified bellowing: "There was more than astonishment in it, it was horror; shock; agony eyeless, tongueless; just sound. . . ." Jason's apathy and resignation vanish as this old focus of his festering resentment presents itself. In Jefferson, at least, Jason will still be able to control and abuse his own family, or at least Benjy and the Negro children who depend on him for a living.

With a backhanded blow he hurled Luster aside and caught the reins and sawed Queenie about and doubled the reins back and slashed her across the hips. He cut her again and again, into a plunging gallop, while Ben's hoarse agony roared about them, and swung her about to the right of the monument. Then he struck Luster over the head with his fist.

"Dont you know any better than to take him to the left?" he said. He reached back and struck Ben, breaking the flower stalk again. "Shut up!" he said, "Shut up!" He jerked Queenie back and jumped down. "Get to hell on home with him. If you ever cross that gate with him again, I'll kill you."[6]

In the 1945 "Compson appendix," Faulkner has recorded what finally happened to all the Compsons: Caddy, Benjy, and of course Jason. Jason's career was touched on also in *The Mansion*. In some ways the later life of Jason resembles the later life of Flem Snopes. Jason discovers that he is not in Flem's league when he sells Flem the remnant of the Compson Mile as the site of the proposed "Snopes Airport." After his mother and Benjy are dead and the Negroes scattered, Jason can begin to spend his money on himself. Once the outward symbols of the injustice he feels has thwarted his life are removed, he loses some of the savage intensity of his reaction to life and his fellowmen. Like Popeye, Jason is actually a criminal, although not openly so. He has committed fraud, embezzlement, and blackmail. Like Flem (who was once an arsonist), Jason is clever, or at least lucky, enough not to be caught at it. In time he becomes a cotton buyer and is well-off. Perhaps this is what society must do eventually; if it cannot eliminate the menace and the evil (as with Popeye), then it must find a way to tame and contain that menace.

Flem

Between *The Hamlet* in 1940 and *The Town* in 1957, there is a lapse of seventeen years and a considerable difference in attitudes, both on the part of Faulkner toward his creature Flem and of Flem himself. At first glance, these changes in Flem may appear to be fundamental and genuine, but more careful analysis will show that he has changed only outwardly. He has learned to trim his cloth to the dignity of his newly advanced station in life. But Flem has the wrong relation to Nature and to Man, and in this he is incapable of change. Like Popeye and Jason, he is incapable of coming into a right relation with Nature and Man because he is basically incapable of love.

On the surface, the middle-aged Flem who is concerned with being a bank president and Baptist deacon in Jefferson appears to be somewhat "humanized," but this is merely a shift in technique. For the first time in his life, his public reputation is a matter of tangible value to him. His instincts and attitudes are the same; in the primary sense he is no more capable of love than he ever was, since he cannot conceive of human beings except as instruments or pawns to be used for his own ends. In short, what Flem is practicing is not humanitarianism but hypocrisy and affectation. This becomes evident in *The Mansion*.

Flem Snopes, particularly in the more savage presentation found in *The Hamlet,* is a ruthless and grasping young man who is clawing his way to the top. On the practical, realistic level of day-to-day human life, he is simply a heartless businessman who has never been bested in a trade. On the philosophical and theological level, he is satanic in the precise Miltonic sense: he knows how to turn the impulses and weaknesses of human beings against themselves and to lead them to their own downfall. He demonstrates a fully matured technique for leading the unwary into temptation and then exploiting the opportunity when they fall. This is an important distinction, because it indicates in Flem a power and capacity for evil far beyond that of Popeye and Jason Compson. As noted, Popeye's capacity for evil, aside from his willingness to do evil, consists only in his pistol; without his pistol he is helpless. Jason shows a certain eagerness to slap or beat those weaker than himself, but his capacity for harm is limited to the inflicting of his sadistic impulses on those who cannot retaliate. This may have serious consequences, as when he drives his niece into nymphomania, but, primarily, persons outside his reach are out of danger from him. Flem is exceptional in that he turns human impulse and emotion to his own profit and moves utterly unconcerned over the human wreckage that occurs.

Human values aside, this shift in technique is startling enough, but in the light of Flem's subsequent history, we can see it as a distinct point in the great transition from barn-burner to financier. In the early stages of *The Hamlet,* however, the prime constituent of Flem's success is a total indifference to social values and social responsibility. Everyone in Frenchman's Bend knows that, given the need or even the opportunity, a Snopes will do anything. Even worse, a Snopes does not care who knows it. Charity, altruism, or good deeds aside, the majority of humanity has vanity or hypocrisy enough to hide its wickedness if possible and makes due allowance for the opinion of the community. Flem is defined by this precise difference, this alienation from the community. His alienation is symbolized in a number of striking ways. The first and most obvious is his physical appearance.

Anyone may be unlucky enough to be born with eyes like stagnant water or a broad, flat face as uncommunicative as a pan of dough. Anyone may have a paradoxical, tiny, predatory nose like the beak of a hawk, designed perhaps by a maniacal humorist or simply clapped down as a "frantic and desperate warning." Flem's facial features are what they are; what really sets him apart both as symbol and literal fact is his soft, squat body. In Frenchman's Bend, a man may be as powerfully built as Eck Snopes or Houston or as wire-drawn as Ab or Mink, but his body is visible evidence of the hard work he does. Flem appears to have avoided all work, even as the son of a desperately poor tenant farmer. Like Jody Varner, this softness is evident not only in the physique but in the clothing they both wear. When we see Flem for the first time, he is already dressed in cheap grey trousers, a soiled white shirt, and a cloth cap. All other men in Frenchman's Bend (except the Varners) wear overalls. This difference, this isolation, is self-chosen and self-proclaimed. Flem's alienation extends even to his own family. In Ratliff's version of the De Spain barnburning, Flem has helped Ab set the fire, but arson is too crude, too unprofitable a means for Flem to employ for very long. The present study has detailed elsewhere Jody Varner's awkward attempt to exploit Ab's family and his panicked reaction when he discovers just what kind of a barn-burner he has hired. Flem intercepts Jody at a point where they cannot be seen from the house. When the secret interview is over, Flem is a member of the Varner enterprises, even though Jody, Will, and the rest of the world may not know it yet.

The relation Flem holds to Will Varner is characteristic of his particular talents. Will despises Flem but sees his usefulness, his undeniable business superiority to Jody, whom Will has always regarded as a fool. The threat of arson may terrify Jody, but Flem knows that arson is like a stick of dynamite—once it is used, its potency as a threat is ended. Will Varner *is* the law in Frenchman's Bend, and anyone who burned his property would be shot or lynched. Unlike Ab, Flem sees there is no profit in arson;

rather than burn the Varner property, he will watch his chances to take it over. What he offers Will is not a threat but an intelligent coalition of mutual interest and profit, which is why they are so soon observed doing business together. Seeing it from the outside, the community can only speculate on the actual sequence of Flem's rise in the world, his growing supervision of Will Varner's cotton-gin, ledgers, and cashbox. Before long, Flem is dealing in blooded cattle and cash loans at a very high rate of interest.

The next phase of Snopesism begins as the horde of other Snopeses descends on Frenchman's Bend. Flem no longer remains in the store; his place is taken by the rapacious I. O. Snopes. The pattern has emerged; people, occupations, professions, exist for one purpose: to provide a métier—suitable or unsuitable—for Snopeses. What the community is seeing is "not the petty dispossession of a blacksmith, but the usurpation of an heirship." Here, too, the community can only speculate on the exact relationship between Flem's cousins and the employment that is within his gift. He is as quick to exploit or destroy a relative for profit as anyone else. The first such occasion is the encounter with Ratliff, the goats, and the idiot Isaac Snopes. The sacrifice of Mink Snopes takes place when Flem sees his opportunity to get rid of Houston by letting Mink kill him. He then gets rid of Mink, a Snopes who is dangerous because he will not subordinate his emotions to profit, by allowing him to draw a life sentence. The relationship which most combines usurpation and exploitation occurs when he is given Eula Varner in marriage. More men than Ratliff mourn the giving of this bucolic Venus to the crippled Vulcan, Flem; yet the symbolic values underlying the event are perfectly "just" in the Aristotelian sense. Flem takes the prize because he is self-aggrandizing and ruthless enough to take it, provided it is something he can use. He does not care that Eula is carrying Hoake McCarron's child, since what Eula and Hoake have done has nothing in common with Eula's utility for Flem. Flem is himself impotent, and "impotent" here is freighted with the full symbolic ambiguity of its various meanings: he knows nothing of the right use of human beings. What every other young man (and some not so young) in Frenchman's Bend has lusted for and brawled over, Flem acquires, but only for business and investment purposes. The course of the Snopes trilogy will show how he uses her and her daughter Linda as well.

Such absence of pride or shame or simple human compassion seems to indicate an emotional impotence to match that physical impotence. This colorless, negative lack of emotion seems at times to suggest a human adding-machine, a personality without personality. At times Flem seems to resemble Percy Grimm in the contrast between negative personality and terrible action. Still, there is the evidence of the ritual clothes he wears, and constant reference is made to the tiny black bow tie he assumes when he comes to work for the Varners. All this is enough to suggest a monstrous vanity and pride that at times breaks out into sadistic action; action that must be called sadistic because there is no especial profit to be gained from it. Once we are aware there is room for vanity under his unswerving devotion to the profit motive, many puzzling aspects of Flem's behavior become comprehensible. The climaxes of Flem's conduct toward his kin and neighbors demonstrate how this vanity is satisfied within the operations of the profit system. One such climax occurs when he returns from Texas accompanied by Buck Hipps and the herd of savage, unbroken spotted ponies.

The entire episode of the spotted horses indicates the extent to which Flem will go to get money, but it illustrates also his instinctive grasp of the kind of folly and foolishness that men are capable of and the predicability of profit to be gained from the manipulation of these impulses to folly.] It is typical of Flem that he takes no outward active part in either the handling or the selling of the savage animals, and in fact, Flem denies any relationship to the horses or the money at all. This episode, in its pattern of temptation and weakness, is discussed more fully in the chapter on Ratliff, who is the only man who makes any attempt to tease the men of Frenchman's Bend out of their foolishness. Flem enters the picture only when he takes the five dollars from Mrs. Armstid, the last money she has in the world. Buck Hipps refuses to take the money, giving it back to Mrs. Armstid. Henry snatches it from her and gives it to Flem. Buck then tells her she can get it back the next day from Flem. The loafers at the store, including Rat-

liff, watch her as she comes to ask Flem for the money. Flem
says Hipps took it all. Past hope, past even the possibility of hope,
Mrs. Armstid waits in the silence of the beautiful spring day for
Flem or someone to tell her what to do. At last Ratliff speaks
to remind all of them why she is there.

"How's Henry this morning, Mrs. Armstid?" Ratliff said. She
looked at him, pausing, the blank eyes waking for an instant.

"He's resting, I thank you kindly," she said. Then the eyes died
again and she moved again. Snopes rose from the chair, closing his
knife with his thumb and brushing a litter of minute shavings from
his lap.

"Wait a minute," he said. Mrs. Armstid paused again, half-
turning, though still not looking at Snopes nor at any of them. Because she cant possibly actually believe it, Ratliff told himself, anymore than I do. . . . Snopes came out of the door, carrying a small
striped paper bag and approached Mrs. Armstid. "Here," he said.
Her hand turned just enough to receive it. "A little sweetening for
the chaps," he said. His other hand was already in his pocket, and
as he turned back to the chair, he drew something from his pocket
and handed it to the clerk, who took it. It was a five-cent piece. . . .
He turned his head slightly and spat again, neatly past the gray gar-
ment, onto the road. . . .

"You're right kind," she said. . . . The clerk in the doorway
cackled suddenly, explosively, chortling. He slapped his thigh.

"By God," he said, "you cant beat him."[7]

Once Ratliff has been taken in by the Old Frenchman Place
scheme and is neutralized for a time, Flem loads the wife who is
not really his wife and the child who is not his child and his other
worldly goods into the wagon for the move to Jefferson. He has
"used up" Frenchman's Bend and is now on his way to open up
the new territory for pillage and exploitation. We are still no
more privy to Flem's secret heart than we ever were, but he drives
three miles out of his way to see Henry Armstid still digging away
in the land Flem sold him. Flem has just publicly bested Ratliff,
got rid of the worthless plantation, and made a handsome profit.
Why savor the final destruction of Henry Armstid? Perhaps it
is to show the spectators how a master does it. Each day there
is a crowd to watch Henry digging himself back into the earth.
The crowd watches Flem drive up and looks with him as two
half-grown boys attempt to slip up to the trench where Henry is

working. Flem watches with the others as Henry stumbles after them and falls.

> . . . beyond the fence the people watched him in a silence so complete that they could hear the dry whisper of his panting breath. Then he got up, onto his hands and knees first as small children do, and picked up the shovel and returned to the trench. He did not glance up at the sun, as a man pausing at work does to gauge the time. He came straight back to the trench, hurrying back to it with that painful and laboring slowness, the gaunt unshaven face which was now completely that of a madman. He got back into the trench and began to dig.
>
> Snopes turned his head and spat over the wagon wheel. He jerked the reins slightly. "Come up," he said.[8]

Seen in this light, Flem's actions become somewhat explicable. When he gives Mrs. Armstid the nickel's worth of candy for the children he has robbed, she says apathetically, "You're right kind," and he spits past her into the road. Against this should be set the unveiling of Eula's monument, when Linda is forced to sit in the car, defenseless, to see the brutal, taunting inscription, so that Flem can spit and say: "All right. You can go now." As Ratliff explains it, Flem at this point should have everything he wants and be satisfied. But he is not; he must force a young girl who is not even his own child to endure the taunt and say: "I humbly thank you, Papa, for being so good to me."

A Snopes Coda

When Flem Snopes drives the wagon away from Frenchman's Bend at the end of *The Hamlet* and arrives at the beginning of *The Town,* he is a red-neck usurer who has got as far as some money and a half-ownership of a back-street lunchcounter in Jefferson. At the end of *The Town,* Flem is president of the bank; he is an *arriviste* who has arrived. Almost two decades lie between, and during that interval Flem discovers not merely what he wants from life but the means to implement it. In the subsequent two decades spanned by *The Mansion,* Flem's achievement is recapitulated, and the process of retribution is prepared for.

In many ways the last two books make clear what Faulkner affirms in a note prefixed to *The Mansion,* that it is "the final chapter of, and the summation of, a work conceived and begun in 1925." As always in Yoknapatawpha, an understanding of any segment of the Snopes trilogy is helped by knowledge of the other parts. This point is underscored sharply by the experience of reading *The Mansion* and then returning at once to *The Hamlet* to begin the cycle again. In the process of such re-reading, many points that were once dim appear sharp and clear. One instance is the clownish vision of Flem in Hell which Ratliff spins for himself just after Flem is married to Eula Varner. Flem has come to Hell, carrying his straw suitcase, to redeem his soul that has been in escrow there. It cannot be found, and the Prince of Darkness is told that Flem refuses to leave.

'What did you offer him?'
'The gratifications.'
'And—?'
'He has them. He says that for a man that only chews, any spittoon will do.'
'And then?'
'The vanities.'
'And—?'
'He has them. He brought a gross with him in the suitcase, specially made up for him outen asbestos, with unmeltable snaps.'[9]

Leslie Fiedler has recently suggested that we regard Flem Snopes with his straw suitcase and asbestos tie as a comic parody of the Faust figure.* Marx's maxim that history repeats itself as comedy is offered as the inspiration for the creation of Flem, since Thomas Sutpen is a Faust figure of fully tragic proportions. In spite of grave reservations about the degree to which Faulkner might feel bound by a maxim of Marx, I should like to offer an alternative myth, one which also is tragic in its earlier Yoknapatawpha version. Near the end of *The Mansion*, using the author's third-person point of view, Faulkner inserts the following casual observation: ". . . there had already been a new Snopes living in Jefferson for going on two years . . . named Orestes, called Res. That's right, Orestes. Even Charles's Uncle Gavin didn't know how either." "How" in this context means "How could any Snopes ever be named Orestes?" More to our purpose would be to ask "Why?"; why not Philocletes or Ther-

---

* Certainly there is insight to be gained from such a comparison. In Ratliff's imaginary interview between Flem and the Prince, the fact emerges that Flem did leave his soul in the Devil's keeping but that "it wasn't no big one to begin with" and now it cannot be found.

sites? I should like to suggest that, on a symbolic level at least, the entire Snopes trilogy can best be understood by reference to the Orestes myth.

In a purely casual and offhand way, Faulkner has scattered the names and terminology of mythology throughout his work. Moving backward from *The Mansion* to *The Hamlet,* Eula Varner is called the bucolic Venus of Frenchman's Bend, suggesting "some symbology out of the old Dionysic times—honey in sunlight and bursting grapes, the writhen bleeding of the crushed fecundated vine beneath the hard rapacious trampling goat-hoof." She is married off to the clever but crippled and impotent Flem, who resembles Vulcan, especially when he is set down in the specific milieu of the coal-fired boiler of the Jefferson power plant. Flem is cuckolded by Manfred de Spain, a martial hero who brazenly flashes about, encased in a gaudy machine trimmed with brass. Flem almost fashions a personal monument out of old pieces of brass but decides eventually to fashion a net to turn the adultery of Venus and Mars to his own ends. The Venus-Mars-Vulcan myth verges into the Orestes myth when Flem begins to use the patterns of insult and injury to rise in the world.

In the *Oresteia* of Aeschylus, Orestes is a troubled young man compelled to kill his mother, who, for reasons of jealousy, love, and revenge, had murdered his father in a shameful and degrading way. Orestes is urged on by his sister Electra and condoned and defended by Apollo himself. In the Snopes trilogy, Linda has only a hesitant and indecisive Gavin Stevens to help her. Using the dedicated but childlike Mink as her instrument, she brings about the death of her putative father, who had subjected her mother to a shameful and degrading death not for love or jealousy or any recognizable emotion but for his cold and insatiable need to become president of a bank. Once more, Faulkner has powerfully demonstrated his awareness of social forces, of the detailed ecology of a community. *The Hamlet* demonstrates the seismic effect of the onslaught of Snopeses on Frenchman's Bend. In *The Town,* the process of Flem's take-over of Jefferson is continued, but the focus narrows to concentrate on Flem, his rise to power by means of his wife's adultery, and his own skillful ability to manipulate community feeling. In *The Mansion* there is the unmistakable stamp of that quality found in all major Faulkner fiction, which is in part a sense of extension: the ability to raise a private and local fiction to the level of universal and timeless myth. In the closing sections the Faulknerian tragic sense asserts itself as a powerful foreboding, as Gavin and Ratliff keep vigil, waiting for the blow of fate, retribution, to strike.

On the level of modern realism, the subject matter of the trilogy is the classic triad of money, love, and death. The process of action throughout is the response of Flem to the environment that confronts him with these phenomena and the corresponding response of the environment to Flem. Much of the brilliance of treatment lies in the simultaneous handling of Flem as both object and abstraction, in the sustained conflict between abstraction and the demands of human life. Essentially, Flem is a creature who consistently injures human beings in the pursuit of an abstraction and who yet must be brought to the bar of judgment as a human being himself. The technical difficulty of such an extended presentation is solved by keeping Flem always at a distant remove from the reader, revealing him primarily through the more or less baffled speculation and comment of such genuine human beings as Ratliff and Gavin Stevens. The simultaneity of concrete and abstract can be seen also in the subtly controlled and unobtrusive symbols. Not since *The Bear,* perhaps, had Faulkner employed objects that are so completely at all times both thing and significance. There are Flem's tie and white shirt. Again, there is money in all its complex manifestations as coin, paper, motivation, usury, and force. What begins as the exaggerated importance of a five-cent piece becomes Mrs. Armstid's last five dollars, which turns into a figurative twenty-dollar gold piece and the means of financial ascendancy. When Mink is released from Parchman, he receives three distinct sums of money: that from Linda, the ten dollars given to all released convicts by the State of Mississippi, and, most important of all, the remnant of the sum sent anonymously by Montgomery Ward Snopes. For literal and symbolic reasons, Mink must divest himself of Linda's money and be robbed of that from the State. The stolen ten dollars are replaced by ten more (with which he buys the pistol) through the agency of Brother Goodyhay, a profane ex-Marine top-sergeant, now an unordained minister, who has had a direct experience of God.

ii.

In the brief exchange between the Prince of Darkness and his assistants, two words should be noted: "spittoon" and "vanity." One is an obvious reference to Eula and an ironic, left-handed comment on Flem's own sexual impotence. Mr. Faulkner has used "spittoon" as a violent and savage term for a woman who is outraged and used without even the semblance of love or decency. At the point in *The Bear* at which young Ike McCaslin is discovering that his grandfather, old Carothers McCaslin, fathered a child on his own near-white daughter, Ike cries out, *"But there must have been love. . . . Even what he would have called love: not just an afternoon's or a night's spittoon."* As for "vanity," one of the clichés in regarding Flem is to imagine him without emotions entirely, without the capacity for emotion, even vanity, and to feel that this incapacity is one measure of the cold, frog-like horror of the man. In the more direct and savage presentation of *The Hamlet,* Flem is a flat character whose monstrous and heartless actions seem to grow from one source only, his violent and rapacious love of money. As episode follows episode—the circumstances of his marriage to Eula, the spotted horses, his treatment of the Armstids—the conviction grows that Flem was born with some terrible inadequacy of the soul; that being unable to feel, he is unable to apprehend the anguish he creates. He seems to lack particularly the capacity for pride or shame. Yet there are the white shirt and the snap-on bow tie. Mrs. Armstid's last five dollars and the inscription on Eula's monument will confirm what these signs had hinted: Flem has already demonstrated a monstrous, sadistic vanity to those perceptive enough to sense it.

iii.

Just before her suicide, Eula reveals the fact of Flem's impotence to Gavin Stevens and says, "Be careful or you'll have to pity him." The reader of *The Mansion* must issue himself a similar warning; be careful or you will find Flem and Mink approaching the condition of tragedy. Somewhat earlier, Gavin remarked that money has cost Flem everything. Flem is in the tragic pattern because he gambles everything on the pursuit of a personal ideal, mercilessly exploiting or destroying anything he finds in his way. His fatal flaw is not a defect of self-knowledge, as it is with Oedipus or Macbeth. It is an inadequate or defective knowledge of others, his basic inability to love, to understand the nature of the human heart, that causes him to commit the unnecessarily sadistic actions he commits. From the comment of Gavin and Ratliff, the reader can understand if not sympathize with the terrible need of someone who is less than nothing to become something tangible and unassailable. This need compels Flem finally to unpin his symbolic twenty-dollar gold piece, the final trump card that is the threat to expose the old scandal of Linda's illegitimacy and Eula's continuing adultery. Eula chooses suicide as the only possible course to free Linda; what Flem cannot be forgiven is the inscription on the monument over Eula's grave, the carved defenseless taunt for the world to see forever: "A Virtuous Wife Is a Crown to Her Husband Her Children Rise and Call Her Blessed."

In the altered perspective of *The Mansion,* Mink Snopes is seen as forced into the treachery and violence of Houston's murder by the combination of his economic poverty, his own small stature, and his being a Snopes. His problem is that he cannot reconcile himself to, cannot submit to, the idea of being valued less than other men. When Will Varner awards Houston his judgment, Mink pays in the only way he can, by hard labor at fifty cents a day. When he has had all that manhood can endure, he shoots Houston dead from ambush. At his trial for murder, he does not resent judge, jury, or his sentence; he is too busy looking for Flem. When the judge orders him to plead, he replies: "Dont bother me now. Cant you see I'm busy?" This is not arrogance; it is his certainty that Flem will come in to honor the clan obligation to save him. When the life sentence is passed, his will hardens on two objectives, or perhaps a single one: to do nothing to jeopardize an early release, so that he may return to kill Flem that much sooner. He devotes to this aim the same unflagging concentration that he gave to Houston's fence posts. When Montgomery Ward Snopes turns up in Parchman, glib and persuasive in the assurance that Flem has prepared the escape, Mink is doubtful and knows better. When the trap is sprung, including as it does the needless added humiliation of the bonnet and dress, five men with pistols and blackjacks are required to subdue Mink. He bears no rancor toward Montgomery Ward, realizing he too is Flem's victim. He says: "Hidy . . . I reckon you'll see Flem before I will now. . . . Tell him he hadn't ought to used that dress. But it dont matter. If I had made it out then, maybe I would a changed. But I reckon I wont now. I reckon I'll jest wait."

In this way his additional twenty years at Parchman begins. Nothing is changed, since there is nothing he did not know before. Only toward the end, under the death threat from the escapee Stillwell, does he put it all into the hands of God. Within a year, Stillwell is dead under circumstances that suggest the miraculous, and Linda's petition for Mink's release can be drawn up. He emerges frail, old, unfamiliar with the changes in the world since 1908, yet he is able to find his way to Brother Goodyhay and Memphis. He somehow is able to elude anyone who might recognize him and so is able to walk into his cousin's house and this time say, from no ambush, "Look at me, Flem."

One of the minor miracles of *The Mansion* is the sense of transformation, of almost imperceptible change, that infuses it. In retrospect, the signs and portents of Linda's fate were clear much earlier. Ratliff's finely drawn speculations on the circumstances of Linda's begetting show that she was destined for some distant function she alone can fulfill. Throughout the bittersweet relationship with Gavin in *The Town,* the word he most often applies to Linda is "save," by which he means actual removal from the sphere of Snopesism. It is then that she seems most troubled, most vulnerable, most in need of some sort of decent life, a life that Eula is trying to provide, ultimately by killing herself. Once Flem has said, "Now you can go," Gavin arranges Linda's opportunity to go from Jefferson into the world, to find whatever happiness she can. She finds a great deal: a total, encompassing love with Barton Kohl and a sharpened, developed passion for justice that involves her in all sorts of hopeless causes. She returns from Spain widowed and deaf. So long as she has Negro educa-

tion to improve or another anti-fascist war to win, she can smother
the cry of her mother's voice from her shameful grave, *Why
didn't you revenge me and my love that I finally found. . . . had
you no love of your own to teach you what it is?* Still, the pattern of destiny and retribution is at work. Barton Kohl must die
so that Linda can return to Jefferson and her appointed function.
When there are no lost causes left, she has Gavin draw up the
documents for Mink's release. Toward the end, as she prepares
to drive away to what may easily be her death, her life has become
a Chekhovian tragedy of waste, as her mother's was, a final bit of
wreckage of the house that Snopes built.

The final, definitive word on Flem's obsessive rise to the top
is spoken inside an automobile parked on a forgotten dirt road
deep in Frenchman's Bend. Ratliff is gently probing Gavin's
moral consciousness, painful as it is, compelling him not merely
to see Linda's involvement in Flem's death—the process of "Give-
me-lief"—but the justice and moral appropriateness of that involvement. "So this is what it all come down to. All the ram-
shacking and foreclosing and grabbing and snatching. . . . maybe
there's even a moral in it somewhere, if you jest knowed where
to look." Gavin's reply is bitter and succinct: "There aren't any
morals. . . . People just do the best they can." Ratliff says,
"The pore sons of bitches." Gavin replies: "The poor sons of
bitches."

This bit of statement and response is the final utterance of a
choral pattern—a basic summation of the meaning of human existence—that echoes and re-echoes throughout the later pages of the
trilogy. There is Miss Reba's passionate outcry: "All of us.
Every one of us. The poor sons of bitches." There is the cold,
seething, intransigent benediction which Brother Goodyhay ha-
bitually speaks: "Save us, Christ. The poor sons of bitches."
Most important of all, the response of Gavin and Ratliff at this
juncture makes clear a pivotal earlier comment by Montgomery
Ward Snopes, which could have been meant for Mink but now
clearly applies to Linda Snopes Kohl:

I was probably pretty young, when I realized that I had come from
what you might call a family, a clan, a race, maybe even a species, of
pure sons of bitches. So I said, *Okay, okay. . . . that's what we'll do:*

*every Snopes will make it his private and personal aim to have the
whole world recognize him as THE son of a bitch's son of a bitch.
. . . But we never do it. We never make it. The best we ever do
is to be just another Snopes son of a bitch. All of us. . . . So the
one true bitch we had was not a bitch at all but a saint and martyr,
the one technically true pristine immaculate unchallengeable son of a
bitch we ever produced wasn't even a Snopes.*[10]

1. Robert Penn Warren, *At Heaven's Gate* (New York: Random House, 1959), p. 250.
2. William Faulkner, *Go Down, Moses* (New York: Random House, 1942), p. 294.
3. William Faulkner, *Sanctuary* (New York: Modern Library, 1932), p. 6.
4. *Ibid.*, p. 378.
5. William Faulkner, *The Sound and the Fury* (New York: Modern Library, 1946), p. 322.
6. *Ibid.*, p. 336.
7. William Faulkner, *The Hamlet* (New York: Random House, 1940), pp. 361-63.
8. *Ibid.*, pp. 420-21.
9. *Ibid.*, p. 173.
10. William Faulkner, *The Mansion* (New York: Random House, 1959), p. 87.

11.

FAULKNER AND TRAGEDY

IN ANY CONSIDERATION of tragedy, we must begin with a major
admission and a major assumption. The admission is this: there
is no final definition of tragedy; there never can be. The assumption grows out of the admission; only on the basis of our imperfect and limited definition of tragedy per se can we attempt to
evaluate the possibility of tragedy in the modern world. We
must, for the moment, beg the question of whether tragedy can
be defined at all.

Among most of the commentators on tragedy, however, it is
possible to find a wide agreement concerning certain attributes
which tragedy and the tragic hero must meet or live up to. The
history of these statements and counter-statements is a fascinating
one, but in this study the temptation to pursue it must be firmly
resisted. I wish to suggest only one point at this time: sooner
or later all definitions come down to that curiously non-objective
point first established by Aristotle: "Tragedy is an imitation of an
action that is serious, complete, and of a certain magnitude; in
language embellished with each kind of artistic ornament, the
several kinds being found in separate parts of the play; in the form
of action not of narrative; through pity and fear effecting the
proper *katharsis*, or purgation of these emotions."[1]

Katharsis, the proper purging of the emotions of pity and
fear in the beholder. We may argue as long as we wish about the
attributes of the hero and the requirements of the plot, but at the
end, tragedy, in order to happen at all, must take place in the

consciousness of the beholder. There may be plays upon the boards and pity and fear in human beings, but unless the pity and fear and the purgation of them are brought about by the spectacle as seen, there can be no tragedy. This qualification, taken in conjunction with the now well-established idea of the communal or group nature of the origin and staging of tragedy, brings us to one inescapable conclusion, well-documented by the critics of the age we live in: the scarcity of tragic literature in our time is not primarily the fault of the writers but of the times themselves, of humanity as it now is, of the "climate of opinion."

What is the climate of opinion we live in? What are its most discernible aspects? At least there is no shortage of comment on this subject. I would like to say only that I think the entire corpus of belief—conscious and unconscious, stated and unstated—can be summarized as the Myth of Cosmic Pessimism. The general implications of the myth are discussed in the Introduction to the present volume. But its philosophic basis is briefly this: in the light of scientific knowledge, there is little hope for either the individual human being or the planet itself. The individual man, however heroic or talented, cannot preserve himself beyond death. If the human race does not destroy itself in the near future with thermonuclear devices, then sooner or later it will vanish in the inevitable death of the solar system. Never before has eschatology been so gloomy and at the same time so unanswerable in its pronouncements.

But, it may be argued, how does this affect the ordinary human being; how is he concerned with the "world which Science presents for our belief"? But we know he is affected by such considerations. The scientific estimate of Man has penetrated every area of human activity: economics, government, jurisprudence, human relations. Science in its disinterested search for "truth" has established that man is not a slightly imperfect angel but rather a highly educated monkey. Among the firmly established minor myths in the folklore of psychology is that of behaviorism: man is merely a helpless bundle of conditioned reflexes, and his will is in no way free. Man is only a chance agglutination of molecules, an accidental by-product of the evolutionary process. To summarize quickly other aspects of the present climate of opinion, we might list the general acceptance of the naturalistic-deterministic view of the cosmos, with the corresponding loss of religious faith and of the sense of the human individual as a being with dignity and importance of his own, capable of shaping his own destiny.

We all know where the present estimate of man comes from. In its literary aspect, the Myth of Cosmic Pessimism is an outgrowth of Naturalism. Naturalism, as we know, is merely the literary result of a scientific cause: the scientific discoveries of the second half of the nineteenth century, the work of the Darwins, the T. H. Huxleys, the Marxes, the Freuds. Not content with upsetting the cosmos, destroying God, and reducing Man to the status of mere unthinking matter, they then retreated into death themselves, leaving us the rubble of civilization to wander in or clear up as best we may.

But bad as the present climate of opinion is, our concern is not with it but with tragedy. If the last few pages are a reasonably accurate account of our present attitudes, what do these concepts do to the possibility of tragedy? Here again, there is plenty of comment. Two well-known authorities on the subject could be cited at this point: Joseph Wood Krutch in *The Modern Temper* (1929) and Alan Reynolds Thompson in *The Anatomy of Drama* (1946). Their two studies are consonant with the general consensus—that in such a climate of opinion, tragedy is impossible. Man has such an abysmal estimate of himself that even if a writer could be found to produce a tragedy, no one would take it seriously.

A summation of these estimates only more strongly reinforces the social concept of tragedy and makes plainer the fact that it is the audience that shapes the climate in which the tragedy must live. Bypassing for a moment the question of whether an individual writer is now capable of writing tragedy at all, we come to the fairly certain conclusion that he would have no audience capable of apprehending his meaning. This is true not only for tragedy written in and about our time but by extension also for those masterpieces of vanished ages which all critics have agreed are tragic. Except for a handful of somewhat "special" individuals, who have some appreciation of these matters by virtue of their highly specialized literary training, modern man completely lacks the tragic spirit. One implication of this impasse is even more depressing: the writer cannot hope to create work that is tragic, simply because he is himself a part of that same audience, that same climate of opinion, which is completely unsuitable for tragedy. In such a climate, where man has so negative an opinion of himself, it may well seem that the creation of tragic literature is impossible. Historically, we know that as civilization begins to slide over into decadence, tragedy disappears.

In a universe as bleak as ours now is, where Man at last has sufficient knowledge, ample means, and apparently the will to destroy not only the whole of humanity but all life and probably the planet as well, a wistful hankering after vanished literary values may seem irresponsible. So it would be, except that in some highly tenuous but quite inescapable manner the two problems are entangled with each other; indeed, one wonders if at bottom they may not be the same. The death of the tragic spirit and the question, "When will I be blown up?" both derive from the same ground: Man's own present estimate of himself.

Difficult as it may seem, in the light of history and the current situation, one contention of this study is that, far from being impossible, the creation of tragic literature has taken place in the present context. Our situation, involving as it does the probable extinction of Man as we know him if not of humanity altogether, certainly seems "tragic" enough. Can nothing be made of a spectacle so appalling? The tragic literature of our time is centered in tragic protagonists who in their symbolic and symptomatic aspects stand for all humanity caught in the coils of the other great myth of our time: the Myth of Cosmic Chaos. One other contention of this study is that, far from abnegating tragedy, the times are ripe for it.

ii.

In a world situation thus defined, how could literature that is authentically tragic be created? What possible manner or means or approach could the writer devise? It seems to me that there are three possibilities. If I have correctly understood the commentators already quoted, the lack of tragic sensibility in our time is a part of the abysmal estimation that modern Man has of himself. I suppose it requires no elaborate documentation to show that on every hand individuals of all kinds are saying that we cannot continue as we are, that we must change or perish. Many of the more thoughtful agree that the key to the entire problem lies in just this area of Man's estimate of himself. For instance, the Neo-Thomists suggest that we begin, quite logically, by returning to pre-Copernican cosmology and restoring the earth to its rightful place in the center of the cosmos. This is the first necessary step, they argue, in raising Man's estimate of himself, in allowing him to believe that anything about himself, as an individual or in the mass, could possibly be of any consequence.

Others take a somewhat different approach to the same general problem. Since we have already mentioned Mr. Krutch's devastatingly honest evaluation in *The Modern Temper* (1929), several instructive comparisons may be made by placing beside it his *The Measure of Man* (1954). I cannot here do even partial justice to the later book, more than to say it refutes the prevailing estimate of Man, particularly those aspects of it based on the "irrefutable" evidence gathered by the social scientists. Against the ever more firmly established notion that man is "nothing but" the sum of those things the scientist can "prove" about him, Mr. Krutch returns the verdict of "not proved." After an extensive discussion of the theories of Darwin, Marx, Freud, *et al.*, he goes on to trace the effects of those theories on modern Man, particularly as the theories have been expounded by the more passionate and less cautious disciples of those prophets. Documenting his case heavily, Mr. Krutch shows what is now becoming generally recognized: that these "scientific" conclusions are based on evidence that is fragmentary and that a true scientist—a chemist or a physician, for instance—would regard as far from conclusive or even demonstrable. Since most of the "methods" were devised for measuring those qualities which machines, rats, and humans have in common, perhaps their usefulness is limited to just those qualities. Mr. Krutch's quarrel is with the unwarranted assumption (which solified into myth and then hardened into dogma) that Man is "nothing but" what these "methods" can demonstrate about him. We must find the "road back"—must re-establish the humanity of Man and persuade him to believe in it.

This is one way. Granted this restoration of human beings to their humanity were possible, we might look for the creation of authentic tragedy as soon as man had learned again to respect himself. But it would be idle merely to wait for this millenium. I wish to suggest attitudes a little less static. I want hopefully to assert that Man has been just a little bit human all the time, even though he may have thought of himself as merely a rat or a machine or the sum of his conditioning.

If this small area of humanity has endured, as I think it has, then we may go on to suggest the other two methods of achieving a modern tragedy. The first method mentioned above requires a waiting for Man to "come up to" an appreciation of tragedy. The second method involves attempting to arouse the tragic response within Man as he now is, as does the third. Again and again we are forced back to the social aspect of the tragic requirement. The spectacle must arouse pity and terror in the beholder. If no modern individual is acceptable as a protagonist, capable of those actions in which strength, pride, and arrogance hurtle him onward to death and destruction, actions the beholder can believe in, then we must look elsewhere.

The tragic response is essential, and it might be possible to create a tragic protagonist who lives in an age more remote, more heroic, more mythical, with which the spectator feels a more emotional, deeper identification. Ultimately, it is in the deepest recesses of the psyche that the tragic emotion, which is a response to myth, takes place. One point this study seeks to make is that the American Civil War, at least for Americans, is such a period; is most deeply charged with myth; is indeed the only truly "tragic" war we have ever been involved in. I assume it is axiomatic that this is true as far as general public interest goes; this at least requires little documentation. One might cite merely the disproportionately large number of novels (both "literary" and "popular"), of movies, of television dramas, that use this conflict as foreground or background. Perhaps only in this remote and mythical age does it seem possible that men could will by deliberate choice to undertake heroic actions. Yet, and this may be a most significant point, that age is not really remote in either time or place. In the South and East, at least, we still reside near some of the historic places, and, until a generation ago, many families could speak of grandparents who had actually lived in the middle of it all. Somehow Scarlett O'Hara and Jeb Stuart and a bitter, fratricidal war that matched brother against brother and expended greatness far out of proportion to the reasons the war was fought have all got mixed up in the public's head. And it makes no difference at all if it never happened quite the way the myth has it; myth is all the better if it is not true. The Civil War has captured the public mind as no other war has. I suppose we need not remind ourselves that the "events" used by Sophocles and Shakespeare were for the most part far more remote from the writer's own time.

Yet, is this enough? To depend, however legitimately, on the glamour that time throws on a departed age? The third method involves one of the real cruxes of this study. We must delay listing all the requirements the tragic hero must meet until a later chapter, but we may now ask: is there no way in which the artist can take a human being of our time and endow him with tragic status, to show his nobility, his humanity, his dignity, his willingness to "press back against the pressure of reality," his drive toward self-definition and self-revelation, his tragic reconciliation with a death brought on by his choosing to persist in a line of conduct that is right but that must inevitably bring him to destruction? Is there no way the writer can make us feel the terrifying pull of those elements of blood-guilt, irrationality, violence, and death not because we have a willing suspension of disbelief or an intellectual, "literary" appreciation but because we feel it almost against our will deep in the place where irrationality and violence lurk in all of us? Can the writer not create for us that tragic lift that comes when the human spirit triumphs over irrationality and death and it is almost as if we too had been purged of such madness and excess? I think he can. I think William Faulkner has done so, with at least one completely modern tragic protagonist.

iii.

To what extent have the critics been aware of the tragic element in the writings of Faulkner? The "melancholy and incredible" history of Faulkner criticism has been mentioned in the

Introduction to the present book. There the point was made that from Faulkner's first publication in 1924 until George Marion O'Donnell's essay, "Faulkner's Mythology," in 1939, it was all but impossible to find any competent or even responsible criticism at all. After 1939, the tide began to run the other way, and once the solid interpretative work of O'Donnell, Warren Beck, Delmore Schwartz, Robert Penn Warren, and Malcolm Cowley had been done, the literary value and philosophical content of the Faulkner canon could be assessed.

As early as 1933, Andre Malraux had, perhaps from the vantage of a more distant and sophisticated point of view, observed in *Sanctuary* "the intrusion of Greek Tragedy into the detective novel." O'Donnell spoke of the Sartoris world as tragic and found in the rise and fall of Sutpen "an action of heroic proportions." ". . . the ritualistic purgation of the doomed house by fire . . . is as nearly a genuine tragic scene as anything in modern fiction." Warren Beck referred to the South's "tragic history" and concluded that "a reader whose sensitivity and courage approach Faulkner's own can scarcely find anything melodramatic or titillating in such books as *Light in August* or *Absalom, Absalom!* but will rather experience that catharsis of pity and terror which comes only of great literature, and which can be conveyed only by a temperament of genius, proceeding from a humane point of view. . . ."[2]

Vincent Hopper spoke of Sutpen's tragic flaws. W. M. Frohock said flatly: "Faulkner's vision is essentially tragic. . . . As with the Greeks, the sign of evil is the violence it brings forth." To those who objected to the violence, he replied: "Not all tragedy is luminous like the *Oedipus*. Some is dark with irrational fear, like the *Bacchae* of Euripides, in which a mother in religious frenzy helps tear apart the body of her own son, thinking him to be an animal, and appears before the spectators bearing what she still thinks is an animal's head. The quality of Faulkner's vision . . . seems to me to approach the Euripidean. . . . If we read him as though he were a tragic poet, many difficulties disappear."[3]

Cleanth Brooks in *"Absalom, Absalom!*: The Definition of Innocence" called Sutpen a heroic and tragic figure and related his "innocence" to that of Oedipus and Macbeth. Speaking finally of Faulkner's achievement, he said: "*In Absalom, Absalom!*, it is tragedy that he has given us."

This new estimate would seem to be in direct opposition to the earlier critical reception of Faulkner's work, which accused him of deliberately choosing cruelty, lust, crime, horror, violence, and so on, for their own sake. I suppose it need not be said that in the opinion of the present writer the later attitude is the more correct one.

We might, of course, simply let the case rest there. But the purpose of this study is to establish the matter and manner of Faulkner's tragic accomplishment. I do not for a moment wish to suggest that Faulkner is primarily interested in writing tragedy to prescription. There has probably been no modern writer who cared less what the professors said of his work. And, as we know, literature ground out in conformity to a set prescription for writing tragedy has almost without exception failed to become tragic. Tragedy is autochthonous and mantic, and set prescriptions for these conditions cannot be made; they must be achieved in another way. One is reminded of Jane Harrison's admission: "Great things in literature, Greek plays for example, I most enjoy when behind their bright splendors I see moving darker and older shapes." It is this kind of infinitely extended suggestiveness, the waking of universal echoes, that the better work of Faulkner so conspicuously has and that the work of so many modern writers —for instance Arthur Miller—so conspicuously lacks.

It is not the purpose of this study to draw the heroes of Faulkner on the rack of one or another Procrustean theory of tragedy and demand that they fit it. It will, rather, use the much lazier method of hindsight: begin with the *fait accompli* of the response and the emotion which the better work of Faulkner arouses in the reader and attempt to account for it.

Commentary on the tragedy of the Greeks and Elizabethans has been brilliant, none of it more so than that written in the present century. We all know by now the criteria the classic tragic hero must meet in order to qualify. He must be a human being like ourselves but exceptionally fortunate and reasonably good and humane, who through an error of judgment or flaw of character plunges to catastrophe. Aristotle was only the first of many to realize that the fall is more meaningful when it is brought about at least partly by the actions of the hero himself and is an outgrowth of his own misguided efforts toward virtue. He must above all be free; free to will his own actions. But beyond all these aspects of character or plot and the convincing creation of them, the critics still return reiteratively to the same point: *katharsis* is the ultimate criterion for measuring tragedy, but it is a condition of the beholder, not the writer. The question for the modern artist again becomes, "How?"

The answer is simple to state, at least in theory. The modern tragic hero must be one whom all modern readers, each locked in the subjective prison of the individual self, can not merely see as believable but with whom they can identify and whom they can accept as typical of both the age and themselves. Only in this way can the beholder achieve the belief that is necessary to any response at all, much more those responses of pity and terror in an age which has long ago grown too calloused for pity and to which terror, the real terror of momentary atomic vaporization, is a commonplace. How then can the modern hero be made both typical and heroic? How can the writer compel belief?

It is safe to say that both writer and reader believe in nothing, at least at first. This condition is the final triumph of nineteenth-century scientific skepticism. The lives of all of us, from intellectual to illiterate, may be defined as a constant process of testing, of searching for values, since we accept nothing at face value. In short, the overwhelming, shattering problem is not Hamlet's whether to be, but *how* to be, the discovery of a way to be, on any basis at all. The problem of the individual is one of definition—an all-embracing one—because literally everything must be defined from scratch, and to do this one must begin at the beginning: the definition of self. The modern hero will find his failure a failure to achieve self-definition, and his *hamartia* will be the persistence in a gravely mistaken estimate of his personal relationship to the cosmos. Conrad's Stein has stated it very well:

"That is the question. . . . How to be! How to be. . . . We want in so many different ways to be. . . . This magnificent butterfly finds a little heap of dirt and sits still on it; but man he will never on his heap of mud keep still. . . .

And because you not always can keep your eyes shut there comes the real trouble—the heart pain—the world pain. . . . I tell you, my friend, it is not good for you to find you cannot make your dream come true, for the reason that you not strong enough are, or not clever enough. Ja! . . . Very funny this terrible thing is. A man that is born falls into a dream like a man who falls into the sea. If he tries to climb out into the air as inexperienced people endeavor to do, he drowns. . . . I tell you . . . the way is to the destructive element submit yourself, and with the exertions of your hands and feet in the water make the deep, deep sea keep you up. . . ."[4]

This is one reason why much of the shrill dissatisfaction with modern literature is so pointless. Literature has changed because the world has changed. When the writer attempts to rely on responses based on historical literary content and emotion, he is almost certainly doomed to failure. When the great myths of mankind, certainly among our most inalienable possessions, are presented, they must be presented in their historical form, as history. The artist attempting to employ the legitimate, perpetual human constants they contain must restate them in completely modern terms, as Joyce has done. He must find what T. S. Eliot in another connection has called the objective correlative, and never more so than when attempting to arouse the emotions of pity and terror. Mr. Eliot has spoken rather plaintively on this subject in describing the difficulties of staging his play *The Family Reunion,* a modern retelling of the *Oresteia.* The problem was the elementary one of presenting the Furies on stage.

Reducing the fact to its bluntest form, modern man does not believe in the Furies. But within an entirely different system of folklore, he does believe quite strongly in guilt, obsession, sudden violence, retribution, and death, or so we are told. The aspiring tragic artist must find ways to embody these beliefs.

In the Introduction, there is a discussion of form in modern literature and of the "difficulty" of modern literature in general. But form and its attendant difficulty and the concern of the artist with it aside, we come to the question of achievement, which we must remember is the final test: response in the reader. Is great modern literature a failure? Dissatisfaction with it is chronic, but the fact remains that almost anyone who in maturity reads through the tragic unwinding of the history of a Karamazov, a Raskolnikov, a Bazarov, a Jim, a Kurtz, a Joseph K., or a Willie Stark will confess to a sense of overwhelming compassion and an almost inconsolable feeling of loss. The heroes of Faulkner are of that company, and I think it is only the combination of subjectivity and bad criticism that causes us to fail to know the feeling for what it is: pity and terror, the twin poles of tragic *katharsis*.

In a world as fragmented as our own, it is not surprising that a major artist should have to wait decades for recognition. In such a fragmented society, in which the artist must face the problem of form as well as the problem of an audience that does not understand him, the job of the critic is very simple: he must do everything he can to bridge the gap. He must strike through the mask in order to make clearer to the reader what he hopes and believes the author meant to say. In the present case, this critic hopes to tear aside the mask to reveal the living face of the tragedy that is there.

1. Aristotle, *Poetics,* VI, 2 (trans. S. H. Butcher).
2. Warren Beck, "Faulkner and the South," *Antioch Review,* I (Spring, 1941), 94.
3. W. M. Frohock, "William Faulkner: The Private versus the Public Vision," in *The Novel of Violence in America* (Dallas: Southern Methodist University Press, 1950), p. 123.
4. Joseph Conrad, *Lord Jim* (New York: Modern Library, 1931), pp. 213-14.

12.

COLONEL JOHN SARTORIS:
THE CLASSIC TRAGIC HERO

In no other case, perhaps, is it more necessary for the critic to strike through the mask than in the case of Colonel John Sartoris. His statue is prominent on Faulkner's map of Yoknapatawpha County, and his presence is in the background of many of the novels and stories. Evidently he is a creation of some importance in Faulkner's consciousness. But the only work, so far, in which he appears in anything approaching a full-scale presentation is *The Unvanquished,* admittedly not one of Faulkner's best novels. And *The Unvanquished* is an *Oresteia,* not an *Agamemnon;* the protagonist is Bayard, not his father.

The critics, by and large, have tended to dismiss the novel as trivial (with the exception of those defenders of the Left who shouted with alarm at the dangers inherent in moonshine-and-magnolia fiction). But the epithet "trivial" was in some respects quite fair.

Perhaps it helps place what is bad in the novel to recall that all of it, with the very significant exception of "An Odor of Verbena," first appeared in *The Saturday Evening Post* or the old *Scribner's.* Faulkner was to tell almost the same story of two boys and an old lady again, and much more badly, in *Intruder in the Dust,* and the objections which have been validly taken to that novel will apply, though much less strongly, to *The Unvanquished.* In the early sections of the older novel there are the encounters of Bayard and Ringo with the Yankee invaders, which are the purest Thomas Nelson Page with overtones of Mark Twain and Sut

Lovingood's tales. The sections in which Granny and Ringo, armed only with a parasol and some forged orders, succeed in stealing countless thousands of mules from the Federal army often threaten, and more than threaten, to fall into the purest farce. They also happen to be about as funny as anything written in our time.

It is unfair, certainly, to dismiss an entire critical generation on the basis of one novel or even one novelist. Yet most of the critics refused to see that behind the fooling, admittedly concealed and implicational but stubbornly obtruding in every scene, was, in capsule, an epic fable of the most moral and tragic proportion. Granny's story, which ends with her death, is the working-out of crimes she committed for the best of reasons. Her story foreshadows the career of Colonel Sartoris, who, of all Faulkner's creations, most clearly fulfills all the criteria of the traditional classic hero, doomed to persist in his own virtues until they become monstrous vices. Only in Bayard do we have the hope of a solution of the tragic dilemma.

But, to repeat, perhaps part of the failure to see Sartoris in the round does grow out of the indirectness of the presentation. Like Sutpen's ghost, who had only Miss Rosa Coldfield's voice to haunt where a more fortunate ghost would have had a house, John Sartoris, properly speaking, does not even have a novel of his own to haunt. In some ways he is already like his own statue in Jefferson, remote and inscrutable. We must reconstruct him, as we do Sutpen, from the profound effect he has on other people, who have never been able to forget him, and from the legacy of his influence, which, like John Brown's body, goes marching on. The job of the critic is to clear away a few trees; then we may be able to see the forest.

In a primary sense, *The Unvanquished* is another version of one central Faulkner myth: the corruption of innocence. This theme is evident in every section of the story; under the pressures of the times, each character commits actions he or she knows are wrong, and the wrong never goes unpunished. Granny begins by lying, proceeds to forgery and stealing, is swept into the current of criminal violence, and is killed. Colonel Sartoris and Drusilla begin in defense of hearth and homeland against the invader.

Sartoris employs all his resourcefulness, intelligence, and daring in the command of his regiment but in the end becomes too accustomed to the atmosphere of violence and is reduced to the killing of carpetbaggers and former friends. Ultimately, the love of violence destroys him as it does Drusilla. Bayard and Ringo begin by shooting at Yankees (and kill only a horse), but they end by pursuing Grumby until they are able to kill him, nail his body to the compress wall, and cut off his right hand to bury on top of Granny's grave.

But the significant fact which must be hammered home about all these actions is that they begin in the noblest kind of human love and human loyalty. I strongly suspect that Faulkner deliberately depicts these actions at first as completely untainted by any notion of self-profit or self-aggrandizement. Granny, Bayard, and Ringo defraud the Federal government not for themselves but for the starving widows and children of the countryside, in direct contrast with Ab Snopes, who steals only for himself. When Bayard and Ringo commit their barbaric mutilation of Grumby, it is a drastic but deserved execution for the needless shooting, in cold blood, of a helpless, elderly woman who was loved and respected by the entire countryside.

But all these actions are, nevertheless, violent. They are extra-legal and have implicit in them a defiance of order and due process. They are what is known in Spanish America as *personalismo*. In keeping with the central Faulkner myth, the character whose innocence has been destroyed must do one of two things: repair his loss of innocence or himself be destroyed. In all the novel only Bayard, aided by his legal training and the moral support of Aunt Jenny, is able to lift himself outside the stream of violence. As noted before, Bayard's basic problem is that of Orestes: in spite of the pressures of tradition, community, relatives, and friends, he must find a way to bring the chain of bloodshed to an end. Edith Hamilton has suggested that the Greek myths dealing with heroes who destroy monsters (Perseus and the Gorgon, Theseus and the Minotaur, Oedipus and the Sphinx) are allegories of the advance of civilization and justice, the substitution of law and order for the violence and *personalismo* of the semibarbaric chieftains of Homeric and pre-Homeric times.

This is what Bayard succeeds in doing, if only partly. He brings to a stop the violence that is his family's curse, even if the violence does break out again eventually in his twin grandsons.

All this seems clear enough, at least in the last chapter of the book. Perhaps the humor itself, the very excellence of the fooling, is what put the critics off in the earlier parts. Almost any humorous scene will serve to illustrate the moral content, but perhaps one of the early chapters, where the ratio of the farcical is highest, should be used as a demonstration. For example, we might look at the episode in which Bayard and Ringo attempt to ambush the Yankee soldier but succeed only in killing a horse.

Bayard and Ringo, both aged twelve, have just seen for the first time in their lives a Yankee soldier. They run frantically back to the house and lift the heavy, archaic musket from over the fireplace. Holding it between them like a log, they run back in time to fire at the cavalryman from ambush. Too late, they discover they have taken on a whole regiment of cavalry. They fling down the gun, and in the familiar Faulkner technique of depicting violent action in terms of distorted perception, they run desperately toward the house that seems to drift ever farther and farther away. They run into the house screaming, "We shot him, Granny! We shot the bastud!"[1] They hide, literally, under Granny's hoop skirts while the enraged troopers search the house, and Granny protects them in the only way she can: by denying she has ever seen any children at all. Even in their terror Bayard and Ringo are remembering that Granny has never whipped them for anything except lying.

As the colonel comes in, the sergeant and the men are busily combing the house; the colonel asks by whose authority and why. The sergeant says because United States troops were fired on. The colonel remarks that the assassination of one horse is hardly sufficient reason.

Like something behind a screen in a Restoration comedy, the action is taking place on several levels at once. There are Bayard and Ringo, aged twelve, glaring at each other under Granny's skirt, who cannot see Granny or the sergeant or the colonel; the sergeant, who does not suspect the boys are in the same room with him, but is violently certain they are somewhere about; Granny, who knows very well where the boys are but wishes she didn't; and the colonel, who guesses at once where the boys are but is too much the gentleman to say so.

Over the aggrieved protests of the sergeant, the colonel sends the troops away, and, after making it quite clear he knows where the children are, begs Granny's pardon for disturbing her. After Granny has fainted and been revived, her first words are:

"Bayard," she said, "what was that word you used?" Then, after she has prayed for forgiveness for telling the lie and supporting the two boys in their lie, she washes out their mouths with soap for using the dirty word. (Later on, when other Yankees come and burn the house, she uses the word herself.)

I trust the implication is sufficiently clear. Within the high burlesque of the two boys hiding under the hoop skirts of an old lady, the pattern is established. Granny, for the first time in her life, has told a direct lie. She has done the bad thing for the good reason, and the process of corruption has begun. In other hilarious scenes to follow, she will discover that in collaboration with Ab Snopes she can defraud the Federal army of several hundred mules and large amounts of food and clothing. It works well for a while, but in the end Ab Snopes persuades her to try once more; this time they must work with a notorious horse thief named Grumby. Bayard and Ringo are against it but are overruled. Granny goes to keep the rendezvous in the abandoned cotton compress, ordering the boys to wait outside. When they break in at last, she has been shot and killed.

After the murderer has been pursued by the two boys and an old man, caught, and himself killed, it is Ringo, who throughout the novel is Greek chorus to the action, who makes the fitting comment on Granny's life and death.

"Yes," I said. And then we both began to cry. We stood there in the slow rain, crying. We had ridden a lot, and during the last week we hadn't slept much and we hadn't always had anything to eat.

"It wasn't him or Ab Snopes either that kilt her," Ringo said. "It was them mules. That first batch of mules we got for nothing."[2]

The inclusion of such a long digression in a study which pretends to be concerned not with the novel but with John Sartoris can be justified only on the plea that it demonstrates something worth showing. It is my hope that the digression demonstrates the technique and intent of the author.

As stated earlier, we have in the small-scale example of Granny a precise paradigm for the tragic development of John Sartoris, and by extension, a pattern for the Faulknerian tragic hero in general. Granny's death is the direct result of wrong actions taken for the best of reasons. To protect children, to save her home, and to succor widows and orphans, Granny begins by lying, then proceeds to misappropriation, forgery, and fraud. Her death comes when she is unable to break off the pattern of her new habits.

ii.

Sartoris is a hero who is distinctly un-modern. That is to say that the crises and involvements which confront him are seldom those which imperil a present-day protagonist. Perhaps those semifeudal qualities inherent in the Old South have something to do with it, but at any rate, it seems to me that he fulfills every requirement the classic tragic hero must meet. To a marked degree, he has the quality of self-knowledge, so conspicuously absent in Sutpen. Virtue, nobility, valor, he has in abundance. His tragic pattern is much like that of Creon, Lear, Macbeth, or Coriolanus. Convinced of the unshakable rightness of what he does, he persists, in pride and arrogance, in his objectives. Too late, he sees the inevitable outcome of his actions but in seeing them accepts fully the consequences of those actions.

Placed as he is in his social pattern, his fortune and "nobility" are assured, in the formal sense; but far more impressive is his literal and actual ability to lead, command, and bend men to his will, best demonstrated perhaps by the fantastic loyalty he commands not only from children and slaves but from substantial men of affairs and even, when building his railroad, from financiers. We see his "heroic" qualities through the eyes of Bayard, who is twelve years old at the time.

Then we could see him good. I mean, Father. He was not big; it was just the things he did, that we knew he was doing . . . in Virginia and Tennessee. . . . He was not big, yet somehow he looked even smaller on the horse than off of him, because Jupiter was big and when you thought of Father you thought of him as being big too.

. . . you said, 'Together they will be too big; you won't believe it.'
So you didn't believe it and so it wasn't. . . . Then I began to smell
it again . . . that odor in his clothes and beard and flesh too which I
believed was the smell of powder and glory, the elected victorious
but know better now: know now to have been only the will to endure,
a sardonic and even humorous declining of self-delusion which is not
even kin to that optimism which believes that that which is about to
happen to us can possibly be the worst which we can suffer.[3]

Fortunate as his position in life is, he is fully capable of the
aristocrat's frugality and parsimony in the protection of his own.
He endures the Spartan life of war and is not afraid to sweat and
strain alongside Bayard, Ringo, Loosh, and Joby to build the
stockpens and hide the cattle. But he has more than this: he has
grace, wit, intelligence, and some learning, in the formal sense.
Above all this, he has an ironic self-detachment so conspicuously
lacking in his contemporaries. But at the heart of it is the beginning of corruption. Power is always corrupting, and only
the very, very strong can resist that kind of corruption. This
corruption is hinted at as early as the formation of his first cavalry
troop, at the beginning of the war. Sartoris is recruiting, and
those incredible McCaslin twins, Uncle Buck and Uncle Buddy,
now past seventy years old, want to go too. Sartoris tries to
point out, not unreasonably, that they are a little old for this.
The twins then threaten to form a company of their own. When
this does not persuade Sartoris, they threaten to call an election
of company officers and demote him from the position of command.
Stung to the quick, Sartoris agrees to take one of them.

This is, of course, his fatal flaw: the classic sin of *hubris*.
Later on, in the war in Virginia, the habit of arrogance becomes
so strong that the regiment does vote him out of command, and
he returns to Mississippi to form his own force of irregulars to
harass the Yankees. This is not actually the equivalent of
Achilles sulking in his tent; his family and friends can even see
much to commend in his defending his own neighborhood rather
than fighting for Jeff Davis a thousand miles away. But the
pattern is already there; Sartoris must have his own way, he must
command and will not submit to anyone else.

Few, I say, can resist the corruption of power. The habit of
command is like drink or drugs. Dangerous as they are, their

sudden removal is even more dangerous. In the vacuum so created, anything may happen. Bayard is the narrator of the story, and between the Bayard of twelve who begins the book and the Bayard of twenty-four who closes it, there is an immeasurable difference. As a child of twelve he responds to the myth: the galloping, the dust, the yelling, and the glittering of brandished sabres. Now he knows better.

Because little by little John Sartoris has lost that "sardonic and even humorous declining of self-delusion" which he once had. The habit of command dies hard. With feverish haste, he throws himself into the rebuilding of his house, not a better house perhaps than the one the Yankees burned but certainly more grandiose. When Reconstruction begins, there are the night-riders to be organized. When the carpetbaggers prepare for the first election in which Negroes will vote, Sartoris warns them he will not allow it to take place. On election day, he and Drusilla delay their wedding long enough to kill two of the carpetbaggers—an old man and a boy—and with the aid of the troop hold an election of their own. Not quite the same as raiding Yankee armies, perhaps, but better than nothing.

In the Faulkner canon, one of the major symbols for the corruption of innocence is the onset of finance capitalism, which "denudes" the countryside, and involvement with the machine, the agent of dehumanization. The next step in the deterioration of John Sartoris is entirely predictable. He forms a partnership with a man named Redmond to build a railroad. They soon quarrel, and Sartoris is able to buy Redmond out for far less than Redmond put in. Redmond did not see combat during the war; he had some sort of appointment with the Confederate government dealing with cotton. He could have got rich on graft but took none. Sartoris knows Redmond is honest and decent, but even after the railroad is all his, he cannot seem to leave Redmond alone. When Redmond announces for the legislature, Sartoris runs against him, constantly and needlessly slurring Redmond's honesty and courage. Even George Wyatt, an intensely loyal member of the old troop, asks Bayard to talk to his father, but Bayard has no opportunity to do so. Sartoris wins in a landslide.

Apparently Sartoris has everything—economic power, political

power, a devoted family, the fanatic loyalty of most of the countryside.   But all this has failed to fill the vacuum, and the inward
corruption has its outward manifestations.   One example is when
Sartoris kills one of his own troopers, his fellow Confederate in
the war.   This is during the building of the railroad: perhaps the
man meant to rob him, perhaps not.   At any rate, Sartoris shoots
first and asks questions later.

iii.

Ideally, perhaps, the moment of reversal and recognition should
come all at once, as it does for Oedipus or Othello.   But with
Colonel Sartoris, the process is gradual.   Somewhere in that
process he has realized his own hollowness, his complete corruption.   Drusilla, his wife, is quick to detect it also.   She has,
Bayard thinks, an affinity for violence which enables her to sense
a commitment for it or against it in others.   She has shared the
violence and rebellion of war and Reconstruction, and being a
woman, now forbidden to participate, she lives vicariously upon
the violence she can engender in others.   Sensing that her husband
is finished, she offers without the slightest hesitation the ultimate
violence she can commit to her stepson, Bayard.

Then she spoke.   "Kiss me, Bayard."
"No.   You are Father's wife."
"And eight years older than you are.   And your fourth cousin
too.   And I have black hair.   Kiss me, Bayard."
"No."
"Kiss me, Bayard."   So I leaned my face down to her.   But she
didn't move, standing so, bent lightly back from me from the waist,
looking at me; now it was she who said "No."   So I put my arms
around her.   Then she came to me, melted as women will and can,
the arms with the wrist and elbow power to control horses about my
shoulders, using the wrists to hold my face to hers until there was no
longer need for the wrists; I thought then of the woman of thirty, the
symbol of the ancient and eternal Snake. . . .[4]

Bayard tries to tell his father.   But this is the day of John
Sartoris' triumphant landslide victory over Redmond.   At dinner,
he rouses a little:

. . . not to talk himself but rather to sit at the head of the table
and reply to Drusilla as she talked with a sort of feverish and glittering

volubility—to reply now and then to her with that courteous intolerant pride which had lately become a little forensic, as if merely being in a political contest filled with fierce and empty oratory had retro-actively made a lawyer of him who was anything and everything except a lawyer. Then Aunt Jenny and Drusilla rose and left us and he said "Wait" to me who had made no move to follow. . . . Then I stood again like soldiers stand, gazing at eye level above his head while he sat half-turned from the table, a little paunchy now though not much, a little grizzled too in the hair though his beard was as strong as ever, with that spurious forensic air of lawyers and the intolerant eyes which in the last two years had acquired that trans-parent film which the eyes of carnivorous animals have and from behind which they look at a world which no ruminant ever sees, perhaps dares to see, which I have seen before on the eyes of men who have killed too much, who have killed so much that never again so long as they live will they ever be alone. I said again, "Father," then I told him.[5]

But the expected explosion does not come off. With the politi-cal victory, the process of corruption has run its course. The John Sartoris who might have killed for a word or a glance says merely:

"You are doing well in the law, Judge Wilkins tells me. I am pleased to hear that. I have not needed you in my affairs so far, but from now on I shall. I have now accomplished the active portion of my aims in which you could not have helped me; I acted as the land and the time demanded and you were too young for that. I wished to shield you. But now the land and the time too are changing; what will follow will be a matter of consolidation, of pettifogging and doubtless chicanery in which I would be a babe in arms but in which you, trained in the law, can hold your own—our own."[6]

But the corruption is not quite complete. There remains the one quality which gives Sartoris his tragic status: his own quietly ironic awareness of his corruption—the realization that his acts of audacity, daring, and violence have, in the lack of any legitimate direction or objective, turned inward and have devoured not only himself but his Mississippi House of Atreus as well. Apparently the realization is complete, because he accepts the consequences of his actions and, like Oedipus or Othello, imposes his own punishment. ". . . and now I shall do a little moral housecleaning. I am tired of killing men, no matter what the necessity nor the end. Tomorrow, when I go to town and meet Ben Redmond, I shall be unarmed."[7]

If the symbol of corruption is the violence it brings forth, then the character of each of the actors in the tragedy is established by his individual response to that violence. With remarkable compression, Faulkner sets up the responses in a series of brief tableaux: George Wyatt and the old troop drawn up and waiting as Bayard comes home; Sartoris in his coffin with sabre and plumes; Drusilla in her yellow ball gown under the bright candles, trembling with ecstasy as she holds out to Bayard the pistols, the formal weapon of ritual murder; the troop again drawn up in the square as Bayard goes to face Redmond in the law office. Drusilla, Ringo, George Wyatt, and all the old troop are eager to kill Redmond, in sharp contrast to Bayard, who, like Orestes, knows that he must find some way to stop the chain of killing. Bayard recalls that Drusilla and Aunt Jenny are identical in being Confederate bride-widows of the same age, yet it is Drusilla who demands violence from Bayard and Aunt Jenny who is his sole support in his repudiation of it.

It well may be that morals are only mores. No one would suggest that, either in grandeur of conception or excellence of presentation, Faulkner's Agamemnon tragedy is the equal of the version by Aeschylus. But, in all humility, I think it can be pointed out that Faulkner's is the morally superior. Consider, for example, the heroes of the action. Both are arrogant, overbearing egotists, but where Sartoris fights and kills, at least it is for his own house and people. Whatever his faults, he is gentle and kind to those who love him. If Homer is to be trusted, it seems doubtful that anyone ever loves Agamemnon or, indeed, if anyone can— a loud-mouthed braggart who sacrifices his own child to insure the success of his freebooting expedition to Troy, who seldom fights, and who returns home with his spoils and his concubine only to be trussed up and stuck like a pig in his bathtub by his outraged wife. Or, contrast Orestes with Bayard, the Orestes of Faulkner. Aeschylus' Orestes seems more interested in his father's throne than anything else and quickly succumbs to the pressures that cause him to kill his mother in revenge of his father's murder. He relies on Apollo to get him off the hook of retribution. Bayard, pressured by the expectation of the community, Drusilla's promise of her body, and the crushing, accumulated weight of his tradition, defies them all and walks unarmed into the office of Redmond to be shot at twice, in order that the chain of violence and bloodshed can be broken.

iv.

Like Cawdor, nothing in the life of John Sartoris so commends him as the leaving of it. Each in his own way, the actors in the drama speak their farewells. In an almost formal parabasis, they one by one attest their grief. Ringo throughout has functioned as Greek chorus to the action, but now he too has been ruined by the violence and has turned sullen and almost vicious.

Ringo was waiting; I remember how I thought then that no matter what might happen to either of us, I would never be The Sartoris to him. He was twenty-four too, but in a way he had changed even less than I had since that day when we had nailed Grumby's body to the door of the old compress. . . . He was sitting quietly in a chair beside the cold stove, spent-looking too who had ridden forty miles (at one time, either in Jefferson or when he was alone at last on the road somewhere, he had cried; dust was now caked and dried in the tear channels on his face) . . . looking up at me a little red-eyed with weariness. . . . We spoke one time, then no more:
"We could bushwhack him," he said. "Like we done Grumby that day. But I reckon that wouldn't suit that white skin you walks around in."
"No," I said.[8]

George Wyatt and the other members of the old troop are waiting as Bayard and Ringo arrive in the middle of the night.

Wyatt met me, I halted the mare, I could look down at him and at the others gathered a few yards behind him with that curious vulture-like formality which Southern men assume in such situations.
"Well, boy," George said.
"Was it—" I said. "Was he—"
"It was all right. It was in front." . . . then he spoke again:
"We'll take this off your hands, any of us. Me."
". . . You're young, just a boy, and you ain't had any experience in this kind of thing. Besides, you got them two ladies in the house to think about. He would understand, all right."
"I reckon I can attend to it," I said.
"Sure," he said. . . . "I reckon we all knew that's what you would say."[9]

But Bayard knows that he has to do it in his own way. No matter what the others may think, Bayard is not going to kill Redmond. No one understands his motives except Aunt Jenny.

"You are not going to try to kill him. All right."
"All right?" I said.
"Yes. All right. Don't let it be Drusilla, a poor hysterical young woman. And don't let it be him, Bayard, because he's dead now. And don't let it be George Wyatt and those others who will be waiting for you tomorrow morning. I know you are not afraid."[10]

Caught as he is under the pressure to take revenge, Bayard hardly trusts himself to give way to the grief he feels:

. . . now I looked at him. It was just as I had imagined it—sabre, plumes, and all—but with that alteration, that irrevocable difference which I had known to expect but had not realized—the nose, the hair, the eyelids closed over the intolerance—the face which I realized I now saw in repose for the first time in my life; the empty hands still now beneath the invisible stain of what had been (once, surely) needless blood, the hands now appearing clumsy in their very inertness, too clumsy to have performed the fatal actions which forever afterward he must have waked and slept with and maybe was glad to lay down at last . . . which had now surrendered that life to which his intolerant heart had fiercely held. . . . maybe I should have said "Goodbye, Father," but did not. Instead I crossed to the piano and laid the pistols carefully on it.[11]

After he has faced Redmond, he returns to the old pasture where years ago he and Ringo shot at the Yankee. He does not attend the funeral, and after it is all over he can go back to the house again.

There was just one light in the hall now and so it was all over though I could still smell the flowers even above the verbena in my coat. I had not looked at him again. . . . I did not see him again and all the pictures we had of him were bad ones because a picture could no more have held him dead than the house could have kept his body. But I didn't need to see him again because he was there, he would always be there. . . .[12]

The most intense response comes from Drusilla. Once before, she had said:

"There are worse things than killing men, Bayard. There are worse things than being killed. Sometimes I think the finest thing that can happen to a man is to love something, a woman preferably, well, hard, hard, hard, then to die young because he believed what he could not help but believe and was what he could not (could not? would not) help but be."[13]

But when Sartoris is dead, Drusilla cannot imagine any possibility other than Bayard's going at once to kill Redmond.

Drusilla now . . . her voice whispering into that quiet death-filled room with a passionate and dying fall: "Bayard." She faced me. . . . again the scent of the verbena in her hair seemed to have increased a hundred times as she stood holding out to me, one in either hand, the two duelling pistols. "Take them, Bayard," she said, in the same tone in which she had said "Kiss me," last summer, already pressing them into my hands. . . . "Oh you will thank me, you will remember me who put into your hands what they say is an attribute only of God's, who took what belongs to heaven and gave it to you. Do you feel them: the long true barrels true as justice, the triggers (you have fired them) quick as retribution, the two of them slender and invincible and fatal as the physical shape of love?" . . . she removed the two verbena sprigs from her hair in two motions faster than the eye could follow, already putting one of them into my lapel and crushing the other in her other hand while she still spoke in that rapid passionate voice not much louder than a whisper: "There. One I give to you to wear tomorrow. . . . the other I cast away like this. . . . I abjure it. I abjure verbena forever more; I have smelled it above the odor of courage. . . . How beautiful you are: do you know it? How beautiful: young to be permitted to kill, to be permitted vengeance, to take into your bare hands the fire that cast down Lucifer. No; I. I gave it to you; I put it into your hands; Oh you will thank me, you will remember me when I am dead and you are an old man saying to himself, 'I have tasted all things.' "[14]

Verbena is Drusilla's symbol for courage. She always has a sprig of it about her; she wore it when she rode as a trooper with Sartoris, because, as she always said, it is the only scent you can smell above the odor of the dust and the horses and the courage. When she realizes Bayard is not going to kill Redmond she becomes hysterical, because to her this can only mean a lack of courage. After Bayard has faced Redmond down, forced him to run away by the sheer force of his unarmed courage, he returns, only to find that she has gone away forever. But not without recognizing that Bayard had deserved the symbol of courage after all.

So the stairs were lighted quite well. . . . I saw her open door (that immistakable way in which an open door stands open when nobody lives in the room any more). . . . So I didn't look into the room. I went on to mine and entered. And then for a long moment I thought it was the verbena in my lapel which I still smelled. I thought that until I had crossed the room and looked down at the pillow on which it lay—the single sprig of it . . . filling the room, the dusk, the evening with that odor which she said you could smell alone above the smell of horses.[15]

Like Orestes and Hamlet, Bayard has the duty of revenging a beloved and heroic father. In each of the three cases there is strong pull of conflicting human impulse: the grief engendered by the assassination of a beloved father and the wish that the crushing weight of carrying out another murder in turn can be avoided, even though community and code demand it. Each will resolve the conflict in the way he must, and each, significantly enough, makes the ultimate decision himself. It is John Sartoris, Bayard's father, who leaves the clearest indication of what must be done. Agamemnon's case calls for matricide on Orestes' part, and the ghost of Hamlet's father clamors again and again for revenge. Only Sartoris is able to say to his son: "I am tired of killing men, no matter what the necessity nor the end."[16]

1. William Faulkner, *The Unvanquished* (New York: Random House, 1938), p. 30.
2. *Ibid.*, p. 211.
3. *Ibid.*, pp. 10-11.
4. *Ibid.*, p. 262.
5. *Ibid.*, pp. 265-66.
6. *Ibid.*, p. 266.
7. *Ibid.*, p. 266.
8. *Ibid.*, pp. 248, 251.
9. *Ibid.*, pp. 267-69.
10. *Ibid.*, p. 276.
11. *Ibid.*, pp. 272, 277.
12. *Ibid.*, p. 291.
13. *Ibid.*, p. 261.
14. *Ibid.*, pp. 273-74.
15. *Ibid.*, p. 293.
16. *Ibid.*, p. 266.

13.

JOE CHRISTMAS: THE HERO IN THE MODERN WORLD

—Aristotle has not defined pity and terror.—said Stephen
Dedalus—I have. Pity is the feeling which arrests the mind
in the presence of whatsoever is grave and constant in human
sufferings and unites it with the human sufferer. Terror is
the feeling which arrests the mind in the presence of whatsoever is grave and constant in human sufferings and unites it
with the secret cause.—

IT IS APPROPRIATE THAT Joyce's Stephen Dedalus should formu-
late this definition, for, different as he is from Joe Christmas, they
are alike in being heroes who are distinctly modern and who must
make their way in a cosmos that is violent, chaotic, and absurd.
Stephen's plight is only slightly less desperate than Christmas',
and Stephen's motto *non serviam* is very close to Christmas' rigid
determination not to submit to those forces that compulsively
attempt to shape him to their will.

Sutpen and John Sartoris, especially when viewed in their
dynastic patterns, are tragic heroes in the grand and completely
tragic mold, partly because, of course, they are located in a remote
and more "heroic" time, when presumably there existed that scope
of action and choice large enough for heroic gestures.

But even assuming Faulkner's possession of a tragic sensibility and granting him the ability to shape it into art, how can the
very long jump to Joe Christmas as tragic hero be made? There
are perhaps two possible approaches to this question, and perhaps
both of them should be used: to what extent is Christmas authen-

tically tragic by traditional criteria, and to what extent can it be shown that he is tragic by some entirely modern, different set of criteria? To oversimplify vastly, the modern protagonist should be one who is typical of the age and not so remote from typical human beings as to make emotional identification difficult for the spectator. In some highly symbolic fashion, the modern hero must typify the major myths and major problems of our century. In a cosmos where all is chaos and all standards have disappeared, he will very likely be destroyed as a result of his failure to define himself correctly in relation to that cosmos. Lastly, he must somehow embody the perpetual human constants which are the property of any age. Bypassing for a moment this very interesting second possibility, let us examine Christmas in the light of traditional, classic tragic criteria. At first glance, this procedure appears unpromising.

Granting his acts of persistence, his arrogance and pride, how can Christmas be called noble? How can he be said to be illustrious in rank and fortune? Above all, how can a human being so conditioned, so utterly predestined to violence and death, ever be called free: free to choose and free to act or not act? It is my belief that this reservation is precisely the point.

ii.

Aristotle awarded the palm for classic tragedy to the *Oedipus Tyrannus* of Sophocles. If this is not quite the same thing as saying Oedipus is the most perfect example of the tragic protagonist, perhaps he will do for comparison. Everyone knows his tragic story, at least in outline, for it is one of the ironies of history that he has given his name to the folklore of psychology. In that same folklore, we in the modern world give tacit agreement to the belief that human free will is all but impossible. In the Greek world, once the oracle had spoken, who was ever so hopelessly "pre-destined" as Oedipus?

But, as everybody knows, that is not it at all. Oedipus becomes tragic only because he does strive against the prediction. Resolved to know, he goes to the oracle himself and hears the dire prophecy repeated. His mistake is in believing that by running away he can circumvent the dreadful events. His *hubris* lies in thinking he has escaped by his own strength and cleverness and in boasting that such is the case. But we know what he does not know, that far from escaping his destiny, he has run full tilt to meet it. When we first see him he is *tyrannus,* "first of men," a king who has made himself king by strength and cunning. But there is more dramatic irony: the tyrannos who killed the sphinx and assumed the throne and the queen is really the rightful ruler of Thebes, the true son of Laius. His confidence still unbroken, he is convinced he can save Thebes again as he did before. He pronounces the curse on the unknown polluter of the city, and as the process of ferreting out the guilty one goes on, Oedipus' search becomes one of finding his own identity. As the dark hints begin to accumulate, he boasts of his contempt for prophecy; his father is still alive and his mother is far away. As the flawlessly plotted action unfolds, there comes the crushing peripeteia: all along he had been nearer home than he knew.

We could say that Oedipus' fault lies in trying to beat the rap. But again, everyone knows that his tragedy has to mean more than that; that this expenditure of human striving and achievement and suffering has to stand for something grave and constant in the eternal human condition. It is very true that his is the classical *hubris,* the sin of pride and arrogance and over-confidence in his own ability. But far more to our purpose, we can say it is a failure to achieve self-knowledge, a failure of self-definition. Oedipus is saddled with an incredibly horrible, inevitable future. He has not asked for it and has done nothing to deserve it; it is all "decided" before he is born. But he persists and demands to know the truth. Bernard Knox has noted how in the Greek original there is the constant, cruelly ironic inter-running of *Oedipus, oidi* ("swell," as with pride or arrogance), and *oida,* "I know," a word that is often, too often, in Oedipus' mouth. At the beginning of the play there is too much that he does not know, and at the end there is too much that he does. It is in the interweaving of guilt and innocence, in the willing of his own actions, in the god-like insistence on knowing *who* he is and the crushing ruin that this knowledge brings him, that the tragic glory of Oedipus lies.

Consider another hero. About his birth there is mystery also.

He too is spirited away as an infant because dreadful things are whispered about him, and he too is brought up by foster-parents whom he leaves hurriedly for fear he may have killed his foster-father. In a direct way, it can be said that his very begetting caused the death of his real father. He brings terrible shame, agony, and death to his real mother. After a great deal of wandering, he returns to that part of the world which, unknown to him, is the scene of his begetting and birth. Early in life he was given a free choice of two lines of conduct, one of which would have removed all danger from him. He persists in the other because it is necessary to the terms of his own definition of himself. He lives connubially with an older woman, who, as a result of his drive toward self-definition, dies a horrible death. The fearful rumors about him break out afresh. There is an old, mad visionary who claims to have special insight into the truth about him, and as a result, his fellow men are convinced he is a ritual pollution in the community. Pursued by them, he is harried for days and is eventually sacrificed in a particularly horrible ritual murder. He has been saddled with a terrible, inevitable curse. He did not ask for it and does nothing to deserve it; it was all "decided" before he was born. The second hero is, of course, Joe Christmas.

iii.

If the fall of Oedipus comes as a direct result of his terribly mistaken idea of who he is and his insistence on finding out, then the death of Joe Christmas is a result of his insistence that he already knows who he is and his persistence in the demand for the right to be himself, to live on the terms of his own self-definition. To state the paradox in another way, the classic tragic protagonist such as Oedipus, Othello, Hamlet, or Macbeth rejoices in an existence that allows him a superb scope of action in which to achieve self-realization, including self-knowledge, even though in this same drive toward self-fulfillment he destroys himself. The modern tragic protagonist, the hero of a Dostoyevsky, a Conrad, a Kafka, a Faulkner, a Hemingway, or a Warren, must use all his intelligence, his strength, his luck, merely to travel the tightrope between Cosmic Chaos on the one hand and Cosmic Absurdity on the other. He can trust in nothing, hope for nothing, and accept nothing at face value until he has put it to the test. He may have heard of determinism, but he does not believe in it; in the face of those joyous theories of self-exculpation formulated by present-day psychology and sociology that presumably give the individual the right to scream, "It's not my fault! It's not my fault!" his preference is much nearer the dreadful freedom of the existentialist: since existence is prior to essence, the individual is totally free and totally accountable for his own view of things, for with total freedom comes total responsibility.

In the case of Joe Christmas, Faulkner takes pains to make this freedom absolute. Here we must be blunt: previous critical opinion seemed almost never to be aware of that freedom. Partly because, one supposes, the term "conditioning" is now a household word, it was decided that Christmas is the helpless victim of his own conditioning. But surely it is obvious that the wellspring of all his actions is his refusal to surrender to that conditioning.

One of Faulkner's clearest strokes of genius is in leaving the question of whether Christmas has Negro blood unanswered. We, no one, will ever know if he has it or not. If he does have it, the percentage is very small, something that not only adds to the irony but leaves him free to "pass" if he chooses. Although he is, largely through the efforts of Old Doc Hines, putatively a Negro child at the orphanage, he is adopted and brought up as a white child by the McEacherns. ("He don't look no more like a nigger than I do," says a white character.) This is probably the most crucial point in the book. Christmas is free to choose what he will be, and his freedom is infinite. Precisely as Oedipus, he must find out who and what he is. One remembers a scene in the orphanage: Old Doc Hines is recalling how the five-year-old Christmas begins following the Negro yard-boy around:

. . . until at last the nigger said, 'What you watching me for, boy?' and he said, 'How come you are a nigger?' and the nigger said, 'Who told you I am a nigger, you little white trash bastard?' and he says, 'I aint a nigger,' and the nigger says, 'You are worse than that. You dont know what you are. And more than that, you wont never know. You'll live and you'll die, and you wont never know. . . .'[1]

But he must know, as with his determination to keep his own name. And because he is free, he cannot ever passively acquiesce.

He cannot let others tell him how or what to be. All his life, people attempt to force him to be what they insist he must be: McEachern's beating him to inculcate worship of the Moloch-Jehovah; Mrs. McEachern's sickening attempts to make him as cringing as herself; Joanna Burden's final insistence that he "become a nigger." His method is active. In the fifteen years of wandering he tries life as a black man living with Negroes and as a white man attempting to live with whites. But ultimately he chooses to be neither—he will simply be himself. Until the very end, the community cannot decide what he is; their deep distrust grows from his refusal to declare himself one or the other in a social pattern in which this is the most important distinction of all. He will insist on his right simply to be; he has defined himself and has fought hard for the definition. The murder of Joanna Burden and his own death are the fruits of that insistence.

Granted he has freedom and choice; what about rank and fortune? The modern hero, like Oedipus and Macbeth, makes his own. Christmas' distinction lies in the strength of his proud, ruthless, arrogant, cold self-sufficiency, as rigid as that of a Richard or an Ahab and more adequate to the strain placed upon it than Macbeth's. As with any modern hero, the simple fact that he is still alive may be as much good fortune as he can expect. It is far more important to prove he is typically human.

Part of the difficulty in understanding Christmas again lies in the form and structure of the novel. The sequence of telling is such that he is first seen as the utterly sinister alien and is revealed early in the book as a brutal murderer. It is only as the flashbacks begin to unfold and we see him as a child and youth that we are made aware of his simple humanity. He is presented for the most part at a distance, and his inmost thoughts and feelings are not often enough open to us. However, at rare intervals a momentary flash of insight will give a total revelation: for instance, we see the denial of love and belonging in the orphanage and the beatings by McEachern. The effect of these is of course cumulative, but the moment of revelation comes when Christmas hears his name will be changed:

"He will eat my bread and he will observe my religion," the stranger said. "Why should he not bear my name?"

The child was not listening. He was not bothered. He did not especially care, anymore than if the man had said the day was hot when it was not hot. He didn't even bother to say to himself *My name aint McEachern. My name is Christmas* There was no need to bother about that yet. There was plenty of time.[2]

We are shown the idyllic relationship with Bobbie, the stunted and no-longer-young waitress who is a working prostitute in her spare time. His slipping away from the McEachern farm at night to be with her is part of his program of defiance, but it is truly, at least at the beginning, the adolescent's first tentative, awestruck discovery of the body of the beloved and all its possibilities. Again, before the dawn of the day on which he will murder Joanna Burden, when the pressures that will compel either murder or complete surrender are building past endurance, he muses on the past:

... it seemed to him, sitting on the cot in the dark room, that he was hearing a myriad [of] sounds of no greater volume—voices, murmurs, whispers: of trees, darkness, earth; people: his own voice; other voices evocative of names and times and places—which he had been conscious of all his life without knowing it, which were his life, thinking *God perhaps and me not knowing that too* He could see it like a printed sentence, fullborn and already dead *God loves me too* like the faded and weathered letters on a last year's billboard *God loves me too.*[3]

His humanity, and perhaps even his own completely tragic awareness of his situation, is revealed in that incredible week in which we run with him while he eludes mobs, sheriff, deputies, Lucas, and bloodhounds. All that has gone before in the novel is brilliantly recapitulated as Christmas, still wrapped in the rags and tatters of his self-sufficiency and pride, works himself slowly away from the violence of the attack on the Negro church toward his tragic reconciliation with his fate, his acceptance of the price and the risk of the human condition. The incidents of his life which have "pre-destined" him toward the proud denial of his own humanity are echoed. Aware, as perhaps never before, of the simple joy of merely being alive and breathing, he watches another day begin:

It is just dawn, daylight: that gray and lonely suspension filled with the peaceful and tentative waking of birds. The air, inbreathed, is like spring water. He breathes deep and slow, feeling with each breath himself diffuse in the neutral grayness, becoming one with loneliness and quiet that has never known fury or despair. 'That was all I wanted,' he thinks, in a quiet and slow amazement. 'That was all, for thirty years. That didn't seem to be a whole lot to ask in thirty years.'[4]

"That didn't seem to be a whole lot to ask. . . ." No, it is not—simply the right to live and be one's own self, to expect perhaps a little peace, a little love; but knowing the price. (Who now hears the far-off echo of Thomas Jefferson: "We hold these truths to be self-evident . . . ?") But Christmas' dilemma is the truly tragic one: he is caught not between right and wrong but between right and right. Rejected, feared, hated, he has sought and been proud of that rejection and fear; but pushed too far he has gone too far, and unable to reconcile conflicting responsibility, he has committed a brutal murder.

Now he must go back. But it is impossible to go back, only forward. He must accept responsibility for the freedom of choice he exercised in his actions and pay the price of that freedom. But because he is truly tragic, he will not practice a mere passiveness and wait for the men with the dogs to come up and shoot him. He will actively seek his human reconciliation: his problem is how to begin to get back inside the human community. It is not easy; he has been isolated for too many years. He waits in the dawn for a farmhouse to come alive and the men to leave for the fields. Then he approaches the farm wife, who recognizes him, and quietly, from a respectful distance, he asks: "Can you tell me what day this is? I just want to know what day this is."[5]

Even though the white woman sends him away, the symbolism is clear. He wants to begin again by reaccepting the limitations of one of the most human and communal inventions: time. The next step involves a basic human need and social ritual. Having violently rejected the offer of food on a number of symbolic occasions, he approaches a Negro cabin to ask for a meal.

He was sitting at a table, waiting, thinking of nothing in an emptiness, a silence filled with flight. Then there was food before him, appearing suddenly between long, limber black hands fleeing too in the act of setting down the dishes. It seemed to him that he could hear without hearing them wails of terror and distress quieter than sighs all about him, with the sounds of the chewing and the swallowing. 'It was a cabin that time,' he thought. 'And they were afraid. Of their brother afraid.'[6]

He has made his first gestures, but it is not enough. He stops two Negro children and a Negro man to ask again the day of the week. They fear him as wildly as do the whites and reject him also. So, having shaved himself as carefully as he can with the razor, the murder weapon, he strikes across country to find his way to Mottstown. Given a ride on a wagon by a Negro youth who does not know who he is, he reviews his life:

. . . he is entering it again, the street which ran for thirty years. It had been a paved street, where going should be fast. It had made a circle and he is still inside of it. Though during the last seven days he has had no paved street, yet he has traveled farther than in all the thirty years before. And yet he is still inside the circle. 'And yet I have been farther in these seven days than in all the thirty years,' he thinks. 'But I have never got outside that circle. I have never broken out of the ring of what I have already done and cannot ever undo,' he thinks quietly, sitting on the seat, with planted on the dashboard before him the shoes, the black shoes smelling of Negro: that mark on his ankles the gauge definite and ineradicable of the black tide creeping up his legs, moving from his feet upward as death moves.[7]

The symbol is perfectly chosen. For thirty centuries or so, the black-white, light-dark, Apollonian-Dionysian, rational-irrational opposition has existed in Western civilization. If this were the only meaning of the symbol, its use would be forgivable but hardly brilliant. It should be remembered that Christmas gleefully exchanged his own shoes for these that had been worn by a Negro woman, to throw the bloodhounds off the scent. (At this stage Christmas, like Oedipus, is "full of devices.") But now, completely alone, he is feared and rejected by both black and white. Urged on by the frantic greed of Lucas Burch and the fanatic madness of Old Doc Hines, the white community considers Christmas a Negro, hunts him as a Negro, and will lynch and mutilate him as a Negro. Continuing to wear the shoes, he looks at that mark "moving upward from his feet as death moves." The murder he committed was the direct result of his refusal to choose, black or white. While choice of action remains (which may not be long), he will *choose* his means of reconciliation. Had he chosen sooner, or had he merely gone away, as he was also free to do, Joanna Burden would not be dead, and he himself would not be about to die. As surely as he sees the blackness (his acceptance of Negro status) creep up his body, so surely his body is sinking into the darkness, the extinction, of death. He walks quietly about the streets of Mottstown until he is captured.

At this point only the last of the tragedy remains to be played out. The reader may decide that Christmas has been unable to sustain his resolution, that his breaking away from the officers only to be shot and castrated by Percy Grimm reveals an artistic defect on the part of Faulkner. But Oedipus and Lear have moments toward the end when the old rage and arrogance blaze out. Antigone, St. Joan, Richard—all have moments when human fear of absolute extinction overwhelms human integrity. The moment is there for a conscious artistic purpose: to give us that ultimate awareness of pity and terror by reminding us that the protagonist is not a hollow tragic mask but a living human being, only a little less lucky than ourselves. There is a further meaning: free to the end, Christmas has held on to his life until this proper moment has come to give it, the moment most filled with reconciliation.

As Gavin Stevens says, no one will ever know what Christmas hoped for from Hightower, but it was the conflict in his blood that let him run but would not let him escape, that made him snatch up the pistol but would not let him kill Grimm with it. (It is Stevens who posits the black-white opposition. Faulkner has never said if there is Negro blood or not.) The meaning has taken on almost universal significance. It is the light-dark opposition that is in the blood of all of us; the savage pull between bright rationality and the darkness so feared by the Greeks, that leads to irrationality and death.

Little else in modern literature has the speed and inevitable onward sweep of the chapter in which Percy Grimm pursues Christmas and kills him. Taken merely as evocative realism, the writing is superb: the shots, the shouting; the blind rushes and clotted confusion of the mob; the added detail of the fire siren, a characteristic sound of our time, screaming the rise and fall of its meaningless message; the early resolution of the pursuit into a

personal contest between Christmas and Grimm. The rendition
of Grimm as a type is as merciless as anything else of the sort
ever done. Grimm is as the embodiment of pure force so often
is: his rather colorless personality and appearance are in ghastly
disproportion to his ability to produce evil and violence. He is
Faulkner's equivalent of the classic Nemesis of the Furies—
machine-like, unerring, impersonal, mindless. Here the problem
of belief is no problem at all.

Still guided perhaps by his irrational hope, Christmas runs
into Hightower's house holding the pistol he has snatched up
on the way. He could kill Grimm easily, but with nothing to
lose by another killing, he does not; this is his final gesture of
human reconciliation. Grimm empties the magazine of his auto-
matic into Christmas' body, but this is not all.

When the others reached the kitchen they saw the table flung aside
now and Grimm stooping over the body. When they approached to
see what he was about, they saw that the man was not dead yet, and
when they saw what Grimm was doing one of the men gave a choked
cry and stumbled back into the wall and began to vomit. Then Grimm
too sprang back, flinging behind him the bloody butcher knife. "Now
you'll let white women alone, even in hell," he said. But the man
on the floor had not moved. He just lay there, with his eyes open
and empty of everything save consciousness, and with something, a
shadow, about his mouth. For a long moment he looked up at them
with peaceful and unfathomable and unbearable eyes. Then his face,
body, all, seemed to collapse, to fall in upon itself, and from out the
slashed garments about his hips and loins the pent black blood seemed
to rush like a released breath. It seemed to rush out of his pale body
like the rush of sparks from a rising rocket; upon that black blast the
man seemed to rise soaring into their memories forever and ever.
They are not to lose it, in whatever peaceful valleys, beside whatever
placid and reassuring streams of old age, in the mirroring faces of
whatever children they will contemplate old disasters and newer hopes.
It will be there, musing, quiet, steadfast, not fading and not particularly threatful, but of itself alone serene, of itself alone triumphant.
Again from the town, deadened a little by the walls, the scream of
the siren mounted toward its unbelievable crescendo, passing out of
the realm of hearing.[8]

They are not to lose it, nor, I think, are we. In Stephen
Dedalus' terms, we feel pity and terror to a degree that is
almost unbearable. One does not know why we feel these

emotions or even less why the tragic spectacle is so compelling. It may be that it is better that we don't know. Certainly,
as Nietzsche claimed, the tragic emotions lurk in the dark, irrational part of the blood, and very likely the rational mind wants
no part of them. "Pity is the feeling which arrests the mind in
the presence of whatsoever is grave and constant in human sufferings and unites it with the human sufferer." This part at least is
no problem. We unite with Joe Christmas because he is the
modern Everyman. In a cosmos where the only constants are
absurdity and instability, we have the right to expect anything
except rationality. Any one of us could become the victim. His
suffering far transcends the time and place and means Faulkner
has used and comes to stand for everything that is grave and
constant in the human condition.

"Terror is the feeling which arrests the mind in the presence
of whatsoever is grave and constant in human suffering and unites
it with the secret cause." The union with the secret cause is almost as terrible as the suffering itself, because it gives a moment
of true insight into ourselves. Part of this insight is perfectly
symbolized in *Light in August* when the injured Hightower, in a
scene that might have come straight out of Dostoyevsky, is working himself toward complete self-knowledge. As the wheel of his
memory turns on and on, he comes to realize that his own cold
selfishness, his absorption in the Confederate grandfather, has
caused his wife's disgrace and death. As the crowd of faces in
his memory struggles to come into focus, one of them becomes
the dead face of Christmas, but the focus is not clear; another face
is struggling with that face, struggling to become clear and be
recognized. Suddenly it emerges: it is the face of Percy Grimm,
gunman, mutilator, avenging fury, lyncher extraordinary. Hightower never saw either of them before the lynching, but their
terrible failure and terrible guilt are somehow directly related to
his own failure to live up to his humanity. Somewhere at the root
of the secret cause of things as they are, we are all related; we are
all involved. We are all responsible because we are all a part of
mankind. So far as the rational mind goes, the union with the
secret cause is a moment of awareness, of realizing that grave
and constant human suffering is truly constant. Once we achieve

this awareness, the acceptance of the tragic human situation, with all its absurdity and irrationality, becomes possible, and with the acceptance come the emotions of peace and tranquility.

Yet the union with the secret cause has another side, which is less commendable. This emotion, which we are not so willing to let swim up to conscious awareness, can be curtly put as "There but for the Grace of God. . . ." The hero has fallen, but we, for the moment at least, are safe. Let society pick its victims as it pleases, so long as the victim is not I. It is in just this area of playing upon our deep, instinctual fears and misgivings that Faulkner has succeeded in achieving a favorable comparison with classic tragedy. It was impossible to put the Furies believably on the stage, but Faulkner found the perfect equivalent in the lynch mob, which one way or another elicits a strong emotion in all of us, or better still, a mixed one. In an age in which the very name of Oedipus has been explained away, tamed and embalmed in the clinic, in which almost no one can truly feel why Macbeth should think the murder of a king so much worse than any murder, and in which no one believes in the absurdity of an ancestral curse, the beholder is simply asked: "Did Joe Christmas inherit a curse?" Or rather, it is not necessary to ask, since we know. Faulkner has used the subconscious fear of mutilation and distrust of miscegenation that lurks in all of us, the love of and response to violence and death, the simultaneous love and hate of the loved one, to arouse these emotions or their equivalents in us. We love the violence and evil because we acquiesce in them. No doubt these emotions are despicable, but no doubt the emotions aroused by the spectacle of what Oedipus did were despicable also. The doctor who tamed the legend of Oedipus and rechristended it a complex only found out very late what the Christian world had known all along: when there are guilt and filth in the human psyche, the only possible remedy is to cast them out.

iv.

This chapter has dealt only with the analysis of Joe Christmas as a modern tragic protagonist. It has hardly mentioned the many other excellences of *Light in August,* leaving until a later chapter the cases of Joanna Burden and Hightower, who are also classic examples of the tragedy of isolation, strongly underlining the case of Christmas.

Tradition tells us that the Greeks demanded that each trilogy submitted in the great dramatic contests be accompanied by an outrageous and lewd satyr play, which preferably would burlesque the very elements and events just presented as tragedy. Perhaps some such comic relief is essential. After the human emotions have endured all they can, after the *katharsis,* something has to sustain us until we can touch earth again. Perhaps this is one explanation of the bawdy, almost folksy humor of the Lena-Byron episode in the last chapter of *Light in August,* so often dismissed with bewilderment or anger as an artistic botch. The direct experience of pity and terror is a little like being caught up in a cyclone, or to use another metaphor, like being at the heart of what goes on in a thermonuclear explosion. In contemplating the question, "When will I be blown up?" the author of *Light in August* has always been willing to risk a small side bet on Mankind. This risk and this faith are also a part of the tragic paradox. The Greeks knew, as did the Elizabethans after them, that, in contemporary terms, once the mushroom cloud has blown away and the fallout has ceased to fall there is always the continuing residue of humanity. It, as the author would no doubt say, will endure.

1. William Faulkner, *Light in August* (New York: Modern Library, 1950), p. 336.
2. *Ibid.,* p. 127.
3. *Ibid.,* p. 91.
4. *Ibid.,* p. 289.
5. *Ibid.,* p. 290.
6. *Ibid.,* pp. 292-93.
7. *Ibid.,* pp. 296-97.
8. *Ibid.,* pp. 406-7.

14.

THOMAS SUTPEN: THE
TRAGEDY OF ASPIRATION

In the beginning is the word.

IN ALL THE HAUNTED, TRAGIC WORLD of Faulkner's imagination, there is no book so haunted as *Absalom, Absalom!* Either by instinct or design, he has made it, of all the novels and stories, the most epic, the most poetic, and the most essentially dramatic— dramatic because, more than any of the others, it is built on words and voices and nothing else. This is literally true. Both John Sartoris and Christmas are assigned a time and place in Yoknapatawpha; we hear them speak in their own persons. In *Absalom, Absalom!*, the beginning is curiously like a dramatic reading in which the actors come out in street clothes and sit at a plain table and begin to speak. Thus Sutpen exists only in the voices; he has his being only in reports of those who were told something by someone else.

In terms of pure form, this procedure equips Faulkner with a flexible medium that need not be anchored to any point in time or space. The way is therefore left clear for a complete freedom of development. The writer can make the hero, the story, and the narrators anything he wishes, since all of them can be defined only in terms of what the speakers remember, what they say, and the way in which they express reaction to events which exist now only in memory and must be reconstituted from memory. In the expression of their reaction and in the way in which they modify their reactions as discovery follows discovery, they too become emotionally involved and swept up into the pattern itself and reveal themselves as well. One by one, the author stage-manages the speakers forward: they each step inside the circle of the spotlight and say their piece. Each is like a spiritualist medium, evoking a ghost for his own purposes. At first Sutpen is one of a "barracks-full" of ghosts, undifferentiated and undefined, which the bored Quentin consents to be told about only for politeness' sake, a ghost who haunts Miss Rosa Coldfield's obsessed, impassioned voice ". . . as if it were the voice which he haunted where a more fortunate one would have had a house." Gradually, as the passion of what Miss Rosa is saying grows on Quentin, the ghost emerges:

Out of the quiet thunderclap he would abrupt (man-horse-demon) upon a scene peaceful and decorous as a schoolprize water color, faint sulphur-reek still in hair clothes and beard, with grouped behind him his band of wild niggers like beasts half tamed to walk upright like men, in attitudes wild and reposed, and manacled among them the French architect with his air grim, haggard, and tatter-ran. Immobile, bearded and hand palm-lifted the horseman sat; behind him the wild blacks and the captive architect huddled quietly, carrying in bloodless paradox the shovels and picks and axes of peaceful conquest. Then in the long unamaze Quentin seemed to watch them overrun suddenly the hundred square miles of tranquil and astonished earth and drag house and formal gardens violently out of the soundless Nothing and clap them down like cards upon a table beneath the up-palm immobile and pontific, creating the Sutpen's Hundred, the *Be Sutpen's Hundred* like the oldentime *Be Light*.[1]

This is the classic technique of the empty stage—the two planks and a passion—out of which, as the various voices tell and retell what they know or must believe, the tragedy is born, a work that ranges over greater areas of meaning and extension than any other work in the Faulkner canon. But this freedom and extension of meaning is not obtained without a corresponding disadvantage. The work is "difficult," as any modern work is apt to be difficult, and the difficulty is compounded, deriving as it does from two simultaneous factors: the method and the meaning.

The novels considered so far in this section of the study have been presented in an order of increasing difficulty, so far as matters of form and structure go. In *The Unvanquished*, the form is simple chronological sequence, opening when Bayard is twelve and ending when he is twenty-four. In *Light in August,* Faulkner employs the technique of spiral form. With some oversimplification, spiral form can be defined as the technique of covering again and again the important point or cruxes of the work but always at higher and higher levels of understanding. Thus, early in the novel we learn that Joanna Burden was murdered and that Christmas was lynched for it. It is much later, only after a series of revelations and successive insights, that we learn the true nature of the relationship between them and the events that lead to her death. In *Absalom, Absalom!* the difficulty is greater in that, besides the necessity for gaining more information, the information when it does come is in the form of highly subjective personal reports, and we must learn how to evaluate them as we go along. But, as revelation succeeds revelation, the level of understanding progresses upward. *The Unvanquished* presents no problems to the reader and requires only a sympathetic response to be successful. In *Light in August,* the reader becomes more deeply involved as he identifies with Christmas' efforts to earn the right to his own self-definition. In *Absalom, Absalom!* there is a major problem. The reader must answer for himself the central question of Sutpen—what he really was, what emotions drove him, why he committed his seemingly inexplicable actions. From a third-hand, totally outside position, we must get inside the major protagonist. The method is invocation. The ghosts are invoked by a series of widely different mediums: Miss Rosa, frantic and eager; Mr. Compson, cynical, ironic, and mildly curious; Quentin, reluctant, then interested, and at last involved beyond recovery.

In *Light in August* the spiral employed by the author is cylindrical; that is, once the points or cruxes are established, the circle of reference moves upward but does not widen out. In *Absalom, Absalom!* the spiral is like an inverted cone, which with every recrossing or recounting of an event goes ever wider and wider into implication and expansion. In *The Unvanquished,* the essential action takes place within the community, the town of Jefferson. In *Light in August,* also, the important matter is the conflict between the community and Joe Christmas. In *Absalom, Absalom!,* the subject of the writer is cosmic; it is the law and structure of the universe itself that Sutpen is in conflict with.

As Vincent Hopper has stated, Sutpen is "a satanic hero in the precise Miltonic sense that he dared to 'defy the omnipotent.' "[2] The sheer magnitude of Sutpen's grand design requires a matching magnitude of form and content: locale and time-span, geographical spread, and analysis of the meaning of history. The author has used several techniques for increasing the sense of a universal involvement. The events of the novel cover more than a century and range geographically far beyond the boundaries of Yoknapatawpha.

Here too, the technique of pulling in by statement and implication the matter of heroic, epic, and Biblical literature greatly widens and deepens the projection until the figures, particularly Sutpen, become larger than life-size. Tucked away in odd corners of the narrative are barrages of names, places, and incidents. Sutpen is a "widowed Agamemnon" and later "an ancient stiff-jointed Pyramus" and an "ancient varicose and despairing Faustus." His descendants of their various kinds are called "that fecundity of dragon's teeth." There are the obvious references in the names like Judith and Clytemnestra (that was a slip of the memory, says Mr. Compson; it should have been Cassandra). The real Clytemnestra is the vengeance-mad first wife, existing solely in the hope of some monstrous revenge for a monstrous affront to herself and her child. As in Greek literature and the Old Testament, the sign of evil is the violence it produces, which breaks out into dynastic fratricide or sets father against son and son against father. Charles Bon and Henry are like Absalom and Ammon, or an Eteocles and Polynices who love each other but are doomed by the grand design to kill each other. Of all the built-in implications, surely the most moving and most implicational is the title itself. Absalom was the beautiful but forever-lost son of David, a great king who founded an assured dynasty that would one day bring forth the Messiah. This, we will discover, is the compulsion that moves Sutpen: to get a son and found a dynasty. David had many sons to fill his lack, but Sutpen has only one that is acceptable to him. In the fullness of time the Messiah is born, but the Sutpen dynasty ends with the half-witted Jim Bond—the end product of the sons Sutpen got. Thus Sutpen's mad design begins to assume the magnitude of a specific segment of history. Sutpen's failure springs from a defect of human feeling, the simple inability to feel and understand the feelings of others. Faulkner commentary has often rightly shown that Sutpen's racial attitudes are a part of his culture and that these same attitudes destroy the culture as well. What has not been shown is that Sutpen's dream of magnificence is typical of the United States as a whole, is indeed an example of the greatest American myth of all and thus is symptomatic of one national cultural failure.

ii.

In some ways, the discovery of what Sutpen was follows the classic pattern of thesis, antithesis, synthesis. The circumambient language winds through the spiral form, telling first one and then another version of what happened. In all the shifting points of view there are sudden, unsignaled shifts in time and shifts from narrator to narrator. There is an almost impenetrable pattern of relatedness and non-relatedness: those who were actually involved in the events were too involved to be objective; those who were capable of objectivity were too remote from the events. The novel begins at a very high pitch, with the near-hysterical, obsessed version of Miss Rosa Coldfield. Her thesis is that Sutpen was demonic, absolutely and damnably:

"He wasn't a gentleman. He wasn't even a gentleman. . . . fiend, blackguard and devil, in Virginia fighting, where the chances of the earth's being rid of him were the best anywhere under the sun, yet Ellen and I both knowing that he would return, that every man in our armies would have to fall before bullet or ball found him . . . a man who rode into town out of nowhere with a horse and two pistols and a herd of wild beasts that he had hunted down single handed because he was stronger in fear than even they were in whatever heathen place he had fled from. . . . And he was no younger son sent out from some old quiet country like Virginia or Carolina with the surplus negroes to take up new land, because anyone could look at those negroes of his and tell that they may have come (and probably did) from a much older country than Virginia or Carolina but it wasn't a quiet one.[3]

All this and many more pages like it are pure Gothic nonsense. The next account is that of Quentin's father: cool, rational, detached, unillusioned, or so it seems. If his account lacks Miss

Rosa's passion and outrage, it also lacks power and conviction. We know Mr. Compson for a skeptic, but here he indulges in an almost contrary fault—speculation. His contribution adds little to that of Miss Rosa, simply repeating what is already known and underscoring Sutpen's character and personality. He comments on Sutpen's courtship, a process which Miss Rosa has insisted was a combination of sorcery and abduction: "They did not think of love in connection with Sutpen. They thought of ruthlessness rather than justice and of fear rather than respect, but not of pity or love. . . . it was in his face; that was where his power lay. . . . that anyone could look at him and say, *Given the occasion and the need, this man can and will do anything.*"[4]

There is little in this to modify our view. After all, a summary of Sutpen's career is given twice in the first six pages of the novel. We have the story of his life in Yoknapatawpha, but there is no insight, no privileged glimpse into the wild and secret heart. Evidently, a totally new approach should be taken, perhaps at first hand. Such a narrator exists in Quentin's grandfather, Sutpen's only friend in Jefferson. Sutpen's trouble, says General Compson, was innocence. If demonism has no exact antithesis, perhaps innocence will do. In the Faulkner canon, the loss of innocence is usually followed by a predictable development, but Sutpen's history is exceptional. It is not that his innocence is crushed and destroyed but rather that he retains it in a distorted and misdirected form. Up to this point in the novel, Sutpen has been at a distinct remove from the reader; nothing reported of him is apt to generate sympathy. Here the author will do more than merely prepare for Sutpen's moral success or failure; he will make him human. With one stroke, Sutpen will be turned into the child we all once were—the child whose innocence and wish to be helpful are wounded by adult callousness in such a way that the child receives a mortal emotional injury from which it never recovers. Even at age twenty-five or thirty, Sutpen still does not quite understand the process himself. He has suddenly thrust upon him the thing he has to do. It is the last thing in the world he is prepared to do, but he must do it, if he is to live with himself and all the dead who have died to make him what he is and all the unborn yet to come.

Sutpen was born in the mountains of what would later become West Virginia. In the mountains there is a standard of excellence, however limited, which has nothing to do with property or possessions or money. A man is a man, and his manhood is measured by a tangible standard: whom he can whip, fair fight or stomp and gouge; what anvils he can lift; and how much whiskey he can hold. Possessions are few, and no one is so corrupt as to imagine that the ownership of things endows the owner with any particular virtue in the act of owning. But Sutpen, or rather his father, makes the mistake of coming down out of the Eden of the mountains (in which, roughhewn as it is, innocence is still possible) and in drifting backward into the Tidewater. Sutpen never knew that ". . . there was a country all divided and fixed and neat with a people living on it all divided and fixed and neat because of what color their skins happened to be and what they happened to own,—and where a certain few men . . . had the power of life and death and barter and sale over others. . . ."[5]

With the mountaineer's aplomb, he accepts things more or less as he finds them, becoming half-aware in the process of education, geography, race-conflict, and caste. The explosion does not come until the day his father sends him to the big house on an errand, and he is told by a monkey-nigger in a butler's uniform to go to the back door. He is little more than a child, but the mortal insult could not be clearer to him. Under the insolent stare of the house-servant, he feels the shame of his "patched overalls and no shoes." He goes away without haste or anger. It is not at all clear to him yet; he only feels the profundity of the insult. It is all foreign to his experience. He evolves the analogy of the rifle, the only terms in which he can explain to himself what has happened; the problem is to know what he should do. He momentarily considers killing the Negro or the plantation-owner, but discards the idea as meaningless. Realization comes all at once:

. . . there aint any good or harm either in the living world that I can do to him. It was like that, he said, like an explosion—a bright glare that vanished and left nothing, no ashes nor refuse; just a limitless flat plain with the severe shape of his intact innocence rising from it like a monument. . . . this aint a question of rifles. So to combat them you have got to have what they have that made them do what

the man did. You got to have land and niggers and a fine house to combat them with. You see?' and he said Yes.[6]

There follows the account of Sutpen in Haiti and his marriage to the daughter of a rich planter there. When he discovers that the wife can never be "adjunctive to the forwarding of the design," he returns her and most of the property to her father and goes to Mississippi. At the advanced age of twenty-five he must begin again. Cheating the Indians out of a hundred square miles of land, he drives his slaves and the French architect into dragging mansion and formal gardens out of the swamp. This done, he marries Ellen Coldfield. He is prospering; he has the biggest plantation in the county, a son and daughter. Now it is Sutpen who lies in the hammock under the arbor and has a faithful retainer to pour the whiskey. When Henry brings Bon home and Ellen announces Judith's engagement to him, Sutpen inexplicably forbids the marriage. War intervenes, and Sutpen apparently sets Henry to kill Bon. During Reconstruction, with Bon dead and Henry gone forever, Sutpen seduces Milly Jones and then goads Wash Jones into killing him.

The manner of Sutpen's death, especially in the light of his lifetime effort to obtain his "better rifle"—the enormous plantation and the undoubted status that went with it—seems inexplicable. We are returned to a scene in General Compson's office just before the end of the war, in which Sutpen is quietly contemplating his past life, without anger or recrimination, with ". . . that innocence again, that innocence which believed that the ingredients of morality were like the ingredients of pie or cake and once you had measured them and balanced them and mixed them and put them into the oven it was all finished and nothing but pie or cake could come out."[7]

He explains the design he had, the acquiring of a plantation and a family, above all of a son to inherit it all and carry on the name. He reviews the circumstances of his first marriage: the birth of a son, the putting-away of that family, and the new start in Mississippi. From the perspective of what Quentin knows, it is seen that Charles Bon is the son of that first marriage. Shreve now believes Sutpen forbade the marriage because Bon was Judith's and Henry's half-brother and that Henry killed Bon to prevent an incestuous marriage. Now, after the war, both sons gone, all Sutpen has to do is begin for the third time to construct his dynasty. After Miss Rosa proves unwilling to test-breed, he begins the seduction of fifteen-year-old Milly Jones. When she is visibly with child, her grandfather, the pore-white Wash Jones, is still confident that Sutpen will "make it right." When the child is born, Sutpen tells the mother, "Well, Milly; too bad you're not a mare too. Then I could give you a decent stall in the stable." Wash cannot believe that the "Kernel" would treat himself and his family with such utter contempt; he kills Sutpen, the grand-daughter, and the infant as well. Sutpen's arrogance and general demeanor show that he means to goad Wash into killing him, which seems incomprehensible in view of his repeated statement that all he wants is a son.

"Will you wait?" Shreve said. "——that with the son he went to all that trouble to get lying right there behind him in the cabin, he would have to taunt the grandfather into killing first him and then the child too?"

"——What?" Quentin said. "It wasn't a son. It was a girl."

"Oh," Shreve said. . . .[8]

iii.

The wheel has come full circle. The little boy who was in-sulted and sent away has found his better rifle but in getting it has succeeded only in killing himself with it. The circumstances of the pattern are the same: the arrogance and intolerance have pro-duced a deadly insult to Wash Jones, a poor white who is a child in everything except age. But here the insult is direct, man to man; so the plantation-owner in the hammock must be killed to wipe out the insult. The temptation to play on Sutpen's word "design" is a strong one; the circumstances of the pattern are the same. Perhaps the tragedy should end here. But the design Sut-pen has engendered is a tragedy of dynastic pattern, and the "fe-cundity of dragon's teeth" has yet to run its course. The insult to Milly Jones is powerful and direct, and retaliation is equally quick. Still, there is in the Sutpen design a rejection even more terrible and more powerfully symbolic. Quentin and Shreve cannot put out of their minds the image of Charles Bon, Sutpen's repudiated older son—Shreve because he does not know and Quentin because of what Clytie told him on that September night the year before, when the House of Sutpen finally vanished in a holocaust of flame, and what he has not been able to forget for a moment since. Sutpen's forbidding the marriage is understandable enough; the total rejection of a son so personally endowed, so genuinely more aristocratic than the Sutpens is the mystery that must be solved.

The evidence thus far shows that Bon went to the Hundred to meet his father at last, fully prepared not to demand any recognition at all, expecting the barest kind of private recognition and acknowledgment, prepared to accept that and never cross Sutpen's door again. It is just this bare recognition, the simple words "my son," that Sutpen cannot bring himself to give. When four years of war have not solved the problem by killing any of them, Bon feels his father has had long enough. He uses the only lever he has to compel Sutpen to acknowledge him: he writes Judith telling her to prepare for the wedding. Here Miss Rosa's hysterical insistence on Sutpen's demonism seems almost plausible. All the accidents of combat have not killed him; he has somehow intuited the exact moment when Henry is ready to permit the marriage in spite of incest. A demonic coincidence brings him to Henry, whom he has not seen in four years. He tells Henry why the marriage must not take place: Bon's mother had a tinge of Negro blood. Even at this moment, he cannot bring himself to send any word to Bon. As Bon makes clear, that one word, "son," even now, would have been enough. Now he must punish Sutpen in the only way he can, by riding with Henry the thousand miles back to the Hundred, so that Henry will have to shoot him dead at last. Now we know why.

iv.

The rest of the story shows the working-out of the doomed House of Sutpen to the third and fourth generation. Bon has died to prove his right to be called a living human being. Charles Etienne St. Velery Bon seems to live only to fling his infinitesimal tinge of Negro blood in the face of Judith and the rest of the white community. We understand the hysterical response of Miss Rosa and Quentin and the others who have approached too near the maelstrom and could not avoid the knowledge from which they can never recover. Now the series of tableaux of minor personages surrounding the central figure of Sutpen begin to take on meaning. More than the single character Sutpen has come full circle; it is the tragedy itself. Perhaps, as Quentin says, any single act is like a stone dropped quietly into a still pool of water, and no one can ever know when the ripples stop moving. Late in life, Sutpen is described as an "ancient varicose and despairing Faustus." In exchange for the grand design of lands and an established dynasty, Sutpen trades his essential humanity—his soul. In some highly symbolic sense, Sutpen has signed a demonic pact with his blood, if "blood" is seen as freighted with all its possible symbolic and ironic meanings: the blood of Milly and Wash, as well as that of all his children, black and white. The tragic pattern of Sutpen's career began in the innocence of primitive mountaineer virtue, received a mortal and undeserved insult, and resolved to match courage and strength, self-denial and persistence, in the struggle to wipe out that insult. In the tragic waste of such virtues, in the persistence at what ever cost, the tragedy is created. The price of the persistence is robbery, exploitation, and the violation of every human instinct including the withholding of love in a blood relationship—which in the case of Charles Bon cost Sutpen his sons and in the case of Milly Jones cost him his life. Motivated by the insult dealt him in the arrogance of ownership and possessions, he lives his life only to die for inflicting the same insult. The old Oedipus who has been blind since birth still does not see the "mis calculation" of what he has done. All he wants is a son, and the son he is left with is the idiotic, saddle-colored Jim Bond.

As those acquainted with the greatest American tragic literature know, the sin of Sutpen is the unforgivable sin. In the terms of Hawthorne and Melville, he has not only isolated himself from all human commitments, he has committed the worse sin of violating the sanctity of the individual human heart; he has ruined not only himself but the lives and hearts of those around him. The list is infinite: he has abandoned his family in Virginia in leaving for Haiti; he has exploited the Indians, Yoknapatawpha, Ellen and her father; he has denied Bon, driven Henry to fraticide, and bent

Judith to his ends; he has shattered the trust of Wash, seduced
Milly and repudiated her and the child, driving Wash to triple
murder; his legacy lives on in Velery Bon and Jim Bond.   In
view of all this, Miss Rosa's absurd Gothic demonism becomes
sensible and Quentin's "Nevermore of peace. Nevermore of peace.
Nevermore Nevermore Nevermore" is the only possible reaction
to what has happened.

The impact on the present-day reader who is not involved, who
can view the tragedy with detachment and aesthetic distance, is
also explicable. What the reader is experiencing is *katharsis*.
Aristotle was correct in stating that tragic events are most disturbing when they occur within the family or between close
friends; this is only one factor that helps equate the Sutpen dynasty
with older and more traditional tragic creations. All too often,
the commentary on this novel has attempted to limit the frame of
reference it is assigned to. Concentrating attention on the "race
problem," the import is dismissed as terrible but as something
local, Southern, and temporary. To be sure, Sutpen's sin is typical
of his culture, and his downfall is symbolic of the downfall of
that culture. The South is destroyed because it "erected its economic edifice not on the rock of stern morality but on the shifting
sands of opportunism and moral brigandage." On a practical,
realistic, American basis, the story is disturbing because we see
in it a trope of one major American myth. Sutpen is only one
more example of the kind of heroes America had before it created
Horatio Alger, Jr. As everybody knows, in America the path to
virtue and success is clear and simple, and any poor boy may follow it: marry advantageously, get a big house, and found a dynasty. The unspoken corollary is: get it all costs, no matter how.
When the boy Thomas Sutpen, ragged and barefoot, comes to the
door of the plantation house, he is punished for the unforgivable
American crime, the crime of poverty. This crime is unforgivable
because poverty is the result of shiftlessness and well-known
remedies exist for it. The remedy Sutpen attempts is the basis
of his tragedy, which is cosmic in its import. As in *King Lear*
or *Macbeth* or *Richard III,* the very frame of Nature has been
wrenched awry, and blood cries out for blood.

"The South," Shreve said. "The South. Jesus. No wonder you folks all outlive yourselves by years and years and years. . . . except for one thing. . . . You've got one nigger left. One nigger Sutpen left. Of course you can't catch him and you don't even always see him and you never will be able to use him. But you've got him there still. You still hear him at night sometimes. Don't you?"

"Yes," Quentin said. . . .

". . . Now I want you to tell me just one thing more. Why do you hate the South?"

"I dont hate it," Quentin said, quickly, at once, immediately; I dont hate it," he said. *I dont hate it* he thought, panting in the cold air, the iron New England dark; *I dont. I dont! I dont hate it! I dont hate it!*"[9]

1. William Faulkner, *Absalom, Absalom!* (New York: Random House, 1936), pp. 8-9.

2. Vincent F. Hopper, "Faulkner's Paradise Lost," *Virginia Quarterly Review*, XXIII (Summer, 1947), 415.

3. Faulkner, *Absalom, Absalom!*, pp. 14-17.

4. *Ibid.*, pp. 43, 46.

5. *Ibid.*, p. 221.

6. *Ibid.*, p. 238.

7. *Ibid.*, p. 263.

8. *Ibid.*, p. 292.

9. *Ibid.*, pp. 377-78.

15.

THE LEGENDARY SOUTH: TOWARD A THEORY OF EPIC TRAGEDY

THERE IS SOMETHING symptomatic in Quentin's frenzied response to the rise and fall of Sutpen's fortune. Even when we discount his somewhat disturbed condition, there still seems to be more in operation than the bare events would indicate. More is involved than the witnessing of the last scene of the last act of the Sutpen drama. This "something more" is not revealed in *Absalom, Absalom!*—it can only be discovered by turning to another book entirely: *The Sound and the Fury.* The excessiveness of his response becomes understandable only when we know the personal history of Quentin, the history of his family, and the events that will take place on the following June 2, 1910. Countless other examples could be appended to show how character and event impinge or are retold from one book to another and help to create the totality of the Yoknapatawpha Saga—"Wm. Faulkner, sole owner and proprietor."

Malcolm Cowley, in his Introduction to *The Portable Faulkner,* uses a metaphor to describe the process by which the Saga has been built up by the creation of the books and stories which are its various parts. It is, he says, as if Faulkner were cutting his various planks not from a log but from a living tree, which remains undamaged, and continues to grow, and from which new planks can be cut. (Faulkner himself often refers to his cache of raw material as his "lumber-room.") After the various rough planks have been planed and finished, they are fitted into the larger structure of the Yoknapatawpha Chronicle.

I do not wish to suggest that critical awareness of Yoknapa-tawpha as an entity is a new discovery; it has been customary to treat it as an organic whole for some time. Therefore I risk being redundant if I repeat a contention made earlier—that quite aside from form and treatment in a given work, Faulkner's genius, his habits of mind, is more congenial to the purely narrative, the epic, the bardic attitudes in the creation of literature. Thus, the Yoknapatawpha Saga in its final form will more nearly re-semble *The Odyssey* than it will *The Ambassadors* or *Finnegans Wake*.

Throughout the present study, some effort has been made to show the affinity between modern literature and the literature of more ancient times.* The discussion of tragedy, for instance, has relied altogether on the definition of Aristotle. It is unnecessary to mention that literary criticism has gone beyond Aristotle in its discoveries and assertions, particularly in its theories about the nature of tragedy. Today, we would say, tragedy is found in forms and genres not allowed it in Aristotle's *Poetics*.

Many critical terms are used in defining or limiting a specific work of literature. Three are form, presentation, and atmosphere. By form I mean the simple classification by definition: novel, short story, play, and so on. Form and presentation have some relation to each other, and the form may often determine the presentation. By presentation I mean the fashion in which the work comes to the beholder. Novels, of course, are usually read by the individual from a printed page, but plays are intended, at least, for dramatic presentation. Atmosphere is a term that evades exact descrip-tion; for the purposes of discussion I shall limit it to two major possibilities, comic and tragic. It should be obvious from the necessity of the use of such a word as "atmosphere" that I wish to discuss qualities in literature that exist irrespective of the rigidi-ties of a given form; I also wish to suggest that form does not determine either content or atmosphere, as Aristotle seems to be-lieve it does, as when he states that tragedy, to be tragedy, has to exist as "representation, not narrative." The modern world no longer seems to think so. Even so eminent a Homeric scholar

* The reader should be warned once more that these affinities may not have been deliberate and are certainly not to be thought of as categorical, especially in the practice of Faulkner.

as E. V. Rieu has stated that *The Iliad* (an epic in form, of course) is tragic and that it is dramatic in its approach. What Homer did was to create a tragic drama before the Attic theatre had been invented.

This long digression on Aristotle's theory of tragic form is intended only to clear the way for a continued discussion of the atmosphere and significance of the Faulkner canon. So far, in the present study, the analysis has been largely in terms of individual characters in the various novels and stories. In the teeming *dramatis personae* of Faulkner, a few characters seem to stand out larger than life. Large as they are, they are involved in and symbolize something larger still. Even the most minor characters also share in this significance. Perhaps no writer on the contemporary scene has created with such memorable realism such a variety of individual, sharply differentiated characters, as diverse as are, for instance, Sutpen, Quentin and Jason Compson, Lena Grove, Ratliff, and Flem Snopes—even the homogeneous Snopeses have their carefully marked differences. It may be questionable, therefore, to state that all the characters in the Faulkner canon, realistic as they are, are ultimately symbolic.

But, to particularize, consider the case of Benjy Compson in *The Sound and the Fury*. He is a thirty-three-year-old man with a mental age of five: the idiot who tells the story full of sound and fury, or helps to tell it. His characteristics are steadfastness, loyalty, and a constancy toward the things he loves. He is, of course, too retarded to realize these qualities do not pay. With remorseless skill, Faulkner delineates Benjy's career in the world as we know it, and the impact of what happens is unrestful and disturbing, more so than it should be by all the normal standards of literary judgment. We should feel pathos, perhaps, but nothing more. Benjy is a character who by definition cannot be tragic, since he has no freedom, nothing to decide, and no choice of action. Obviously, he has no place to "fall" to, since his uncorrupted innocence is, in the final sense, beyond any harm that can be done to him, and he will never "rise" in any usual sense of that word.

Why then the disturbing emotions that surround him? As the flawlessly arranged parts of *The Sound and the Fury* unfold, it is possible to discern a reason. The various Compsons are sharply individualized; for instance, Quentin, the same Quentin we know from *Absalom, Absalom!* We see him on the last day of his life, the day he commits suicide at Harvard. But Quentin too should be merely pathetic: he is weak, defeatist, and almost completely lacks the will to press back against the pressure of reality. What we respond to is, of course, the sense of tragic waste and loss—the self-inflicted death of so much sensitivity and perception.

Or there is Caddy, the sister whom Quentin loves so much, perhaps too much. She is the prize of them all—the most beautiful, the most fearless, most intelligent of all the Compson children. But she finds nothing to answer her eagerness, her challenges, in all of petty Jefferson, least of all in her family, where no one, not even Dilsey, can seem to provide her with enough stability and love. So she turns to Dalton Ames, drifts eventually into nymphomania, leaves her illegitimate daughter at home, and is last seen as the mistress of a Nazi general.

His brother Jason is everything Quentin is not. More than one commentator has called Jason Compson the most monstrous villain in all American literature. He may be. He is madder than anyone else in the Compson family, and his paranoia is further inflamed by the fact that those of his blood kin he most hates are forever beyond his reach: Quentin and their father and all the ancestral Compsons because they are dead and Caddy because of her forced exile. He can retaliate only upon the weak and helpless ones who remain: his mother, Benjy, his illegitimate niece, and the Negroes.

In all these people, taken as individuals, there is little that could be called tragic in the classic sense. Yet the final section of *The Sound and the Fury* is as completely suffused with tragedy as anything written in the past hundred years. The tragic emotion lies not merely in the juxtaposition of the Easter season against a scene in which there will never be any resurrection, not merely in Dilsey's repeated and repeated "I've seed de first en de last," but in something that includes and exceeds all of it. The explanation, the key, may be found perhaps in the final scene of the novel. Benjy is being driven for his Sunday ride to the cemetery by

Luster in the old wagon pulled by Queenie, the ancient mare.
Benjy is happily holding in his fist a flower with a broken stem.
Luster has been repeatedly warned to drive always to the *right* of
the Confederate monument; in his self-importance and need to
show off, he drives to the *left* of the monument.

> For an instant Ben sat in utter hiatus. Then he bellowed. Bellow
> on bellow, his voice mounted, with scarce interval for breath. There
> was more than astonishment in it, it was horror; shock; agony eyeless,
> tongueless; just sound, and Luster's eyes backrolling for a white
> instant. "Gret God," he said, "Hush! Hush! Gret God!" He
> whirled again and struck Queenie with the switch. It broke and he
> cast it away and with Ben's voice mounting toward its unbelievable
> crescendo Luster caught up the ends of the reins and leaned forward
> as Jason came jumping across the square and onto the step. . . .
> Ben's voice roared and roared. Queenie moved again, her feet
> began to clop-clop steadily again, and at once Ben hushed. Luster
> looked quickly back over his shoulder, then he drove on. The broken
> flower drooped over Ben's fist and his eyes were empty and blue and
> serene again as cornice and facade flowed smoothly once more from
> left to right; post and tree, window and doorway, and signboard, each
> in its ordered place.[1]

Perhaps the symbolism is clear; we will return to it later.
The Compson saga is greater than the sum of the significance of
the individual Compsons. Their family history in turn is symbolic of something in the larger corpus of Faulkner's entire work.

Even the most casual reader of Faulkner soon comes to realize
that the novels and stories form an interlocking and interconnect-
ing whole; that they reinforce and complement each other. This
is the spiral method with a vengeance. Each character of course
justifies his own existence, and any of the stories is capable of
standing alone. But each of them is also a part of the broad base
of the pyramid of significance. What the apex of this pyramid is
can, I think, be demonstrated.

ii.

The present writer is willing to concede full, individual tragic
status to only three of Faulkner's characters. These are the three
already dealt with: Colonel Sartoris, Christmas, and Sutpen.
Yet, as noted in the case of Dilsey and the Compsons, we have the
apparently contradictory situation of tragic effect without an in-

dividual tragic protagonist. A brief examination of some other Faulkner characters may help to clear up the point.

There are the characters like Donald Mahon in the early *Soldiers' Pay*. Mahon returns from the First World War blasted in mind and body. He has only momentary flickers of consciousness and is nothing more than an inert lump of animal matter, not even aware he is dying. Is such a figure tragic? In a series of flashbacks we are shown Mahon as a youth: rebellious, very much alive. By extension he comes to stand for all youth maimed and killed in such a useless fashion.

Another example of a human being on the same approximate level may be the idiot Snopes in *The Hamlet*. An entire section of the novel is given over to his love affair with a cow, including a great deal of high burlesque of situation and the language of courtly love. Some of the rest of the Snopses provide seats for those who wish to watch him at his love-making. Throughout this section of the novel the tone is carefully maintained; the outrageous bawdiness is continued to the end and the narrative is never allowed to break over into pathos. What is there that could be tragic? Very little perhaps, but there is a great deal that is paradoxically beautiful. In the total abandonment of his love for the cow, the idiot has something that the cold and calculating Flem Snopes has never had and never will. The idiot has given himself; he has made a human commitment of himself into a living relationship. Flem is not capable of such a commitment. The idiot thus comes to stand for more than just himself and his cow: he represents perhaps all humanity, however crippled and limited, that takes the risk, the commitment of love, in contrast to those who, however fortunate otherwise, cannot.

In this same class of severely limited or crippled persons, and on an only slightly higher level, may be included Shumann in *Pylon* (who is already dead and knows it) and the jumper and the wife they share; and Tawmy in *Sanctuary* or Young Bayard in *Sartoris,* who cannot endure life without his twin brother John and who, choosing between grief and nothingness, settles for oblivion.

In a slightly different classification are those somewhat intelligent and able persons who are driven mad by outside pressures or the force of evil. I would include Darl (*As I Lay Dying*), Henry Armstid (*The Hamlet*), and Mink Snopes, especially as he is viewed over the forty-year period between *The Hamlet* and *The Mansion*. Darl becomes insane because he is too sensitive to endure the sordid and ambiguous complexity of the world as he discovers it, and Henry becomes insane in his insistence that the world must provide him with at least as much as it provides other men. Mink begins as a hot-headed, murderous bushwhacker who kills from ambush, to be transformed at the end of *The Mansion*, purified by his suffering, into the agent of divine retribution. Characters like these, however twisted, are idealists of sorts, and there is nothing particularly tragic in thwarted idealism. But when idealism is persisted in in the face of all contrary evidence and the persistence leads to the destruction of the idealist, then perhaps the idealism, as such, is tragic.

In somewhat the same classification there are the ineffectual men of good will such as Horace Benbow or Gavin Stevens. Both are lawyers, and with varying degrees of success both attempt to see justice done. Somewhat more important are comic heroes like Ratliff and Byron Bunch. These are figures who are in every way the antithesis of the tragic hero: ineffectual, bumbling, and with the odds severely against them. Nevertheless, they are on the side of the angels and return after every fight, undaunted, to fight the good fight again. And they continue. There are others who do not, others more heroic than they, who perish. But these former figures are aware enough to realize that they survive precisely because they are not important enough for the world to destroy them. It is out of this kind of awareness that the tragic element in the often bitter comedy of Faulkner grows.

Even the villains are tragic. In such people as Jason Compson, Flem Snopes, and Popeye there is the sense of tragic waste, not in themselves but in what they do to others. They are all monsters who have grown away from any idea of what human beings should be. Significantly enough, they are all modern figures, and all have become what they are under the seductions of modern capitalism. They are villains because they are dehumanized: they are involved in no human relationships and feel no human emotions (except Jason, who is divesting himself of them as fast as he can). If this is the direction modern Man is taking, as Faulkner sometimes seems to be saying it is, then perhaps the villains stand for all of us.

The position of Harry and Charlotte in *The Wild Palms* is different. They are trapped between their own desires and the world that will not recognize their right to the fulfillment of those desires. Granted that the desires may be illegitimate and immature, nevertheless their constant sacrificing of comfort and security to keep their love inviolate does constitute a serious and single-minded attempt. Their love and their purposes are the cause of Charlotte's death, but Harry's decision to serve out his life sentence and his choice of the memory of grief in preference to suicide may indicate a step toward self-knowledge and reconciliation.

A very special place is occupied by those women who emerge beyond the fumbling and incapacity of mere humankind into a state of being that seems beyond good or evil, or tragedy itself. In contrast to Drusilla and Narcissa after their corruption, they seem not to need to do harm to any one and seldom seem to need help. One of these is Dilsey, who seems to stand for all the loving and inarticulate suffering in the world. At the last moment we see her, she is both chorus and symbol of the tragic decay of the house of Compson. Yet it is clear she is moving by the action of suffering through abnegation and immolation to the condition of sainthood.

But Eula Varner Snopes and her daughter Linda Varner Snopes Kohl are truly beyond the condition of tragedy. Eula appears first as the bucolic Venus of Frenchman's Bend and is comic; but once mature, she moves untouched through the tumescent orbit of her uncaring, unconcerned career, neither accepting nor rejecting the emotional upsurges her presence generates. At last she kills herself, to leave her daughter "a mere suicide for a Mother, and not a whore." Linda, who is so long the object of Gavin's nervous care and love, offers to marry him, but he cannot ever consider her anything other than his spiritual daughter. So he sends her out into the great world to match the magnitude of her own capacity for it and her passionate concern for justice. This search leaves her a widow and stone deaf. Once more she offers herself to Gavin, who refuses because he knows his own in-

adequacy. She then emerges finally as a terrible, impartial agent
of retributive justice (not blind but deaf), whose last function is
to revenge her mother's death and rid Jefferson of Snopeses
forever.

iii.

If all the *dramatis personae* of Faulkner carry tragic implications, what do those characters who are more nearly tragic in
their own right imply? As we approach them, we find that while
their significance is universal, their locus is always the South. In
this group I would include the tragicomic McCaslins, beginning
with that evil old man Carothers McCaslin, through the dynamically moral Uncle Buck and Uncle Buddy, and following the long
career of Uncle Ike, in his lonely and precariously maintained
morality, through his old age and into the grief and disillusion-
ment of seeing the younger generation repeating the sins of the
fathers that he has devoted his life to atoning for. Closely related
to the McCaslins by blood and by significance are the several
generations of Beauchamps and the unhappy patterns of miscegenation between them.

The usual flaw among the minor tragic figures is pride, which
quite often takes the form of insistence upon privilege or preroga-
tive. One example is Miss Emily Grierson of "A Rose for Emily."
This short story is a complete tragedy in itself and in capsule
presents a pride as presumptuous and monstrous as that of Sutpen. Miss Emily resembles her domineering father so much that
she cannot tolerate direction or contradition. Confronted by the
impending loss of her lover, she refuses to accept the degrading
notion that he could possibly want to leave her. Rather than face
that possibility, she poisons him and sleeps beside his dead body
for thirty years. Thus she defies not only mere human intracta-
bility but even all nature and the laws of the universe, symbolized
by the natural processes of death and decay, as well.

On the positive side, there is the type personified by Saucier
Weddel in the story "Mountain Victory." Returning home from
the war, the ex-major, CSA, requests from a pro-Union East
Tennessee family shelter for himself and his body-servant. The
uniform he has worn, his manners, the vanished way of life he
represents, and his very presence on the spot are all a deadly af-

front to the son of the family, who has been briefly a Union soldier. Weddel is warned to leave by the father of the family but declines to go because his elderly Negro servant has found some moonshine and is too drunk to move. Weddel's sense of responsibility is too great to allow him to go without the servant. Early the next morning, from ambush, the pro-Union son kills Weddel and the servant.

Finally, there are Hightower and Joanna Burden in *Light in August*. They are both examples of the tragedy of isolation, similar to Captain Ahab and Chillingworth in their conviction that they do not need, and indeed do not want, the help of any other human being in the pursuit of whatever goal they have set for themselves. Miss Burden is the descendant of the two Abolitionists who were shot by Colonel Sartoris. She is of New England stock, with the traditional New England spinster's conscience. Her entire life is devoted to welfare work for Negroes. She sees herself as born under the shadow of a black cross. Her only turning away from this singleness of effort is when she takes Joe Christmas for a lover. She conceives the idea of having him attend a Negro college, obtain a law degree, and manage all her affairs. He flatly refuses because in order to do it he would have, he thinks, to "become a nigger." But she persists, and when he still refuses, she attempts to kill him and is killed by him. When her body is found, the head is nearly severed by the razor-stroke and is turned backward. The backward-turned head, as one critic has remarked, is the punishment meted out to soothsayers and diviners in the *Inferno* of Dante. Only God can know the future. The effort to see into (and perhaps even influence) the future was therefore held by Dante to be a very grave sin. Such sinners (who attempted to see forward) are punished in the *Inferno* by having their heads fixed backward for eternity. Essentially, Miss Burden's actions are no different from those of Miss Emily, who also could not allow her will to be thwarted by the mere forces of Nature.

The Reverend Gail Hightower's difficulties grow out of a similar concern with his own obsessions. His isolation from his fellow men and his denial of his responsibilities toward them grow out of his single-minded determination to have what he wants.

What he wants is the right to live in Jefferson where his grandfather, a Confederate cavalryman, was shot dead from his horse in a raid. He is obsessed with the idea of the grandfather and is preoccupied with reconstructing an imaginary life built around the grandfather's accidental presence in Jefferson long ago. He has no real concern or interest other than being present at the window of his study late each afternoon when he imagines he hears the horses of the troop galloping through the town. His church members are bewildered and shocked by his concern with his grandfather, and his neglect of his wife drives her to nymphomania and eventually to a scandalous death. When he refuses to leave the town, he is taken into the woods by masked men and beaten unconscious. But he proves more stubborn than his attackers and in the long run the town decides to ignore him.

His one friend is Byron Bunch, and it is Byron who comes to Hightower and asks him to swear that Christmas was at Hightower's house the night of the murder. Hightower will not do it, even though it may save Christmas from the mob. "I've paid! I won't! I've bought immunity!" is his cry. Too late, when Percy Grimm is pursuing Christmas into Hightower's house, Hightower shouts out the lie that, told earlier, might have saved Christmas' life. But it comes too late, and Christmas is killed in Hightower's kitchen.

Later, when the violence is over and Hightower is going through an agonizing reappraisal of his life, he realizes that his own selfishness has brought on the death of his wife, that his own cowardice and his failure to save Christmas are somehow part and parcel of the guilt of Percy Grimm. In his arrogance, his selfishness and pride, his persistence in his line of conduct, and the fall from the high calling of his office, he is authentically tragic.

iv.

The close involvement of Joanna Burden, Hightower, and Christmas underlines the contention made earlier: that all the characters in Faulkner's *dramatis personae* are interlocked and that their appearance (in some instances) in several different books points to a significance greater than that they have as individuals. As in the case of the Compson dynasty, the whole is

greater than the sum of the parts.   Each individual seems to per-
sonify the tragedy of his family or group.   The crucial question
seems to be now: what do the families stand for?

The real protagonist of all Faulkner's writing, the protagonist
for which the individuals and the families and the dynasties stand,
is the South itself.   Faulkner's canon of novels and stories covers
all phases of Southern history, from before the advent of the white
man up to the present time, but largely it is the period of the War
Between the States and Reconstruction that is dealt with.

Malcolm Cowley has referred to the myth in this manifestation
as "William Faulkner's Legend of the South."   Or, as Faulkner
himself has put it in another connection, "that chronicle which was
a whole land in miniature, which multiplied and compounded was
the entire South."   Briefly recapitulated, the legend goes something like this: The South (particularly the deep South that Faulkner knows best) was settled by men who were unusually strong
and ruthless, as they had to be in order to establish a new country
in the wilderness.   But some of them, the better sort, had a vision
somewhat more graceful, more humane, more idealistic.   Once
the country was civilized, there might have grown up a society
in which liberty, culture, and stability would have been possible.
To some extent, a high level of culture was reached in certain
cities and regions, particularly in such disciplines as architecture
and government (essential in a new country), rather than in literature or music.   This was particularly true in such stable, long-
settled regions as Tidewater Virginia, Charleston, and New Orleans.   Virginia alone, for instance, provided four of the first five
presidents of the United States.

But inherent in the system were the evils that would destroy
it.   Few men are great enough to handle power, particularly the
power of life and death over human beings.   In the early days, men
wise and humane enough, such as George Washington (and later
Robert Lee) might make provision for freeing their slaves, but
later the temptation to make money and wield power became too
great, and the planters became as rapacious as the Yankee slave-
traders who had brought the Negroes in the first place.   The evil
inherent in slavery and miscegenation corrupted the system from
within, and the War and Reconstruction completed the destruc-

tion from outside. Exhausted by the War, strangled by Reconstruction, and divided at home, the South was never able to come
back. The old aristocrats exhausted themselves attempting to
continue the status quo, and the new red-neck class (the Snopes)
was fighting its way up from the bottom, using every means, fair
or foul. The descendants of both kinds, black, white, and mixed,
have reaped and are still reaping the whirlwind.

Assuming the legendary South to be Faulkner's tragic protagonist, it would be interesting to place it alongside those qualities which we find have been traditionally required of the tragic
protagonist and see how the South measures up. That the old
South was fortunate, at least in colonial and ante-bellum times, is
obvious. That it was prosperous (at least for the big planters) is
evident. Its virtue consisted in the possibility of the good life
that it held out and in the cultural hope implicit in the lives of
such men as Jefferson. The flaw was that liberty was denied to
some, while lip-service was given to the ideals of freedom. The
consistency lay in the subborn refusal to change or to compromise,
the fire-eating that led to the premature bombardment of Fort
Sumter. As for courage and strength and determination, the
record speaks for itself. It is still the tactics of Lee and Jackson
that is studied at West Point, and the military psychologists are
still attempting to discover the secret of the kind of morale that
the Army of Northern Virginia exhibited.

As for suffering, the record is evidence for that also; Faulkner's novels are full of it. There remains only the ideal final step
of self-knowledge and reconciliation. In part, for certain individuals, this step has been achieved; as for the rest, evidently the
curse and fatality have not yet worked themselves out. The
reader is simply invited to look at the latest newspaper.

In all of Faulkner's best writing, his major individual characters are symbolic, then, of the larger pattern. Sartoris, Sutpen,
and Christmas are tragic because they are involved in the larger
tragedy of the most tragic period in the history of a major civilization. We can understand now, to some extent, why a character
like Benjy Compson can take on such moving tragic overtones
that we really have no right to feel. The meaning of the closing
scene of *The Sound and the Fury* should be plainer now.

Benjy knows what he loves but also (in his five-year-old mentality) is incapable of apprehending change or growth or of realizing that others change. In the closing scene of the novel, serene and happy, one of the last of the Compsons, he is being driven to the cemetery. When the irresponsible Luster drives to the wrong side of the statue of the Confederate soldier, the agonized reaction takes place. After Jason (the villainous representation of the corruption in the new South) has seized the reins from Luster (indolent, careless, traditional), the customary pattern is re-established by violence. But soon Benjy's eyes are "empty and blue and serene again as cornice and facade flowed smoothly once more from left to right; post and tree, window and doorway, and signboard, each in its *ordered* place" (italics mine).

In the violence, Benjy's illusioned happiness has been restored, but the stem of his single flower has been broken again by Jason, who is ashamed of his brother and only wants him out of the way. I trust the symbolism is clear and the reason for the anguish we all feel. The anguish is for the innocence: at once so helpless and so far beyond the need for help.

In similar fashion, a detailed discussion of each character in the Faulkner canon could be made, relating him to the central symbol of the legendary South. But by this stage of the present discussion, such a process is no longer necessary. Sartoris, in his inability to adjust the dynamics of his morality (courage, persistence, leadership) to the changed conditions of Reconstruction and to find a suitable field for their outlet, is representative of that aspect of the South's history. Sutpen, in his rigid determination to found a dynasty, no matter how, and his refusal to meet the problem, is symptomatic of the South's inability to solve the problem, then or now. Christmas, with Quentin Compson and a host of other present-day figures, represents those who have reaped the sins of the fathers and are still reaping those sins. Hightower and Joanna Burden (whose head turned backward) represent those who are still looking backward, still keeping alive the old delusions to feed the emptiness of their own lives. All of these, then, and all of the novels and stories in the Yoknapatawpha Chronicle, however brilliant they are in their own right, are facets of the larger meaning of Faulkner's work.

v.

Faulkner is not, of course, a popular writer. But he was, until his recent death, the greatest living writer in the English language. His writings do not and never can, perhaps, reach the general public. Much, too much, has already been said about the plight of the artist who must function without a homogeneous culture that shares the same myths. Sophocles did not have this problem, and Shakespeare was able to contain it. The present study is not concerned with the techniques of capturing mass audiences by printed books.

It is doubtful that the literary artist is ever going to enjoy a completely homogeneous culture again. It is certain that no artist in our own time is going to enjoy it. Yet, it is demonstrable that the American Civil War is one of the few areas of myth that the nation as a whole shares. This fact is evident in all media of communication and entertainment, especially motion pictures and television. It is not my contention that Mr. Faulkner's cleverness in "choosing" this subject should be praised; it simply happened to be the subject and region he knew best. He is praised, and rightly, for doing the thing that every writer of genius must do, which is to create unforgettable human beings in whatever time and place he puts them in. Faulkner's emphasis is always on the human.

In the case of John Sartoris, the setting is somewhat romanticized; not everyone finds it easy to identify with a discontented, arrogant ex-colonel of Confederate cavalry who has run out of something to do. Yet he is humanized by being seen through the eyes of an adoring son, and bit by bit, we see him pick up the stubbornness, the arrogance, the inflexibility, of an Ahab or a Creon or a Lear, and, wrapped in the assurance of his own essential rightness, he weaves the net of his own destruction. Thus, we share the son's awareness. The son is there as witness of the suffering, and in his telling it, it becomes our story too.

In *Light in August* Faulkner attempts the task of creating a modern protagonist in the person of Joe Christmas, endowing him with all the absurdities, the tensions, the limitations of the modern age and yet making him heroic. Incredibly, the attempt is not a failure. Christmas is presented unsympathetically, is shown to have a very poor adjustment to what society expects of him, and is revealed as committing monstrous crimes. In his loneliness, his atypicalness, his pride, he somehow is transformed into a tragic Everyman and comes to stand for all of us.

In *Absalom, Absalom!*, Faulkner realizes his most profound tragic creation in Thomas Sutpen, who bestrides the past and present like a colossus and whose influence, in the working out of his demonic will, spans the better part of a century. He has all the tragic virtues with the exception of humanity, self-knowledge, and reconciliation. His milieu is traditional, but his attitudes and actions are modern. In the contrast between what Sutpen wanted and what he got, there is a paradigm for all of us.

Faulkner, in spite of the alleged "difficulty" of his style and the highly ambiguous nature of such concepts as "truth" and "reality" in our own time, has nevertheless managed to convey with great immediacy the humanity of his protagonists. At the same time, he is able to bypass or circumvent many of the labyrinths and blind alleys of twentieth-century literature in order to get at what he has called "the old truths . . . of the human heart in conflict with itself." It may be that this is the explanation for that ultimate satisfaction his work has for his dedicated readers: the ability to express convincingly the archaic, fundamental notions about humanity in a setting acceptable to the habits and expectations of the modern individual. Faulkner's presuppositions and conclusions are, of course, notoriously old-fashioned. He appears to believe, in common with the creators of Oedipus, Macbeth, Hamlet, Lear, and a few others who could be named, that the basic problem of every hero (and every non-hero, for that matter) is the problem of self-definition: you must know who and what you are.

vi.

This study hopefully asserts that Faulkner's true tragic protagonist is the legendary South. Although the present writer has pointed out the "popularity" of the historic South as subject matter, it is by no means contended that the versions we get from Hollywood or the "bosom and broadsword" school of fiction have anything to do with authenticity. The year 1961 was the centennial of the firing on Fort Sumter, and since then there has been a crescendo of celebrations, festivals, pageants, and recreations. Commissions were set up from the beginning to avoid the unpleasantness of conflicting activities in competing communities. The techniques of Hollywood and Madison Avenue have been turned to the task of capturing everything, and it may well be that none of those who actually saw the war saw nearly so much as this.

It may be that in the conjunction of Faulkner and the South we have seen the last possible opportunity for a meeting of the myth and a man able to write about it. What Conrad was to the particular world of sail as he knew it and Melville was to whale-fishery Faulkner has become to the South. Say what we will, the South is finally fading away. Even if Hollywood finds wider screens, even in spite of the last frightened upsurge of racial unrest, the South as a cultural entity, a state of mind, a body of myth, is dying. The latest of Faulkner's books indicate his realization of this and contain what may have been his own valediction to the subject of his finest writing. In *Intruder in the Dust* and particularly in that final section of *Requiem for a Nun* entitled "The Jail," he carefully documents the causes of the submergence of the South as a separate entity in the standardized, mass-production, mass-consumption vulgarity of the present-day United States. He mentions the intrusion of the federal government, the mass media of communication, the automobile, and the deprovincializing effect on young men of military duty in the far corners of the earth. In *A Fable,* he chose an altogether different area of myth to write about, and in *The Town* and *The Mansion,* sequels to *The Hamlet,* he shows that arch-villain, the dehumanized, rapacious predator Flem Snopes, as an outwardly respectable, domesticated conformist, as president of a bank and owner of an automobile. It may be that this is the fate of all of us, since Faulkner remarked at the time that respectability gets us all in the end.

We are taught to believe that respectability is the last refuge of the scoundrel and that society guarantees that this refuge will be impregnable. Yet in *The Mansion* even Flem Snopes finally demonstrates that Old Moster don't joke. With the closing of this trilogy, all major segments of the Yoknapatawpha epic were complete, and the work of a lifetime was finished. There yet remained only *The Reivers,* a lyric flute-song in praise of life and joy, a final affirmation. The writer, the artist, builds and rebuilds, creates and modifies his cosmos, which is a tragic process, since in the very act of building that epic, that cosmos, bringing it into existence, it has already begun to decay. Yet this is no great matter, for in this particular regard it is not the art but the artist's satisfaction with it that matters. Asked in March, 1958, what he felt his goal as a writer to be, Faulkner replied:

I think that a writer wants to make something that he knows that a hundred or two hundred or five hundred, a thousand years later will make people feel what they feel when they read Homer, or read Dickens or read Balzac, Tolstoy, and that's probably his goal. I don't think that he bothers until he gets old like this and has a right to spend a lot of time talking about it to put that into actual words. But probably that's what he wants, that really the writer doesn't want success, that he knows he has a short span of life, that the day will come when he must pass through the wall of oblivion, and he wants to leave a scratch on that wall—Kilroy was here—that somebody a hundred, a thousand years later will see.[2]

I think it safe to assume that this work—these marks against oblivion—is permanent. The man, the moment, and the milieu met, and the creation of a major epic was the result. Like Pip and Ishmael, who fell into the sea and were forever changed, no one who shares the rage of uselessness with Sartoris, who runs in desperation with Christmas in his lonely flight to find human acceptance, who sees with Dilsey the first and the last, or who strives with Sutpen to build an enduring monument with only the dust of merely human materials to work with, will ever be quite the same again. These all too human creations will endure.

BALD HEAD ISLAND
CHARLOTTESVILLE
FREIBURG IM BREISGAU

1. William Faulkner, *The Sound and the Fury* (New York: Modern Library, 1946), pp. 335-36.
2. *Faulkner in the University,* ed. Frederick L. Gwynn and Joseph L. Blotner (Charlottesville, Va.: University of Virginia Press, 1959), p. 61.

INDEX

INDEX

DATE DUE

DATE DUE			
DEC 20			
FEB 10 '65			
APR 27 '65			
5/17			
JUN 2 '65			
GAYLORD			PRINTED IN U.S.A.